Serious Play

Serious Play

The Cultural Form of the Nineteenth-Century Realist Novel

J. Jeffrey Franklin

PENN

University of Pennsylvania Press

Philadelphia

Copyright © 1999 University of Pennsylvania Press
All rights reserved
Printed in the United States of America on acid-free paper

10 9 8 7 6 5 4 3 2 1

Published by
University of Pennsylvania Press
Philadelphia, Pennsylvania 19104-4011

Library of Congress Cataloging-in-Publication Data
Franklin, J. Jeffrey.
Serious play : the cultural form of the nineteenth-century realist novel /
J. Jeffrey Franklin.
    p.   cm. (New cultural studies)
    Includes bibliographical references (p.   ) and index.
    ISBN 0-8122-3484-7 (alk. paper)
    1. English fiction — 19th century — History and criticism.   2. Realism in literature.
3. Literature and society — Great Britain — History — 19th century.   4. Performing arts
in literature.   5. Gambling in literature.   6. Play in literature.   7. Literary form.
PR868.R4F73   1999
823'.80912 — dc21   99-012680
                                                                              CIP

Contents

I

Nineteenth-Century
Discourses of Play and the
Novel as a Cultural Form

> Images of all things in a shadow play of discourse.
> Plato, *Sophist*

Near the end of *Vanity Fair*, Joseph Sedley, having left the safety of England and traveled to the Continent, bellies up to a roulette table beside a mysterious masked woman who turns to him and says in a convincingly French-inflected accent, "You do not play to win. No more do I. I play to forget, but I cannot" (615). The speaker, Madame de Raudon, is also Madame Rebecque of recent fame in a nearby opera house, but the reader knows her as Becky Sharpe. Becky uses play here to denote gambling, but other connotations resonate throughout this novel and, indeed, throughout a broad range of Victorian texts. Despite disclaimers, Becky never forgets and always plays to win, even if winning entails playing with the truth. She has staged this coincidental meeting with Joseph, and the text thus suggests that not every gamble—or textual probability—is determined by chance. Becky is playing at love, speculating on the profit in marrying Joseph, and in this respect her character is part of a nineteenth-century literary tradition that includes as varied a group as Mary Crawford in *Mansfield Park*, Gwendolyn Harleth in *Daniel Deronda*, and Arabella Donn in *Jude the Obscure*, to name a very few. Her multiple names, masquerading, and acting on and off the stage constitute the theatrical play by which many Victorian novels characterize one prevalent model of femininity. The theatrical female character such as Becky Sharpe often activates a dangerous play along the boundary that separates propriety and legality from immorality and "foul play." Finally, Becky's play is of a piece with the play of the text, both the irony by which the reader knows her better than Joseph Sedley does and the

double sleight-of-hand by which Thackeray plays both the ironically removed puppet master and the sincere oracle of truth.

At the most practical level, this book began from such observations as
these, which in turn led to a series of deceptively straightforward questions.
How is play represented in British Victorian texts? In which nineteenth-
century discourses was play a central trope? What ideological interests were
served by the figurations of play in those discourses? How, finally, was play
practiced and represented in this age that generations of critics have stereotyped as peculiarly "unplayful"? Research across a range of nineteenth-
century texts — novels, nonfiction prose, poetry — identified a number of
consistently reproduced and widely circulating Victorian discourses in
which play was a recurring and sometimes central trope. Those include discourses about gambling; stock market speculation, as part of the ubiquitous
discourse of money; drama and theatricality; children's play, in relation to
issues of child-rearing and education; recreation, which the nineteenth century defined especially in opposition to work; and sports and fitness, which
the Victorians first institutionalized in their modern forms. An intensified
effort to develop an adequately explanatory theoretical framework for so
diverse a collection led me finally to the topic of aesthetic theory. Aesthetics
is a domain within which the concept of play is both historically crucial —
indeed, definitive — and extremely problematic for Victorian thinkers, especially realist novelists. I chose finally to focus the current study on Victorian
conceptions of play within three of these areas: gambling, theatricality, and
aesthetic theory. Considered collectively, they provide a multifaceted introduction to nineteenth-century British liberal-intellectual modes of thinking
about, writing about, and living play.

An analysis of the figure of play in any one of these three play-related
discourses easily could provide enough material from nineteenth-century
culture and literature to fill a book. This is in part because play is a concept
that continually threatens to expand to fill any space allowed it, ballooning
into a universalization. Friedrich von Schiller, the first disciple of Immanuel
Kant and one of the siphons for the concept of play into nineteenth-century
British thought, famously writes (in the gendered terms of his time): "For
to declare it once and for all, Man plays only when he is in the full sense of
the word a man, and *he is only wholly Man when he is playing*" (*Aesthetic
Education* 80). At what might be thought the opposite end of the spectrum,
Jacques Derrida writes in no less sweeping terms, "Being must be conceived
as presence or absence on the basis of the possibility of play and not the
other way around" (*Writing* 292). These sorts of claims also characterize

many of the most best-known twentieth-century theoretical treatments of play, such as those written by Johan Huizinga, Eugene Fink, and Jacques Erhmann. Huizinga, for example, writes in his landmark study, *Homo Ludens*, that "civilization is, in its earliest phases, played. It does not come *from* play like a babe detaching itself from the womb; it arises *in* and *as* play, and never leaves it" (173). While critiquing Huizinga's idealizations, Ehrmann too makes claims like this one: "In other words, the distinguishing characteristic of reality is that it is played. Play, reality, culture are synonymous and interchangeable" ("Homo Ludens Revisited" 56). In contrast, I strive to avoid such universalizing claims. At the same time, however, I also eschew the pressure and temptation to conclude at any point what play "really meant" to the Victorians. Rather, I attempt, as far as the familiar dilemmas of historical distance and critical self-obstruction permit, to allow Victorian texts to define their own play. This means allowing for their multiple, potentially contradictory definitions. Thus the picture of nineteenth-century British play that emerges is unavoidably heterogeneous and partial, though not indeterminant in the postmodern sense. I hope that this will not be confused either with lack of focus on my part or with giving in to the essentializing tendencies that I identify in some eighteenth-century, nineteenth-century, and late twentieth-century texts.

One strategy for avoiding essentialization is to return insistently to consideration of specific texts and their representations of specific cultural discourses in relation to identifiable historical events, institutions, and interests. Each of the three main chapters historically contextualizes its readings in this way. The chapter on gambling focuses on what is called "play" by characters and narrators in many Victorian novels, in this case George Eliot's *Middlemarch* and Anthony Trollope's *The Duke's Children*. The analysis situates gambling in relation to events in the histories of recreation and the stock market, the latter of which was experiencing the throes of adolescence in the process of institutionalizing into the pillar of modern capitalist societies. Histories of Victorian gambling practices also provide valuable background, in particular parliamentary regulations on gambling and the subsequent adaptations by the institutions of gambling, which produced the "gambling hell," the race track, and the "turf accountant." The third chapter similarly analyzes novelistic texts — *Shirley* and *Villette* by Charlotte Brontë and *Felix Holt* and *Daniel Deronda* by George Eliot — in relation to histories of the British theater and of antitheatrical prejudice. I analyze the events between the Theater Licensing Act of 1737 and the rescinding of it in 1843 as part of a cycle in British theater history, punctuated by the practices of masquerade and private theatricals, the advent of melodrama, and the "Old Price" theater riots of 1809. That cycle not only brought significant changes to the form of British theater but also was critical to the newly commercializing form of the novel. Finally, the fourth chapter compares representations of aesthetic play in major critical works such as John Ruskin's *Modern Painters* and Matthew Arnold's *Culture and Anarchy* to its figurations in William Makepeace Thackeray's *Pendennis* and Charles Kingsley's *Alton Locke*. These analyses take their context from the history of play as an aesthetic concept, most specifically from its modern origins in Immanuel Kant's *Critique of Judgment* forward through the Romantics to the Victorian period, where it became highly pressurized and sublimated into the very form of what has come to be called, with varying degrees of specificity, "the Victorian novel," "the bourgeois realist novel," "the realist novel," and sometimes simply "the novel."[1]

This book also uses attention to textual and historical details as a means of working toward broader insights about early to mid-Victorian culture (1840s-1870s) and the significance of the realist novel as an integral part of that culture. Regardless of the clichés about unplayful Victorians, play had profound and varied significance within nineteenth-century British culture and society. Play is notable to the extent that it functioned as a primary trope within multiple, relatively discrete domains of discourse. What is more, play links each of these areas to broader, culturally defining issues that Victorian texts frequently express as chance versus necessity, the artificial versus the authentic, or false art versus true art. One way of interpreting this is to conclude that play was simply widely dispersed and "common" in a trivial sense. This study suggests the opposite: that play functioned as a linch-pin concept within the discursive infrastructure by which Victorian society represented itself to itself: common in the sense of "natural" and, therefore, ideologically instrumental. Thus Victorian texts typically represent the figure of play as the mystified kernel at the center of culture, which in turn is mystified as the product of the play of the cultural imagination, which, as I argue, is precisely how Victorian society encoded its most disturbing issues of gender difference, class inequality, social mobility, and capitalist expansion. *Serious Play* works to demystify and decode play and its ideological functions within Victorian literature, culture, and society.

This is not to imply that the figure of play functioned simply or only to recuperate dominant, bourgeois ideology, though it did that as well. Play served a connective or bridging function, tying the demonized issue of gambling, for instance, to the socially pivotal institution of the stock market, and linking both of these to two of the most important issues in Victorian thought: work and money. The effect was to foreground contradictions within the increasingly dominant ideology of finance capitalism between different definitions of "value." Play leads, then, to the culturally defining question of what constitutes true value. Is it inherited money and blood, which effectively privileges chance over merit, as a traditional, aristocratic ideology might maintain? Is it money earned by work—for which play is the supposed antithesis—as one traditional strand of middle-class ideology would argue? Or is it money gained by the play of "speculation," as in fact was becoming the most important source of financial value in society? How does Victorian society square monetary value with moral values?

In parallel ways, the chapters on theatricality and aesthetic theory find the figure of play performing a critical, connective function within the discursive infrastructure of Victorian culture. Theatrical play, for instance, repeatedly leads to questions about subjective authenticity, thereby opening into the pervasive dialectic within Victorian texts of inner versus outer, public versus private. Since the most common theatrical figure in Victorian novels is the theatrical woman, the character who performs—rather than *is*—her self, the issue of authenticity couples *via* the figure of play with the equally pervasive concern over gender identity. The construction of the gendered, middle-class subject in turn ties back to the broader question of the real versus the artificial. Since this latter question is identical to the question to which nineteenth-century realism offered itself as the answer, play therefore links overarching Victorian concerns about domesticity and bourgeois hegemony to the formal concerns of realist novels. Play thus engages the novels read in this study in a precariously reflexive dialogue about their own formal projects and social functions. The mimetic play of nineteenth-century realist novels links the issue of the real in fictional form to the issue of the real (the true, true value) in society.[2] This becomes especially relevant in chapter four on aesthetic theory, which analyzes a debate about art-as-play versus art-as-work, Romantic poetry versus the "prose duties" of the novelist, as *Pendennis* puts it (380). This debate impinges on nineteenth-century critical debates about the relative merits of "realism" as opposed to "romance" or "sensation" and concerns over the professionalization and proper social role of the artist, with unavoidable reference to the novelist. Play therefore proves critical for understanding the role that realist novels constructed for themselves as vehicles for Victorian discourses at the very time when that form was reaching the height of its market penetration as a dominant medium for cultural material.

Thus in this book I read novels and other texts as richly textured cultural artifacts. This does not imply ignoring their qualities as works of literature or abstracting them into a "cultural poetics." On the contrary, I analyze realist novels as representative of one among other historically and socially contingent cultural forms that competed within specific cultural arenas for entertainment market share. This understanding of "cultural form" emerged during preliminary research for chapter three out of a need for a concept more material than "genre" to describe the historical competition that I observed in the eighteenth century between popular commercial theater and the newly important form of the novel. Cultural form might be thought of as a combination of genre, medium, and material, recognizing that "the novel" does not exist as a genre in an abstract form but rather is inseparable from the medium and material in which it is produced and consumed: ink printed on paper bound in serials, or triple-deckers, or single-volume books (which may constitute three separate cultural forms). This concept became central to the architecture and argument of this book as I progressively recognized the extent of the representations within nineteenth-century realist novels of historical competitions between the novel and other cultural forms. Novels stage within their pages discursive contests between figures representing their own realist form and figures representing other cultural forms, specifically the book on political economy, the Romantic poem, the melodramatic theater performance, and the treatise on aesthetic theory (as well as other novelistic forms, such as romance, sensation, or gothic). In this way, nineteenth-century realist novels worked to define "realism" and to actualize the claim of their own form to cultural hegemony. The following list of the characteristics of a cultural form provides an introductory definition.

- Cultural forms entertain and socialize, and the two functions are inseparable. They serve as vehicles for disseminating social discourses. Different cultural forms may by the very nature of their form lend themselves to carrying certain types of information and ideas. Some correlation exists between the formal characteristics that distinguish a cultural form and the ideology that it embodies.
- A cultural form is accompanied by a specific, widely practiced mode of consumption; for example, sitting quietly for hours reading a book in one's hands, standing before a podium listening to a political speech, or sitting in a darkened room full of strangers eating snacks and watching a movie. The mode of consumption produces

identifiable effects on individuals who spend time practicing it, *regardless of the "content" of the cultural form*. The mode, as well as its content, socializes people in specific ways that are different from the socializing effects of other cultural forms.

- Cultural forms compete, first, in a very material and often economic sense: for the number of people who are interested in and willing to buy or otherwise acquire them in order to consume or participate in them. In western postindustrial capitalist societies, cultural forms tend to be produced in proportion to their success in creating demand and coming to occupy a share of the entertainment market.[3]

- Cultural forms compete in the second place for access to definition of the subject, which is never separate from market share. Different cultural forms reproduce different subject positions. The more dominant a cultural form, the more potential it has for shaping the interests, beliefs, and behaviors of individuals in the society.

- Certain cultural forms are more "dominant" than others in terms of their breadth of distribution and consumption. Given the data, dominance could be measured fairly exactly in both size and demographics, for example, the number of teenagers who watch a certain television show, or the number of middle-class women who read novels in 1850s London. A society in which a particular cultural form is dominant is different in specific, significant ways from a society in which another cultural form is dominant.

- Cultural forms have histories; their production and consumption change over time, and it might be possible to assess the size and direction of these changes. For example, as this study shows, the novel partially supplanted the theater as the more dominant cultural form in the first half of the nineteenth century in England. Cultural forms wax, like television in 1950s America or the e-mail exchange in the 1990s, and wane, as in the case of the publicly recited epic poem or the in-home private theatrical.

- Cultural forms are "interested" in the sense that individuals and institutions have interests in producing or consuming that form. The primary interest of any cultural form is to propagate itself. Cultural forms disseminate by generating demand, which means producing consumers, which means fashioning social subjects who in part define themselves by and through their consumption of that cultural form.

These characteristics constitute a preliminary theory of the cultural form. Some of them are commonplace assumptions that often go untheorized and therefore perhaps should be questioned; others are hypothetical propositions with rhetorical value to this study, which will be developed throughout this book.

One of the distinguishing characteristics of the nineteenth-century British realist novel as a cultural form is its relationship to play. That relationship is summarized by one of this book's broadest conclusions: the primary function of the figure of play within realist novels is to signify their Other. This claim applies at three levels of analysis. At the most straightforward level, the novels read here use the figure of play to scapegoat activities, social groups, and ideologies that they portray as antithetical to the dominant discourses of the text. Thus they stigmatize gambling, chance, and associated "bad" sources of value (playing the market, debt or bankruptcy, foul play, for instance) with the figure of play. These then serve as straw figures in juxtaposition to which are defined the "good" sources of value, such as work, social responsibility, or suitable marriage. In general, characters and actions associated with gambling, theatricality, or aesthetic play are demonized as duplicitous, superficial, illusory, selfish, idealized, violent, or carnal, and these act as foils to privileged characters and tropes that are portrayed as sincere, authentic, real, meritorious, sympathetic, domestic, and enduring. At the simplest level, then, the modus operandi of these novels is to expose and then correct the excesses of play as a means of prescribing something that they suggest is the opposite.

This first level of analysis may appear to demonstrate that play simply recuperates dominant, bourgeois ideologies, confirming a critical commonplace that Victorian novels, in content as in form, mainly serve as vehicles for those ideologies.[4] This study throughout complicates both sides of this commonplace, challenging the assumption that a monolithic bourgeois ideology ever existed as well as the assumption that nineteenth-century realist novels straightforwardly or nonreflexively reproduce any single ideology. So, while the novels read here scapegoat play, that is neither their most significant representation of play nor itself straightforward, since play thereby emerges as not simply the opposite but the "negative analogue" of certain ideological pillars of Victorian society.[5] In this way, play marks and makes visible the boundaries of dominant discourse. The text exposes to scrutiny the supposedly critical difference between the privileged figures and the figures of play to which they are juxtaposed. Finance capitalism thus may emerge suddenly as organized gambling on a mass scale; the mask of authentic subjectivity slips up to reveal a casting call of socially contingent roles; realness, through a reversal of figure and ground, may appear as nothing more or less than a construction. The realist text itself simultaneously supports and undercuts the same tenets.

At the second level of analysis, realist novels take play as their Other by using it to characterize other cultural forms. For instance, in the novels of George Eliot in particular gambling comes to signify any approach to representing or interpreting events that allows chance, coincidence, Providence, or fate more explanatory authority than choice, consequence, or logical commonsense probability. Thus this play-related discourse leads to a dialogue within these novels about their own preferred formal strategies in contrast to those that these novelists and some critics of the time attributed to un-realistic novelistic subgenres. Similarly, all of the novels considered in this book apply the figure of play to non-Classical or non-Shakespearean theater, especially melodrama. They repeatedly juxtapose theatricalized figures characterized in terms of their duplicity or exteriority, for instance, to certain other figures characterized in terms of authenticity, interiority, and realness. This emerges as a dialogue in the novel between the figure of the novel and the figure of one of its parent genres, the theater. These two cultural forms, realist fiction and melodramatic theater, were engaged in a quite specific, historical contest for cultural dominance at that very time. The analysis of aesthetic theory finds the same sort of pattern: Victorian play stigmatizes the aesthetics associated with the German Idealism and British Romanticism that preceded it, to which the novels offer as the recommended alternative the aesthetics that typifies the formal strategies of the realist novel itself (which then prove to be linked to the healthier "fair play" that underwrote British colonial expansionism). Thus this contest too is grounded in historical competition between cultural forms, the form of theoretical writing about art and the novel as a form of fictional writing that takes itself as the exemplar of Art as "literature." The traditional distinction between "the ideal" and "the real" to which this competition appeals points to the third level of analysis at which nineteenth-century realist novels designate play as their Other: play as mimesis, not simply a topic in a novel but the novel's enactment of that topic as its form. This conception of play ties the Victorian contest between idealism and realism back to its origins in the Platonic contest between philosophy and poetry and, at the same time, forward to the postmodern contest between theory and literature.

Victorian Play / Postmodern Play

If this were a postmodern text, not just a text written in the era that critics
call postmodern, then it might *perform* its subject of inquiry rather than only
applying to it certain analytical and writing strategies passed down from the
traditions of Classical rhetoric, Renaissance rationality, and Victorian historicism. If I chose to write like a grammatologist or a l-a-n-g-u-a-g-e poet,
I might be able to push writing up to the brink of becoming play or, as
Roland Barthes would say, of playing with itself.[6] The text might mirror
itself, as in Jacques Derrida's *Glas*, or attempt to enact its own topic, as in
Jean-François Lyotard and Jean-Loup Thébaud's *Just Gaming*, or become
rhizomic, as in Gilles Deleuze and Félix Guattari's *A Thousand Plateaus*
(and, recently, in electronic hypertexts). Any of these might seem more
appropriate to my subject matter, but none of these is the approach that I
have chosen in this case to take.

The question of the critic's choice of textual strategies is especially
relevant to the current study because of the conjunction of two inescapably
related facts: this is an analysis of certain discourses of play in the literature
and culture of the historical period that proceeds the current period, and,
second, the intellectual environment of the current period, and therefore of
this study, is heavily conditioned by postmodern theory. As anyone working within this environment knows, post-structuralist theories have produced a pervasive, critical self-reflexiveness by drawing a great deal of attention to issues of signification, which then unavoidably implicate the writing
critic's own textual practice. But, more to the point, there is one salient
feature shared by many postmodern theories that makes the current theoretical environment germane in a very specific way to this book. I will
summarize it for the moment as baldly as possible: *postmodern theories are
about play*. What is more, postmodern uses of play concepts are not independent of nineteenth-century uses of play concepts, the recognition of
which does not require subscribing to a simplistic model of causation or a
teleology. These claims obviously require some qualification and defense,
which will follow. Suffice it to suggest in the meanwhile that the relationship between nineteenth-century discourses of play and late twentieth-
century discourses of play is a very complex and largely unexplored one that
cannot safely be ignored in any study of play performed in the current
period of the former period.

"Play" appears as a pivotal concept, whether untheorized or theorized
as a non-concept, in the writings of prominent thinkers in western philoso-

phy from Heraclitus (circa 500 B.C.) to Derrida. Historians of play such as Johan Huizinga or Mihai Spariosu trace play back to one of its original recorded sources, the aphorisms of Heraclitus, one of the best-known of which states: "Lifetime is a child at play, moving pieces in a game, the kingship belongs to the child."[7] Friedrich Nietzsche, the self-professed inheritor of the Heraclitian formulation of play, was the gatekeeper for that concept into post-structuralist and then postmodern theorizations of it.[8] In one of his several direct responses to Heraclitus, for example, Nietzsche writes: "That which he [Heraclitus] beheld, the doctrine of the Law in the Becoming, and of the Play in Necessity, must henceforth be beheld eternally; he has raised the curtain of this greatest stage-play" (*Age of the Greeks* 114). Nietzsche uses this conception of play as the basis for the terms on which his philosophy is founded, terms such as "the Dionysian" or "the Will to Power." But Nietzsche's play is not the same as that of the other most noted aesthetician of play, Immanuel Kant, who of course is among those whom Nietzsche critiques. As in Nietzsche's writing in general, in Kant's *Critique of Judgment* play is the central underlying concept. In Kant, play does not signify the irrational and unbounded nature of becoming, but rather marks the rational order of the universe according to which an external object can correspond with an internal, subjective state, especially in the experience of the beautiful. This occurs, Kant argues throughout the third *Critique*, as the "*free play* of the cognitive powers": "It is this feeling of freedom in the play of our cognitive powers, a play that yet must also be purposive, which underlies that pleasure which alone is universally communicable although not based on concepts."[9] Play defines the Kantian "*Zweck ohne Zweckmassigkeit*" or "purposiveness without purpose," on which his whole aesthetics rests like an inverted pyramid on its point.[10] As such, play not only designates but *is* the gap between the aesthetic subject and the aesthetic object.

This thumbnail genealogy, which provides a frame for Victorian play between Kant and Nietzsche, suggests that Kantian play is, in a certain sense, the opposite of Nietzschean play, though the two thus also are integrally linked. This is only to highlight the heterogeneity of play concepts. No unified or continuous historical progression exists among play concepts. At the same time, however, a reading of the most noted theories of play across two thousand years finds it frequently functioning at the most general level in a consistent way or, perhaps more accurately, occupying a similar space: that of the gap, the abyss, the third term, the "not" (or "[k]not," as a deconstructive theorist might suggest). Whether one is reading Martin Heidegger, Hans-Georg Gadamer, Eugene Fink, or James Hans, for example, play ultimately is that which constitutes a gap, whether it be the ontological gap between being and becoming, the metaphysical gap between self and other, the epistemological gap between subject and object, or, most recently, the post-structuralist gap between signifier and signified.[11] Partly as a result of this aspect of play, theorists have tended to posit it as that which by definition resists definition, is the resistance to definition, is, finally, the indefinable. Thus, while being relied upon to provide the ultimate support for entire philosophical systems, play more often than not has escaped direct analysis.

In the realm of eighteenth-century aesthetics, this means that play indicates the place called "and here God must step in." Kant admits, if reluctantly, that the necessary guarantor of the *Zweck ohne Zweckmassigkeit* is God, just as other aesthetics of the time — such as the *je ne sais quoi* — also require God as their ultimate referent.[12] At least since Nietzsche, however, this post has been vacant, or rather has been *the* vacancy. Following Nietzsche, post-structuralist and then postmodern theorists made this very place (or nonplace, as the case may be) the focus of their investigations. One need not subscribe to a familiar, simplistic reading of Derrida's notion of *jeu* as "free play,"[13] for instance, in order to observe that all of his coined words — *différance*, trace, supplement — are not only play-derived but are synonyms for play as Derrida himself understands it.[14] This is evident throughout his writing and is acknowledged directly in several places, as here in "The Double Session": "Is it by chance that all these play effects, these 'words' that escape philosophical mastery, should have, in widely differing historical contexts, a very singular relation to writing?" (*Dissemination* 221). All of Derrida's "play effects," of course, do refer to writing. Writing — the structure of signification itself — is the form of play, the ultimate referent for the play-terms (aporia, indeterminacy, *simulacra,* etc.) coined not only by Derrida but by a range of post- theorists. This point gains particular relevance in analyzing how Victorian novelists constructed their writing as writing, but the immediate point is that even Derrida's philosophy, which is the single most sophisticated and sustained theorization of play yet written, still ultimately leaves play as that which lies beyond analysis. In saying this I only am agreeing (though perhaps for the wrong reasons) with those who might feel compelled to defend the claim that deconstructive or other post- theories escape the pitfalls of western metaphysics precisely by activating play as a *nonconcept* that marks the limits of all signification. As a nonconcept that "escapes philosophical mastery," Derridian play, while designating something that could not be more different from the Kantian idea of God, nevertheless *functions* exactly in the same way as does Kantian play and occupies exactly the same location within its philosophical system as that beyond which nothing more can be signified, the infinite regress of signification.[15] Thus, even while Derrida mounts an extremely convincing critique of Kant's idealism and the idealism of western metaphysics in general, his philosophy and that of many postmodern theorists joins these idealisms at this one seminal and disseminating point: play.

After all, Derrida's correction of Kantian play with his own play is in some important ways a reenactment in reverse of Plato's correction of the play of Heraclitus and of the Sophists. In the *Republic*, Plato mounts his famous attack on "imitation" in art, especially poetry, as being the most dangerous "form of play" (*Republic*, Book X, 827). In *Sophist*, Plato's speaker, Stranger, stigmatizes the Sophist as one who sells his illusory representations of reality in the market for entertainment. The danger of such counterfeit versions of reality, which are cheapened additionally by the marketing of them (and which bring to mind the marketing of and criticisms of both nineteenth-century realist novels and twentieth-century television), is that they will disseminate an unreal, mimetic play: "Then must we not expect to find a corresponding form of skill [among Sophists] in the region of discourse, making it possible to impose upon the young who are still far removed from the reality of things, by means of words that cheat the ear, exciting images of all things in a shadow play of discourse, so as to make them believe that they are hearing the truth?"[16] Derrida's response to Plato in "Plato's Pharmacy" is to counterattack the "Platonic repression of play" by opening up and turning against it the very Sophist play that Plato tried to repress (*Dissemination* 156). Derrida does not so much reverse Plato's understanding of play as he reverses Plato's valuation of it (if then to deconstruct the difference). He foregrounds the other side of play, as it were, which he follows Plato in defining as "writing": "The play of the other within being must needs be designated 'writing' by Plato in a discourse which would like to think of itself as spoken in essence, in truth, and which nevertheless is written" (163). While "writing" here designates writing itself in general, the immediate exemplar of it that Derrida's writing puts forward is his own. Derrida is less concerned (if at all) with defending writing as "literature," which is the form of writing that Plato most specifically attacked for its mimetic play, than he is with producing in the form of his own writing an enactment of the very play that his text simultaneously theorizes. This is the predominant strategy throughout Derrida's *oeuvre*.

Derrida's texts position his type of writing—philosophy or theory—as the writing that, in effect, rescues the writing that Plato othered in his attack on mimetic play. In this way, Derrida repositions "philosophy" over the location where Plato had positioned "literature." This is a brilliant strategic maneuver. Not only does it reclaim a form of play that is anathema to Plato and perhaps to Kant and thereby explodes or appears to explode western metaphysics; it manages at the same time to preserve philosophy by establishing an identity between it and the very play in opposition to which Plato originally defined "philosophy."

Plato institutionalized a discursive dichotomy between literature and philosophy that became a historical contest between cultural forms that persists to the present day. He laid the foundation for "an epistemological split, in our culture, between art as play and philosophy and science as seriousness and morality" (Spariosu, *Dionysus* 129). The persistence and contentiousness of this dichotomy has been demonstrated again in the 1980s and 1990s both within and outside the academy in the "theory versus literature" debate, which appears to be an ongoing politicized subtext if not an overt battle within every university English department in the United States. Derrida's philosophy is for the most part simply not interested in this debate and unconcerned with the question of the relative merits of theoretical as opposed to literary writing, and this lack of concern with maintaining that boundary is what incites certain people. Derrida nonetheless has been a pivotal player in the historical contest between two cultural forms, philosophy and literature.

But the event that brought Plato's argument back to the forefront of modern theoretical concern was the unprecedented burgeoning of aesthetic theory in the eighteenth century. A proliferation of theorists occurred from around the time of the third earl of Shaftesbury's *Enquiry Concerning Virtue or Merit* (1688) through Edmund Burke, David Hume, H. H. Kames, Alexander Baumgarten, Immanuel Kant, and Friedrich von Schiller to the artist-theorists of the Romantic period, especially Wordsworth's preface to the *Lyrical Ballads* and Coleridge's *Biographia Literaria*. This century-long accumulation resulted by the early nineteenth century in the professionalization of the critic—signaled by Coleridge's idea of the "clericy"—and the institutionalization of both modern philosophy and literary theory. What is more, this occurred roughly during the same period that also witnessed the modern institutionalization of "literature" as a sphere with privileged access to the powers of the imagination, a discrete set of cultural forms ("the lyric," "the historical novel"), and its own professionalized practice in the marketplace.[17] The timing of these two occurrences is not coincidental. The discursive dichotomy between philosophy and literature manifests itself at the end of the eighteenth century as a contest between the two cultural forms, that of idealist aesthetic theory and that of "literature." The latter was defined by writers of the time first as what we now call Romantic poetry and then most pointedly in the form of the realist novel.

According to Michel Foucault's well-known account in *The Order of Things*, these events can be understood as part of a shift in the dominant western episteme away from a representational understanding of language toward the modern concern with signification and writing (which J. Hillis Miller, for one, analyzes as the "linguistic moment"). Literature emerges in the nineteenth century as "that which compensates for (and not that which confirms) the signifying function of language," compensates for the "demotion of language" in relation to signification (*Order* 46, 299).[18] At the same time, philosophy and criticism emerge as part of "the new positivity of the sciences of life, language, and economics" (*Order* 244). Foucault's summary of that situation uses terms of particular relevance to this study:

At the beginning of the nineteenth century, at a time when language was burying itself within its own density as an object and allowing itself to be traversed, through and through, by knowledge, it was also reconstituting itself elsewhere, in an independent form, difficult of access, folded back upon the enigma of its own origin and existing wholly in reference to the pure act of writing. *Literature is the contestation of philology (of which it is nevertheless the twin figure):* it leads language back from grammar to the naked power of speech, and there it encounters the untamed, imperious being of words. From the Romantic revolt against a discourse frozen in its own ritual pomp, to the Mallarméan discovery of the word in its impotent power, it becomes clear what the function of literature was, in the nineteenth century, in relation to the modern mode of being of language. Against the background of this essential interaction, the rest is merely effect: literature becomes progressively more differentiated from the discourse of ideas, and encloses itself within a radical intransitivity; it becomes detached from all the values that were able to keep it in general circulation during the Classical age (taste, pleasure, naturalness, truth), and creates within its own space everything that will ensure a *ludic denial* of them (the scandalous, the ugly, the impossible). (*Order* 300)

I do not subscribe fully to Foucault's potentially idealized notion of literature, and I remain sensitive to the possibility that he may uncritically reproduce Plato's categories; nevertheless, my findings are consistent with Foucault's reading of the historical relationship between "literature" and "philology." Literature and theory enter the nineteenth century engaged in a discursive contest — a version of the Platonic contest — over which types of knowledge, definitions of reality, and genres of writing will have truth-telling authority and, what is more, which will be the representative for the play of signification itself. The Victorian novels analyzed here not only represent these discourses, which are discourses of play, but embody and act out this contest at the level of their form. In making these claims, I go beyond Foucault's description of literature, which implies a full retreat into the fictive and an abnegation of truth-telling authority to the newly institutionalized sciences. Nineteenth-century realist novels, by dint of their commitments to realism and what they perceived to be its moral imperatives, claim authority over "the real" in a way that challenges empirical science while at the same time defending a potentially contradictory because idealist claim to the superior status of "literature." In other words, these novels are not satisfied simply with positioning theoretical writing as the "bad" Other in relation to their "good" literary writing; they also strive to supplant theory's supposedly more scientific truth-telling function. Victorian texts participate actively and consciously in the historical contest with philosophy that Plato initiated and that Derrida trumped. My claim is that nineteenth-century realist novels trumped it first, if in limited and specific ways to which I will return. Suffice it to say for the moment that the novelistic texts read here attempt to be "literature" and also to be "philosophy," a strategy that Derrida's writings apply in reverse by positioning "philosophy" over Plato's stigmatized category of "poetry."

As may be apparent, I interpret the literature-philosophy dualism as one expression of a historical contest between different play concepts. This also is the thesis of the most thorough historical analysis of play available, Mihai Spariosu's *Dionysus Reborn: Play and the Aesthetic Dimension in Modern Philosophical and Scientific Discourse*. Spariosu analyzes the history of play as "a history of conflict, of competing play concepts that become dominant, lose ground, and then reemerge, according to the needs of various groups or individuals contending for cultural authority in a given historical period" (xi). He identifies two predominant, discontinuous but recurring families of play concepts: a "prerational" play concept that is traceable to Heraclitus and a "rational" play concept formulated by Plato and those who followed him. "Prerational" play is agonistic and violent, an enactment of power, a "manifestation of ceaseless physical Becoming" that creates the potential for unrestrained freedom, but also is arbitrary and chance-driven (12). Within this paradigm, "mimesis" retains its pre-Platonic meaning, not as imitation but as performance, embodiment, and dissolution of the self-other dichotomy. It is this understanding of play that links the various philosophies of

Gadamer, Derrida, and Deleuze back through Heidegger and Nietzsche to Heraclitus (which is not to deny the links to Kant and Plato as well). By contrast, "rational" play appeals to an order of Being within which both violence and freedom are limited, the play between chance and necessity is rule-governed, and mimesis is bound to imitation. Within this lineage, Kantian play is linked back to Plato and forward both to German idealism and to the "rational" play within certain modern social and natural sciences (for example, Charles Darwin's evolutionary theory, Werner Heisenberg's indeterminacy principle, Jean Piaget's social psychology, and contemporary chaos theory). But Kant and the less "rational" Romantic revolution that followed him also were pivotal within the history of "prerational" play concepts. Spariosu dedicates the first half of his book to following the ramifications of the Kantian revival of play forward to its crescendo in postmodern theory, as he summarizes here:

From a suppressed epistemological prop of philosophy (controlled and regulated by [Plato's] mimesis-imitation), mimesis-play turns once more into an indispensable cognitive tool, a fundamental way of understanding the world of Becoming. In this context, mimesis-imitation also reverses its function: it is no longer an instrument for subordinating mimesis-play to knowledge and truth (as it was in Plato and Aristotle) but is on the contrary an instrument for subordinating knowledge and truth to mimesis-play. Plato's nightmare of bad mimesis, associated with immediate power and violence, finally comes true. In such contemporary thinkers as Deleuze, Derrida, and their followers play is no longer good mimesis, installing Being and Truth; rather, mimesis is (Platonic) bad play, replacing Being and Truth with the eternal play of simulacra. (20)

If Derrida would deconstruct this dichotomy between "good play" and "bad play," then Spariosu also is aware of the risk his analysis runs of essentializing its categories. He works to avoid this by maintaining a recognition of the contingent and context-specific nature of historical occurrences of play while still tracing "family resemblances" between different play concepts over time. On the other hand, Derrida too draws on a similar dichotomy in his critique in *Of Grammatology* of Plato's "metaphysico-theological" logocentrism. He distinguishes between Plato's "good writing," which effaces and interiorizes its status as writing, and "bad writing," which embraces and utilizes its "exteriority," its nonpresence in and as writing (13ff.). These distinctions are crucial in an analysis of Victorian writing, given the fact that critics in every generation since have either praised or ridiculed it as the epitome of unplayful good writing.

This last point prepares a return to the question raised earlier about the critic's choice of writing strategies. Is my writing in *Serious Play* inherently unplayful because it takes play seriously in a sense predicated by western rhetoric and metaphysics? If so, does it therefore blindly reproduce the "good writing," and so ideology, of the culture and texts that it analyzes: nineteenth-century middle-class liberal-intellectual culture and its realism? And, more specifically, how adequate as a description of Victorian writing, especially realist fiction, is the concept of "good writing"? Before addressing these questions directly, I note that even to ask them in these ways is to point to a whole series of related and by now both commonplace and periodically challenged assumptions: that the Victorians were essentially repressive of play; that realism as a genre is inherently unplayful; that this unplayfulness is synonymous with reproducing bourgeois ideology; that some postmodern theorists have seen through this and so liberated themselves from the old-fashioned idea of ideology all together; that the artful play of some postmodern texts is in itself a demonstration of their freedom from the logocentrism of other forms of writing, of which realism would be the extreme case; and, finally, that play thus practiced is inherently liberatory. These assumptions partially define what I will call the *anti-play/pro-play position*.

There is a lengthy and articulate tradition of criticisms that variously elaborate the pro-play side of this position. To summarize briefly, that tradition begins in earnest with Oscar Wilde and the writings of the Decadents on the heels of the more "Victorian" Victorians.[19] In many ways, however, the Decadents fulfill the aestheticism that the Romantics initiated in the wake of Kant and that Victorians like John Ruskin and George Eliot strove in the interim to curb. Then come the reactions against "Victorianism" and revisions of realism by Modernist writers, the critical and artistic revisions of realism by socialist thinkers such as Bertolt Brecht, the dissections of the body of realism by post-structuralists such as the Roland Barthes of *S/Z*, and the dancing on the grave of "mimesis-imitation" by a variety of postmodern theorists. Indeed, one might build on Spariosu's theory to hypothesize a periodicity of discursive contests between competing play concepts that has been cycling along at least since Kant. It could be summarized as follows: Kant's "rational" play is responded to by the "prerational" play of the Romantics, to which the Victorians retort with the "rational" play exemplified by realist fiction, which is countered variously by the "prerational" aesthetics of the Decadents and then the Modernists (not to mention Nietzsche), which is mediated in turn by the American New Critics, for instance, who are superseded most recently by the insistently "prerational" play of postmodern theories and literatures.

This admittedly simplistic model sketches a historical frame within which to situate the period of interest here, the early to mid-Victorian decades. It also suggests an alternate phrasing for the question that motivates this study: what happened to play in the decades between the Romantics and the Decadents? This phrasing recognizes that something *did* happen to play; cultural and societal changes produced different discursive formations within which the figure of play took on specific new intensities and functions. At the same time, this does not endorse the even more simplistic model according to which once upon a time there was true play, then the Victorians came along and repressed it, and since that time play has been making a slow comeback until the postmoderns set it — and us — free once more.

This latter model might be described as the repressive hypothesis of play, with obvious reference to the "repressive hypothesis" that Foucault theorizes in relation to sexuality. The first volume of *History of Sexuality* famously opens with the statement, "For a long time, the story goes, we supported a Victorian regime, and we continue to be dominated by it even today" (3). Critics who either harp on the repressiveness of the Victorians or celebrate the postmodern escape from such repressiveness vis-à-vis play equally contribute to the repressive hypothesis of play. The simplified summary of that position is "the Victorians were not playful, but we are." While I continually strive to complicate that position, showing whenever supportable that the Victorians were more playful than many critics think and that postmodern theorists are less playful than many of them think, I also do not support the opposite position: "The Victorians were playful, and we are not." Either of these positions — "see, we've achieved real play," or "if only we could get back to *that* real play" — perpetuates an idealized definition of play, according to which it is originally, inherently, or naturally free and liberatory. My approach is closer to though not identical to Foucault's in my concern with analyzing the specific ways that play is "'put into discourse'" and how those discursive formations positively generate power in the nineteenth century as in the twentieth (*Sexuality* 11). Thus the third position — "the Victorians were playful, and so are we" (or its converse) — either is utopian (or distopian) or, as I intend it, a recognition that for the Victorians, as for the postmoderns, the turning of play into discourse unavoidably serves identifiable, historically specific interests and institutions.

Again, this is not to deny that social conceptions and practices of play changed significantly between the Decadents and the Romantics. They did. Peter Bailey's *Leisure and Class in Victorian England* documents changes in the area of recreation, for instance, that appear to support the anti-play or

repressive hypothesis. Bailey argues, in short, that an increasing rationalization of recreation and disciplining of it to meet the requirements of industrial capitalism for a house-trained workforce occurred throughout the century.[20] He concludes: "Play was not to be allowed any form of special
license; rather it had to be firmly and unequivocally integrated with the rest
of life and securely anchored in orthodox morality. Ideally—rationally—
recreation was an adjunct and complement to work" (94). Terry Castle's
Masquerade and Civilization similarly draws conclusions that support the
anti-play position, describing the eighteenth-century practice of masquerade in ways that are consistent with the discourse of theatricality analyzed in
chapter three. Castle documents a sudden decline in masquerades after the
French Revolution and a domestication of the figure of masquerade in
subsequent fiction. This conclusion seems reasonable enough to anyone
who has read Jane Austen's *Mansfield Park* or studied the fate of "private
theatricals" in the early nineteenth century.

The danger of the anti-play/pro-play position lies, however, in essentializing either "play" or "the Victorians," as occurs, for instance, in perhaps
the most famous historical study of play, Huizinga's *Homo Ludens*.[21] Huizinga concludes in a way that appears to lend strong support to the anti-
play position: "The nineteenth century seems to leave little room for play.
Tendencies running directly counter to all that we mean by play have become increasingly dominant. . . . But the great currents of its thought,
however looked at, were all inimical to the play-factor in social life. . . .
Never had an age taken itself with more portentous seriousness. Culture
ceased to be 'played'" (191–92). But Huizinga's treatment of play is pre-
determined by a subscription, on the one hand, to a rationalistic model that
replicates aspects of nineteenth-century bourgeois ideology and, on the
other hand, to an agonistic model that replicates aspects of traditional aristocratic ideology. The former model, as interpreted by Huizinga, dictates a
simple dichotomy between play and "reality," which is assumed to be preex-
isting and constant. As Jacques Ehrmann argues, Huizinga and other midcentury play theorists essentialize play in one (or both) of two directions,
treating it as either a degraded or a sanctified domain separated from "everyday reality." Huizinga further assumes a progressive teleology for play,
according to which "civilization arises and unfolds in and as play" throughout what is presented as a continuous human history (i). However, his
measure of "civilization" turns out to be "virtue, honour, nobility and
glory" as exemplified by the rituals of gentlemanly combat (64). As society
has suffered "democratization . . . of fashion" and "world-wide bastardiza-

tion of culture," these practices have waned, and so has "civilization," according to Huizinga, though this claim directly contradicts the initial teleological assumption (193, 205). Huizinga, then, while still useful in any study of play, serves as a cautionary tale against both teleological and apocalyptic narratives, which he unintentionally demonstrates are the same thing. He fails to see that there is no monolithic "culture" or universal definition of "play." Culture did not cease to be played in Victorian England; rather, it was played in ways specific to the conditions of a particular society.

Both sides of the anti-play/pro-play position run the risk of essentializing play. After all, the two sets of assumptions underlying that position—those about the recuperativeness of nineteenth-century realism and those about the liberatory nature of postmodern theory—are part of the same discursive complex. This observation is simultaneously so obvious and yet so infrequently made that it seems to indicate a possible case of ideological naturalization carried to the point of cultural amnesia. The point, stated for the moment as bluntly as possible, is that the most specific Other for the majority of post-structuralist and postmodern theories is nothing other than nineteenth-century realism. Post-structuralist theories are centrally concerned with the problems of signification contingent upon what Plato called "mimesis," and realism is the primary example of mimetic art among twentieth-century critics. Barthes and Derrida testify alike to this in the frequency and tenacity with which they both return to the problems of mimesis. Barthes confronts nineteenth-century realism again and again in such works as *S/Z*, *The Pleasure of the Text*, and *The Rustle of Language*. This is logical both historically and conceptually, since nineteenth-century realism is a dominant cultural form of the immediately preceding period and also is the single most thorough embodiment of and engagement with the problems of mimesis prior to the twentieth century and perhaps even to this day.

But my argument about the linkage between the play of nineteenth-century realist fictions and the play of late-twentieth-century theoretical writings does not depend on whether the latter takes the former as its object or topic. Quite the contrary. Postmodern theorists such as Deleuze or Baudrillard who have little or no interest in nineteenth-century realism but base their entire theoretical systems on play-derived terms are perhaps even more locked in the historical contest between play concepts. The most commonly shared strategy among postmodern theorists, who otherwise are unique and diverse, is to activate a form of play as the means of escaping logocentrism. Yet, at the very moment that this move promises to step outside all dualities, the taking of that step is, by its own definitions, contingent upon a final dichotomy between the "rational" play that supposedly characterizes logocentrism and the "prerational" play activated to undo it. One can leap into the abyss of play and wander among the infinite oscillations of indeterminacy, but if one does this in writing as a critic and not on the wall as a schizophrenic, then one unavoidably continues to participate in discourses of play that hearken back to before Plato. Fighting play with play perpetuates play.

By deconstructing the frequently assumed gulf between nineteenth-century realism and twentieth-century theory, I am suggesting that both periods and genres of writing are centrally concerned with issues of representation and signification that impinge upon the problems of mimesis. Mimesis as defined from Plato forward is the nut to crack at the center of representation, if not signification as well, François Rastier observes: "The concept of realism continuously and obsessively traverses all western reflection on the arts, from Plato to Breton. It merits particular attention, because it molded aesthetic practices themselves. Far from being a simple descriptive or episodic category (in the sense of nineteenth-century realism) the concept of realism determines the representational function of the arts, up to and including surrealism" (80).[22] It is ironic and disturbingly appropriate, then, when critics treat realism as a passé area of inquiry in the age of proliferating simulacra and the advent of virtual reality technologies, especially if the dismissal comes from a critic who also is engaged in disseminating a play-based theory for which realism is the unrecognized Other.[23]

For historical as well as theoretical reasons, nineteenth-century realism is the necessary Other of postmodern theory to an extent that generally is not recognized (and might be denied categorically) by more than a few postmodern theorists. The types of play othered (but also used) by Victorian texts bear strong resemblance to the types of play advocated and practiced by many postmodern theorists. Postmodern theory is in a sense as much the Other for Victorian realism as mimetic realism is the Other for postmodern theory. This is not to slight the analytical advances and paradigm-shifting significance of post-structuralist and postmodern theories, which after all supplied some of the tools by which I have been critiquing them and analyzing play. Nor is it to tout Victorian playfulness (though I will try to give the Victorians their due in this regard), because in certain practical ways the cliché holds. It simply is to return to the assertion with which I began this introduction, but now with somewhat more grounds for making it: any analysis of either Victorian play or postmodern play is in danger of being shortsighted if it neglects consideration of the other. The key to the connection is the play of mimesis.

The Realist Novel as Play Space

In a limited and perhaps obvious sense, the realist novelist is the Sophist of the nineteenth century, marketing her claim to present the real through a form that instead only represents "images of all things in a shadow play of discourse" (*Sophist* 977). Nineteenth-century realist novels raise mimetic play to a historical high point, enacting what may be the culmination of mimesis in its formal refinement throughout the century toward a more thorough elision of the author and effacement of the text's fictional status. The novel as such is constructed by and as play, Plato's nightmare of "bad play." On the other hand, it would not be fully accurate to claim that novelistic realism enacts pre-Platonic, performative "mimesis-play," as defined by Spariosu. Indeed, in another and equally limited sense, novelistic realism is the exemplar of Platonic "rational" play with its concern for redirecting the power, violence, chance, and Becoming of Dionysian "mimesis-play" toward Apollonian knowledge, truth, necessity, and Being. Where, then, is the point between these two extreme understandings of mimetic play that more adequately describes what nineteenth-century realist novels do?

Answering this question, or even phrasing it in the way that I have, requires some debunking of the recent critical consensus, exemplified, for instance, by Nancy Morrow's *Dreadful Games: The Play of Desire in the Nineteenth-Century Novel*. Morrow writes in relevant terms that the "emphasis, in the Realist novel, on human reason can be tied to the absence or suppression of the play spirit in so many fictional worlds: excessive rationalization undermines the spontaneity and freedom inherent in the playful exchange of desire" (170). Leo Bersani argues along similar lines in *A Future for Astyanax* that while "the eighteenth century offers numerous examples of a playful subversion" in its literary characters and plots, "[r]ealistic fiction serves nineteenth-century society by providing it with strategies for containing (and repressing) its disorder within significantly structured stories about itself" (58, 63). Although Morrow and Bersani are rigorous and convincing, a critical problem with these and related studies is the underlying and often unacknowledged assumption that somehow, some-

where there was, is, or could be play that is not contained within a form and
a form that is not contained within a society. As Jacques Lacan, Michel
Foucault, and D. T. Suzuki each argues, from extremely different perspectives, human desire is never free of context (and I could add Thomas
Hardy, among others, to this list). To recognize this is not to imply that
nineteenth-century realist novels do not strive to contain disorder, because
of course they do, nor is it to claim (at least not yet) that they are inherently
more playful than, say, late-twentieth-century performance poetry. It is only
to say in the first instance that they *have* a form and that like all forms,
including avant-garde and postmodern ones, they reflect social order and
impose an order on social discourses. Novelistic realism operates somewhere between the extremes of entirely "monological" discourse — the ser-
mon or the traditional philosophical treatise, for example — and the utter
formlessness of desire conceived in the idealistic way implied by Morrow or
Bersani.

One approach to a more complete understanding of nineteenth-
century realism is opened by the theories of Mikhail Bakhtin. Novels by
William Thackeray, Charlotte Brontë, and George Eliot, for instance, are
dialogical in the Bakhtinian sense. While they do no consist of a free or
unstructured interplay of voices, neither are they dominated by an "authoritative discourse," one that "permits no play with the context framing it, no
play with its borders, no gradual and flexible transitions, no spontaneously
creative stylizing variants" (*Dialogic* 343). Realist novels allow for play
among different "images of languages" and ideological discourses but
within the form-giving structures of realism and the novel (416). They
operate between no-play and all-play. They therefore enact what Sandy
Petrey describes, in an analysis of Honoré de Balzac's novella *Adieu*, as a
"third way": "Deconstructionists' rush to repudiate realism has posited two
kinds of language, one slavishly subordinated to extralinguistic facts, the
other gloriously independent of everything except its own exhilarating
playfulness. *Adieu* helps inaugurate the realist commitment to a third way, a
form of representation that labours in the world even though it enjoys the
same freedom from referentiality as the most effervescent postmodernisms"
("Balzac's Empire" 36–37). Realist form therefore can convey a recuperative bourgeois ideology as if it were universal truth while simultaneously
advancing a critique of middle-class society. It can enlist the reading subject
in a form and an activity that inculcate social disengagement, and in the
same moment it can offer possibilities for radically destablizing the existing
social order. The "third way" that makes such apparently contradictory
combinations of functions possible is mimetic play.

But to understand mimetic play in this way requires moving be-yond what has become the standard, ideological critique of realism. Doing so is made more difficult by the fact that such critique finds support in the definitions of "realism" offered in the critical writings of prominent, liberal-intellectual Victorians, such as Thackeray, Ruskin, Eliot, Lewes, and Bulwer-Lytton. But their definitions also are far from a "naïve realism" that assumes a "correspondence-theory of truth" or posits "a simple *adequation* between words and things" (Norris, *Derrida* 54). The paramount concern among Victorian writers was not with mirroring nature — though some claims are made in this regard — or even with the real per se; rather, these writers were concerned with *the true*. They defined the true precisely by its opposition to the real, which had connotations of solely empirical realism or verisimilitude (in a sense implied by Spariosu's definition of "mimesis-imitation"). The real/true distinction figures centrally, for instance, in Rus-kin's *Modern Painters*, in Eliot's famous review of that work, in the oft-cited chapter seventeen of *Adam Bede*, in Lewes's "Realism and Idealism," in Thackeray's preface to *Pendennis*, and in Bulwer-Lytton's critical defense of "le vrai" as opposed to the mere factuality of "le réel."[24] Yet the ambition on the part of nineteenth-century realist fictions to be vehicles for truth telling indeed is the ambition to be "philosophy" as Plato defines it, which is to be "good writing" as Derrida critiques it. If this were all that Victorian novels do, then they would be entirely monological and authoritative.

The question about the extent to which realist novels are monological or dialogical — more like propaganda or more like an open dialogue of difference — is both complicated and clarified by reference to the distinction between diegetic and mimetic writing strategies.[25] Traditional philosophi-cal writing is the exemplar of the diegetic approach of direct address to an implied reader (or to an interrogator who marks the place of reception), whereas the realist novel moved increasingly throughout the eighteenth and nineteenth centuries toward a high-mimetic strategy of effacing the narrative apparatus as the means of implying that the text is simply a win-dow onto historical events and real lives. Thus the question about whether realist novels are more authoritative in the Bakhtinian sense than philo-sophical texts might boil down to a question about which writing strategy (or mixed ratio of strategies) predominates in each form and which strat-egy, diegetic or mimetic, holds more pretense to truth telling (and so, by implication, more thoroughly recuperates dominant ideology). Ideological and postmodern criticisms of realism tend to assume that the latter is more recuperative, thus implicitly if perhaps unintentionally siding with Plato.

One of the best-known critiques of mimesis as a truth telling strategy is

Barthes's theory in *The Rustle of Language* of the "reality effect" of the "referential illusion." Barthes writes, "The truth of this illusion is this: eliminated from the realist speech-act as a signified of denotation, the 'real' returns to it as a signified of connotation; for just when these details are reputed to *denote* the real directly, all that they do — without saying so — is *signify* it; Flaubert's barometer, Michelet's little door, finally say nothing but this: *we are the real*; it is the category of 'the real' (and not its contingent contents) which is then signified; in other words, the very absence of the signified, to the advantage of the referent alone, becomes the very signifier of realism: the *reality effect* is produced, the basis of that unavowed verisimilitude which forms the aesthetic of all the standard works of modernity" (148). Barthes applies this analysis equally to the writing of history and of realist fiction, two genres that institutionalized in conjunction with one another during the eighteenth and nineteenth centuries.[26] He thereby reductively obscures important differences between the two. While the preceding passage may partially describe the operations of a historical text, which rests its authority on the fact, it provides an even less complete description of what realist novels *do* to establish truth-telling authority. In the first place, barometers and the like constitute a small part of novels like *Madame Bovary*, even if their signifying function is pervasive. More importantly, if Barthes's point is that the barometer effect is the means by which a text establishes a claim for itself to be, as a unitary whole, a signifier of the "category of 'the real,'" then he has done little more than show how all representational language can be reduced to the signifying function of the word. From that position it is a relatively small step to realize that Barthes's argument applies to all texts of all kinds, in short, to language period. It does not change the nature of signification, for instance, to say, "A barometer in a surrealist novel is not intended to signify a real barometer"; it always already does and does not.[27] Though the barometer effect obviously occurs in realist novels, it is only one of a much broader array of more sophisticated textual strategies, and Barthes has been an important teacher of this very fact. Both the ideological discourses and the truth-telling strategies of realist novels are more complicated than a categorical distinction between either dialogical and monological or mimesis and diegesis can explain.

The second point to make in this regard is that the truth that Victorian novels set themselves to convey is far from unequivocal or essentialized; the ideology that it represents cannot be adequately explained by a formulaic notion of "bourgeois ideology." One of the most pervasive representatives of truth in George Eliot's fiction, for example, is the widely noted Victorian trope of sympathy. At the first order of analysis the figure of sympathy might appear to be aligned with authenticity in direct opposition to play and, therefore, to function straightforwardly as a vehicle for middle-class ideology as typically conceived. But sympathy — like the realism for which it functions as a metonym — is more complicated than this.

In the first place, sympathy is the sign of the negotiability and precarious contingency of social reality, which, as John McGowan observes in *Representation and Revelation: Victorian Realism from Carlyle to Yeats*, is the ultimate referent in Eliot's realism: "The crucial development of Eliot's realism is the shift from a world of objects inertly perceived to human interaction with that world as the 'reality' to which words must 'refer'. . . . It becomes important to stress language's referential abilities precisely because the link between word and referent has become a problem" (134–35). Sympathy is the figure for the social reality to which words must refer, and that reality is anything but fixed.

In the second place, as I show in chapter three, sympathy operates through an effective splitting of the self that occurs as the prerequisite of the ability to identify with the suffering of another. The antecedent for this model is Adam Smith's *Theory of Moral Sentiments* (1759), in which the central concept of sympathy is defined in terms of a universal, internalized "impartial spectator."[28] According to Smith's inherently theatrical morality, the subject is doubly split: *externally* between the self as simultaneous spectator of others' actions *and* performer before society, and *internally* between a monitoring gaze or voice *and* the part of the self that is aware of performing its motives and feelings before this gaze or voice.[29] The subject simultaneously is severed from and joined to itself in one direction and simultaneously severed from and joined to society in the other. In Eliot as in Smith, sympathy ultimately is defined as a state of sustained indeterminacy: oscillation between internal and external, self and other. This variety of truth certainly is not identical to any essentialized presence or "referential plenitude" (Barthes, *Pleasure* 148).

In other words, sympathy is a figuration of play, the very same play that characterizes the realist novel's own mimetic oscillation between the inside and the outside of the text, fictional and factual, ideal truth and empirical reality. Analysis of the function of the figure of sympathy in nineteenth-century novels yields this equation: *realism = (truth = sympathy) = play*. Sympathy is a figure in the realist novel of the novel's own formal artifice. In the same moment, it is a trope for the sympathy that the text positions the implied reader to exercise. The reader exercises this sympathy not only through identification with the "sympathetic" hero or heroine (sympathetic precisely because of his or her ability to exercise sympathy), but also in the very act of reading the novel. The moral economy of sympathy balances self-distancing (and distancing from social action) against identification with the (self as) Other. The Other in this case is a fictional character or world, which in turn emblematizes through the thematic of sympathy an abstraction called "the wholeness of society," namely, culture. The ability to identify-with-while-remaining-distanced-from is one for which the reading of realist novels is the peculiarly suited training. Through this series of textual strategies, the realist novel's form directly enacts its own thematic and positions readers to participate in that enactment.

To claim that novels are "unaware" of this series of textual strategies is to practice critical and historical condescension. Bersani verges on doing this when he writes that "fiction unexpectedly — and, I think, unintentionally — points to its own status as purely verbal artifice by the ways in which it demonstrates the persistence of significant structures in modern life" (*Astyanax* 66). It is his "unintentionally" that I take exception with. Instead, I argue in line with Ann Jefferson when she writes: "In contrast to Barthes, Bakhtin is suggesting that there is nothing naïve about the language or codes of fiction, so that in analysing plot, character, authorial style or representational devices in a novel one always has to bear in mind the possibility that the text is conscious, if not critical, of the languages of which it is composed. The novel's capacity for self-criticism should accompany our examination of its every aspect" ("Intertextuality" 238). Jefferson draws here on Bakhtin's theory of the *"auto-criticism of discourse,"* which he argues is a "primary distinguishing characteristic of the novel as a genre": "Discourse is criticized in its relationship to reality: its attempt to faithfully reflect reality, to manage reality and to transpose it (the utopian pretenses of discourse), even to replace reality as a surrogate for it (the dream and the fantasy that replace life)" (*Dialogic* 412). Appropriately enough, another term that is analogous to "auto-criticism" in Bakhtin's writing is "play."[30] The figure of sympathy is one example of the nineteenth-century realist novel's "auto-criticism," one of the ways in which novels not only acknowledge an awareness of their textual artifice but also make that awareness a defining characteristic of their form. Far from only forwarding themselves as "good writing," the novels that I read in this book utilize their textual status and "exteriority" as "bad writing" very much in the Derridian sense (*Grammatology* 14ff.). To deny novels the use of their own textual strategies is precisely to ignore how post-structuralist theory has enabled us to see that the Victorian novel never was meant to be nor ever was read simply as a window on reality or a monological truth.

Far from trying to eradicate play, as critics traditionally have argued, nineteenth-century realist novels are bent on the infinite promulgation of play, their own play. They strive to disseminate the play of their form *into society*. Having written this and having worked throughout this chapter to break down the barriers that many critics assume separate realistic from postmodern writing, I now want to redouble that motion. While the dissemination of their formal play is the means by which realist texts unsettle, critique, and reshape dominant social assumptions, that play is at the very same time the aspect or mechanism that is most recuperative of dominant ideologies. What is more, this same logic applies equally to postmodern texts, though I cannot take the time here to substantiate that claim beyond the groundwork already laid for it. My point is that realist novels are equally as subversive *and* as recuperative as postmodern texts, *and in precisely the same way*: by disseminating their own textual play. The novels read here do this simultaneously at four levels: the word, the thematic image of society, the construction of the reader, and the cultural form.

Realist novels instigate play in the first place at the level of the word. Bakhtin analyzes the dialogical word as the site of intersection of overlapping utterances, which means something very different from simply saying that a word has multiple connotations. The "living word" contains "alien words about the same object"; between the word and its object and between the word and its speaker there is "an elastic environment of the other" (*Dialogic* 276). The word embodies the multiple and potentially contradictory social contexts from which its meanings resonate, as well as the ideological valences attached to each of those contexts of meaning. The word is the meeting place for the history of its uses and, at the same time, the conversation place for all of the various voices that use it at the historical moment in which it is used. If not forced to serve an authoritative discourse, the word becomes saturated with the play of uses and voices it contains, "penetrated by this dialogic play of verbal intentions that meet and are interwoven in it" (277). Surrendered to the intentions of other voices, given to the use of characters like Lucy Snowe in *Villette* or Leonora Halm-Eberstein in *Daniel Deronda*, the word may become what Julia Kristeva, following Bakhtin, calls "ambivalent."[31] "Ambivalence" occurs because the "historical word" (and the polyphonic novel it typifies) provides a "space" in which multiple contexts of meaning can converge intertextually: "Each word (text) is an intersection of words (texts) where at least one other word (text) can be read" (66, 74). A dialogical text is "*writing* where one reads the *other*"; therefore, "[d]ialogue and ambivalence are borne out as the only approach that permits the writer to enter history by espousing an ambivalent ethics: negation as affirmation" (39, 40).

This understanding of textual play at the level of the word is distinct from most post-structuralist theories of signification. In *The Pleasure of the Text*, for instance, Barthes celebrates the play of the reader and the "desiring text" in an infinite field of textuality where all "value [is] shifted to the sumptuous rank of the signifier" (65). In contrast, I recognize the play of signification as a prerequisite condition of the play of the *social word*. That recognition rests in turn on a recognition of the materiality of language and of the fact that discourse produces material consequences, makes things happen. These theoretical and methodological commitments align *Serious Play* not with any one school of criticism but rather with a diverse range of Marxist or post-Marxist, materialist, social discourse, and speech-act theorists who nevertheless share a concern with the social word.[32]

In the second place, realist novels instigate a revision of their social context in the image of their own formal play. As my analysis of the figure of sympathy suggests — and to appropriate the terms developed by J. L. Austin in *How to Do Things with Words* — the "constative" truth of realist novels is that truth inherently is "performative": conventional, socially contingent, negotiated through its enactment. Or, as Petrey puts it in *Realism and Revolution: Balzac, Stendhal, Zola, and the Performances of History*, "The fundamental realist discovery [is] that the social resonance of any sign is invariably a performative act in which the absence of a solid referent is irrelevant to the presence of a solid signified" (70). Petrey's point is that the historical work and social functions of language go on not in spite of but precisely because there is no determinate referent. The only referent is "a reality produced by communal agreement to act *as if* denotation were feasible" (*Realism* 6). Further, nineteenth-century realist texts do not avoid or even simply acknowledge this condition but actively exploit it as an opportunity (George Eliot might say a moral obligation) to participate in the construction of social discourses.

And this is precisely what realist novels *do*: they perform a revised version of society into existence by both thematically representing and formally enacting a reality that is similar to but "truer" than social reality. Nineteenth-century liberal intellectuals thought this necessary because they feared that their social reality was too concerned with exploitative relationships, social advancement, material wealth, and the merely empirical truth of facts. A distinguishing characteristic of realism, then, is the extent to which the images of society that it provides are simultaneously *very* like and *very* unlike the predominant understanding of what the social reality is. The gap between the two images of society is the site of play. That play is experienced by readers as an oscillation between the imaginary and the real, the fictional world and the social world in which they sit. One might even argue that the greater the verisimilitude of the literary representation the more intense is the oscillating play between the two. One effect of this is to destabilize the "reality" of reality.[33] This in turn opens society to discursive revision, which is precisely the means by which works of literature contribute to the constitution of social reality.[34] This is a defining purpose and characteristic of mimetic play. In one sense, realism thus understood is the opposite of its conception in the critiques of it mounted by some modernist and postmodernist critics. Indeed, "realism" might best be defined as any cultural form that engages readers in a continuous oscillation between contexts of meaning to which the readers themselves actively contribute.

In the third place, readers continuously participate in this play, moving back and forth between their material society and the fictional society within the novel. Readers simultaneously know that the fictional world is not real *and* feel that it is; at the same time, they know their social existence is real *and* increasingly sense — in the process of reading — that their knowledge of that existence is mediated by signification in a way not unlike the fictional world. Wolfgang Iser's *The Fictive and the Imaginary: Charting Literary Anthropology* is a book-length analysis of this process, which he describes in terms that support the argument here about mimetic play: "Just as the fictionalizing act outstrips the determinacy of the real, so it provides the imaginary with the determinacy that it would not otherwise possess. . . . Reproduced reality is made to point to a 'reality' beyond itself, while the imaginary is lured into form. . . . Consequently, extratextual reality merges into the imaginary, and the imaginary merges into reality" (3). To simplify Iser's terms, "the fictive" can be understood as an oscillating transaction between the text and its social context(s), and "the imaginary" as an oscillating transaction between readers and the text. For Iser, historical readers are the sites where these boundary-crossing transactions take place; readers activate texts just as fictions provide the stage on which the "impossibility of being present to ourselves becomes our possibility to play ourselves," to enact our "human plasticity" (xi, xviii). The fictive and the imaginary are in one sense empty or potential spaces until activated by reading. Each individual, unique reading is the event of the interactive definition of the fictive and the imaginary. The name that Iser adopts for this process is "play."[35]

One use to which Iser applies these concepts is to try to explain the social specificity of writing and of individual readings in relation to the historical continuity of a cultural form: how can a text be both specific to the social context from which it was produced and also "open" to produce new readings within later societies of readers? Iser argues that texts remain "open to the imprint of history," because the oscillating "doubling" between contexts of meaning that takes place in the act of reading "manifests itself as a play space in which all the different discourses come together to form the matrix that enables the text to end up with a potentially infinite variety of relations to its surroundings" (xii, 228). I would both expand Iser's model and make it more explicitly historical. One could revise his notion of "the fictive" to recognize that it is constituted in relation to a specific social context. That context is preserved in an interpreted form in the text's representations of the social discourses of that context, which in turn are reinterpreted by each reader in relation to her own historical context. Similarly, "the imaginary" is constituted from within the social context of the individual reader, which is both historically distinct from and related to that from which the text was written. Readers assess the realism of a text in relation to their own social existence through an incredibly complex, continuous series of iterative comparisons between what might be called the *context of inception* and the *context of reception*.[36] This is the historical nature of play that mimesis disseminates.

Finally, the fourth way that realist novels promulgate their own play is by reproducing themselves as a cultural form. Rather than analyzing as Barthes does the ways in which the "desiring text" disseminates its play within a universal, synchronic structure of signification, I analyze how a specific cultural form propagates itself in very material ways: by contributing to the discourse production and consumption behaviors of a society that it helps create, the society of readers. What Barthes calls the "pleasure of the text" is more accurately reconceived as the pleasures of quite specific reading audiences — consumers of culture — without whom a cultural form such as the realist novel will fail to reproduce itself by failing in the first place to be printed, purchased, and read. The continued existence and success of realist novels depends, then, on the constitution and proliferation of a specific subject position. The subsequent chapters theorize the position of the *reading subject* as one that is inwardly directed and self-reflexive, socially isolated and deactivated, and engaged in the cultivation of the capacity for identification with others. This is the ultimate output of mimetic play.

There is no such thing as a monolithic form called "realism"; rather, what we call "realism" is a bundle of shifting, historically specific, and potentially contradictory textual strategies operating simultaneously at levels ranging from the word to the cultural form. However, all of these strategies — those that produce a seamless experience of "realism" and those that reveal textual self-consciousness or foreground textual artifice, those that obviously recuperate bourgeois ideologies and those that mount a critique against those same ideologies — all of these contribute to the reproduction of the reading subject. The novels that I read in the following chapters stage within their pages contests between figures representing their own cultural form and figures representing other cultural forms, such as melodramatic theater or Romantic poetry. These representations are part of those novels' discourse about their own mimetic play, as well as the acting out of their claim to victory over other cultural forms in terms of control over the play of signification that we call "writing." At the same time, they are part of what is perhaps best described as marketing. In discussing nineteenth-century realist novels, competition for entertainment market share and for the discursive exercise of power within society are inseparable from consideration of mimetic play.

Gambling with Fortuna

At a time when the poor were existing on wages that could be counted in shillings per week rather than pounds, and women could be employed at a penny an hour in the Welsh coal-mines, Harry Hastings lost more than one hundred thousand pounds in the two-and-a-half minutes in which it took to run the Derby.

Henry Blyth, *Hell and Hazard*

Gaming / Gambling

Why is the figure of the gambler, the "player," a common feature of so many nineteenth-century novels? Why does it function pivotally in multiple works by a number of prominent Victorian novelists, notably William Makepeace Thackeray, Charles Dickens, George Eliot, and Anthony Trollope?[1] Scenes of gambling, of course, appear in earlier novels (*Tom Jones* and *Moll Flanders*, for example). However, in the four decades between *Wuthering Heights* (1847) — in which Heathcliff's power depends on the winning of the Heights from Hindley Earnshaw at cards — and *The Return of the Native* (1878) — in which the plot unwinds around the preternatural defeat of Wildeve by Diggory Venn at dice — gambling becomes a figure of more frequent and more intense inspection in the novel. Indeed, "gambling" does not exist as the set of social discourses and institutions by which it still is recognized until the end of the eighteenth century and does not find commensurate literary expression until the mid-Victorian period. This chapter investigates these claims and the questions from which they issue through analysis of gambling primarily in two novels that appeared near the end of this period, George Eliot's *Middlemarch* (1872) and Anthony Trollope's *The Duke's Children* (1880). I situate novelistic representations of gambling in relationship to the gambling practices and gambling legislation of the period and analyze the figure of gambling as part of the Victorian discourse of money, treating it as one among the other channels through which capital was circulated in nineteenth-century Britain. Money in general and gambling in particular were so troubling to the Victorians in part because they emphasized the association between value and values. Thus gambling infiltrated two central Victorian registers of value—work and marriage—functioning as the problematizing link between these two areas and money. Gambling also unavoidably served as a marker for the waves of financial speculation and panic that were endemic to nineteenth-century Britain, and the image of speculation came to be associated disturbingly with moral and metaphysical speculations. The intensity of concern with gambling found in novels of this period like *Middlemarch* and *The Duke's Children* is representative of broader social concerns that were conditioned by specific historical circumstances and, therefore, were not produced by the play of chance alone.[2]

In a literal if limited sense, gambling comes into existence in Britain only near the end of the eighteenth century. The *Oxford English Dictionary* makes this point in its etymology of "gamble": "The vb. has not been found till about 1775–86; the apparent derivatives GAMBLER, GAMBLING . . . occur earlier, and in the 18th c. were regarded as slang. The word is prob. a dialectal survival of an altered form of . . . OE. *gamenian* to sport, play, f. *gamen* GAME." Up until that time, what is now called gambling was more often thought of and referred to as "gaming" and was represented as a distinguishing characteristic of the upper classes. The seventeenth- and eighteenth-century "gamester" was as much or more someone who took part in the typically aristocratic leisure activities of field sports, private theatricals, and chivalric courtship as someone who "play[ed] at games of chance for money or other stake." Gaming was a defining part of a traditional aristocratic ethos; the ability to win with magnanimity, to lose with dignity, and to honor gambling debts without question became one mark of a true gentleman. More than one gambling historian has theorized that "those whose status is based on the aleatory principle of heredity will cultivate it at play" (Downes et al. 14). So meetings on the green baize in part replaced meetings on the jousting green as the arena in which character was to be proved and the regard of providence tested.

Thus discourses about gaming underwent a significant change from around the time of the French Revolution (1789–94), when "gambling" started to supplant "gaming." Historian Phyllis Deutsch marks this change from the parliamentary electoral defeat in 1784 of Charles James Fox; Fox's legendary personal gambling became an emblem in the public's mind of an aristocracy that was placing the nation at the mercy of Fortuna by wagering future prosperity against a ballooning national debt. In its early uses, gambler was defined as a "fraudulent gamester, a sharper," and, secondarily, as "one who habitually plays for money, esp. for extravagantly high stakes" (*OED*). The term was used as often to describe the "stock jobbers" or "stags" who gambled with financial instruments and national economies as to describe those who gambled with cards or dice. In *The History of Gambling in England* (1898), for example, John Ashton wrote: "*Gambling*, as distinguished from *Gaming*, or playing, I take to mean an indulgence in those games, or exercises, in which *chance* assumes a more important character; and my object is to draw attention to the fact, that the *money motive* increases, as chance predominates over skill. It [gambling, as opposed to gaming] is taken up as a quicker road to wealth than by pursuing honest industry, and everyone engaged in it, be it dabbling on the Stock Exchange, Betting on Horse Racing, or otherwise hopes to win. . . . [S]o we either appropriate our neighbours' goods, or he does ours, by gambling with him, for it is certain that if one gains, the other loses. The winner is not reverenced, and the loser is not pitied. But it is a disease that is most contagious" (2). By the mid-nineteenth century, chance and "the money motive" overshadowed the play aspects of gambling; gambler almost completely replaced gamester in the English lexicon (Deutsch 4). By the Victorian period, "the origins of gaming as play were suppressed": "Once gaming was detached from the meaningful world of play [as a culture-specific practice], it lost its ability to focus and valorize aristocratic identity, community, and rank" (Deutsch 229). The nature of antigambling rhetoric likewise underwent revision: "Critics of gaming in the previous century had also criticized those who made play an occupation, but they were as concerned with the abuse of *playful* activity as they were with its uncanny resemblance to adventure capitalism. Victorians who criticized the professionalization of gaming were concerned *only* with its complex relationship to the principles of commerce, money making, and trade" (Deutsch 229). This is consistent with the cultural and social paradigm shift away from a certain, traditional aristocratic ethos — especially after the widely touted decadence of the Regency — toward the characteristically middle-class conceptions of gambling, money, and work that typified nineteenth-century British civil society.

But the figure of gambling-as-play persists, if often to be demonized, throughout Victorian fiction. In *Middlemarch* one reads that Fred Vincy "liked play, especially billiards, as he liked hunting or riding a steeplechase; and he only liked it the better because he wanted money and hoped to win"

(*MM* 229). When Fred's aristocratic pretensions and penchant for gambling are corrected by the combined efforts of Mr. Farebrother and the Garth family, Caleb Garth instructs Fred as follows: "You must love your work, and not be always looking over the edge of it, wanting your play to begin" (543). Here "play" holds all of its connotations, but most pointedly those associated with gambling. When Dr. Lydgate observes Mr. Farebrother's gambling at whist (before it is corrected by the combined efforts of Lydgate and Dorothea Brooke), he is disturbed to see that "the vicar should obviously play for the sake of money" (*MM* 176). When Lydgate himself is later driven by debt to the devices of gambling (and is corrected, ironically and logically, by the combined efforts of Vincy and Farebrother), one reads that "play" had reduced the normally self-possessed gentleman to the semblance of "an animal with fierce eyes and retractile claws" (*MM* 652).

These examples suggest several points that will require further analysis. First, the play of gambling functioned as a boundary marker between different sources of value and particularly in relation to work. Second, gambling was troubling in this regard especially because of its multifold relationship to money. Gambling places the value that money represents under the sign of fortune, chance, fate. What is worse, gambling threatened to reveal its analogical relationship to paper money and to the chancy flow of abstract value in the speculative channels of market capitalism. Gambling appears as exchange for the pleasure of exchange, exchange without conscience, or, as the Duke of Omnium suggests in *The Duke's Children*, "progress without reflection" (*DC* 516). Third, the discourse of gambling is internally conflicted. Fred Vincy's play is condemned by the text because it is too aristocratic; he plays without due regard for the value of money and without appropriately sober concern with the consequences of losing. Fred plays too playfully. Farebrother's play is condemned for the opposite reason. He gambles calculatedly for financial gain, which is antithetical to an aristocratic ethos according to which gambling should be a sign of one's freedom from need. His too unplayful play ("gambling" as opposed to "gaming") foregrounds the prescribed boundary between play and work in a way that brings it into question. The novel seems to suggest that if one could play without erring in either direction, then perhaps play might be acceptable. However, the inhabitants of Middlemarch find it all but impossible to balance on such a slim and precarious middle ground.

Lydgate, for example, starts the novel with a middle-class attitude toward play but with an aristocratic attitude toward money: "Lydgate was no puritan, but he did not care for play, and winning money at it had always seemed a meanness to him. . . . Money had never been a motive to him" (*MM* 176). After marriage to Rosamond Vincy, who trumps his aristocratic attitude toward money, Lydgate swings to the opposite extreme. He gambles in a context—the Green Dragon pub—that admits shady horse traders such as Mr. Bambridge and with a desperation that links him to what Victorian texts typically represent as one of two things: debauched aristocratic play or lower-class gambling fever. A prime example of the former is Lord Grex, whose gambling tragically compromises his daughter Lady Mabel Grex in *The Duke's Children*. A prime example of the latter is Lapodith in George Eliot's *Daniel Deronda*, who likewise tragically compromises his daughter Mirah through compulsive indulgence in "a passion for watching chances—the habitual suspensive poise of the mind in actual or imaginary play" (*DD* 843). After Lydgate receives an education in the bitter necessities of marriage and money, he comments in similar terms to Farebrother (the very person whose gambling he had criticized): "I don't see that there's any money-getting without chance . . . if a man gets it in a profession, it's pretty sure to come by chance" (*MM* 625). The narrator of *Middlemarch* cannot but label this attitude of Lydgate's as "the cynical pretence that all ways of getting money are essentially the same and that chance has an empire which reduces choice to a fool's illusion" (*MM* 641). As any reader of George Eliot would know, her novels strive to show that the different ways of getting money are far from the same and that the play between chance and necessity should be mediated by choice, even when choice cannot change circumstance.

Choice, Circumstance, Chance

> Only in the eighteenth century, in "civil society," do the various forms of social connectedness confront the individual as a mere means towards his private purposes, as external necessity.
>
> Karl Marx, *The Grundrisse*

One of the reasons that gambling is a figure of particular significance in nineteenth-century British fiction is because it unavoidably brings to the fore the issues of free will and determinism that especially troubled Victorian society. These issues have received substantial critical attention, including a recent book-length treatment by John Reed that identifies five "primary reasoned positions" represented in Victorian texts: "(1) materialistic determinism or necessarianism, which concentrated on the law of invariable consequence, or cause and effect; (2) providential order, which allowed varying degrees of human freedom; (3) predestinarianism, which was confined mainly to the more aggressive dissenting religious sects; (4) fatalism, which allowed for the existence of a malign or indifferent principle active in the universe against which free will might or might not be operable; and (5) chance, which assumed no necessary concatenation of events" (*Victorian Will* 402). Reed expresses a critical commonplace in observing that a generalized cultural shift from providential to deterministic thinking occurred throughout the nineteenth century, a shift from (2) and (3) to (1) and (4). George Eliot's fiction in many ways captures that shift, and the deterministic philosophy that her writings come to embrace has a long tradition of analysis.[3] Eliot's "tragic" worldview is illustrated by this assertion from the closing paragraph of *Middlemarch*: "For there is no creature whose inward being is so strong that it is not greatly determined by what lies outside it" (*MM* 811). The telling words here are inward, which introduces the pervasive dialectic of inward and outward, and greatly, which leaves some room, however small, for self-determination. The inward/outward dialectic can be translated as will (or *hybris*) versus destiny (or *nemesis*), but to leave the matter at that is greatly to simplify what is represented much more complexly in Victorian fictions. Eliot's fiction admits of neither extreme; her nonfiction writings argue explicitly against both "free will" and what she called "necessitarianism."[4] Thus George Levine summarizes the doctrine that her writings express as a belief "that the world is rigidly determined, even in cases of human choice, but that man remains responsible for his actions" ("Determinism" 350). Far from attributing deterministic force to the traditional sources — Providence or Fate — Eliot's determinism upholds a "secular and scientific concept of a destiny inherent in the natural laws of an indifferent universe" (Bonaparte 22). This system depends on a causal model and a continuous chronology that links past to present to future.

One typical error made by Eliot's characters, then, is to assume that they can escape their past deeds. In *Middlemarch*, Bulstrode the banker commits this error in assuming that the unethical means by which he accrued his wealth can be cleared by the spiritual ends that he has convinced himself he now is achieving. The text will demand that means justify ends, that the past be justified in the present. Unfortunately for Dr. Lydgate, he becomes embroiled in Bulstrode's inexorably unfolding destiny, again through the medium of money, the same dirty money. Bulstrode sponsors the infectious diseases hospital that Lydgate will head and then, near the end of the novel, again compromises him by the loan of £1,000 under questionable circumstances. The terms used by the narrator to describe Lydgate's perspective on his own intended charity work for the hospital are telling in this regard: "He did not mean to imitate those philanthropic models who make a profit out of poisonous pickles to support themselves while they are exposing adulterations, or hold shares in a gambling-hell that they may have leisure to represent the cause of public morality" (*MM* 145). It is part of the irony of the text that neither Lydgate nor the reader will know for five hundred pages yet that this is a chillingly accurate description of Bulstrode, who "won his fortune" through a speculative marriage and foul play and is attempting to absolve himself through a combination of hospital charity and self-righteous condemnation of others' lack of religious zeal (*MM* 705). It is again both ironic and appropriate that Bulstrode's past is brought back to haunt him in the form of a character whose name is a type of gambling — Raffles — and whom Caleb Garth describes as looking like "one of those men one sees about after the races" (*MM* 507). Truly, as the narrator observes, "Destiny stands by sarcastic with our *dramatis personae* folded in her hand" — folded like manuscript pages, principally, but also like a hand of cards (*MM* 95).

Yet Bulstrode is not damned mechanistically. It is not that he committed certain wrong acts in the past that therefore unavoidably will return to destroy him no matter what else he may do. If this were the case, then there would be a directly linear and utterly inescapable relationship between past and present, which would obviate choice and responsibility. This would be the "necessitarianism" to which Eliot opposed her deterministic creed. Bulstrode's most egregious error, rather, is that he fails in the present to own and learn from those past deeds and thus continues to commit acts of a similar nature without being fully consciousness of doing so. He is who he is because of who he was, but if he could recognize who he was and, as a result, change who he is now (in consciousness), then his past self presumably would lose at least some of its fatal hold on him, or so the logic of the text suggests.[5] Eliot's determinism allows — indeed requires — an attempt at self-creation, which is why reflexivity and self-improvement (education, growth) are so important in her fiction. This reading is supported by Bulstrode's "accidental" contribution to Raffles's death and his subsequent attitude toward that event, as here the narrator comments: "It was that haunting ghost of his earlier life which . . . he was trusting that Providence had delivered him from. Yes, Providence. He had not confessed

to himself yet that he had done anything in the way of contrivance to this
end [Raffles's death]; he had accepted what seemed to have been offered. It
was impossible to prove that he had done anything which hastened the
departure of that man's soul" (*MM* 696). This last sentence is written from
within Bulstrode's character zone and clearly is the character's own rationalization, to which the text's implicit response is: impossible to prove does
not mean innocent. The legal system is not the most important law in
Eliot's novels.

In other words, Bulstrode fails to achieve the reflexive self-awareness
that the "novel of experience" demands, to adopt the terms that Thomas
Kavanagh applies to the eighteenth-century French novel in *Enlightenment
and the Shadows of Chance: The Novel and the Culture of Gambling in Eighteenth-Century France*: "The novel of experience became for its audience the
cornerstone of a new individuality and a new identity. Characters existed
not so much in terms of what they did as in terms of their awareness of the
reasons why they acted as they did. The novel's narrative of choice became
the story of a reflexive self-awareness moving along determined and compelling pathways" (118). Bulstrode therefore fails to represent the type of
individualized subject-position that the novel uses as a vehicle of identification for carrying the reader along its "determined and compelling pathways" (while Dorothea, for instance, succeeds in modeling that position).
Fred Vincy very nearly fails for reasons that might appear to be the same.
Like Bulstrode, Fred banks on providence, as here the narrator wryly comments to the implied reader: "You will hardly demand that his confidence
should have a basis in external facts; such confidence, we know, is something less coarse and materialistic: it is a comfortable disposition leading us
to expect that the wisdom of providence or the folly of our friends, the
mysteries of luck or the still greater mystery of our high individual value in
the universe, will bring about agreeable issues such as are consistent with
our good taste in costume and our general preference for the best style of
thing" (*MM* 224). The particular sign of this condition is, of course, Fred's
gambling. As Felicia Bonaparte writes, gambling is "only symptomatic of a
far more general condition which appears frequently as a blind faith in some
unspecified providence whose personal benevolence, the character believes,
must interfere with the cosmic order on his behalf" (17). Fred's error is in
believing that *character* will manifest itself, as if by magic, in the desired
material outcomes. This is a category error within the logic of the text, a
confusion of inward and outward, self and other, that results from a naïve
belief in the efficacy of individual identity and will. In one sense, then, this is

the opposite of Bulstrode's error, which is to absolve the self's responsibility in reference to a providential other, namely, God. Bulstrode believes that the present can obviate responsibility for the past, while Fred believes that an imagined future can obviate present responsibility. Thus *Middlemarch*, like all of Eliot's novels, describes two reciprocal types of error in this regard. One can err by subscribing to providence (chance, fate, luck, coincidence, or gambling), thereby assuming that one's choices and responsibilities are excused by a blessing or, in the worst case scenario, refused through a curse by a malignant power. Or one can err by subscribing to free will and by thus assuming that one's own desires can be realized independently of circumstance. Both of these positions are symptomatized by gambling of one form or the other.

To say that the former of these two positions overvalues will and that the latter overvalues destiny is to miss the point as represented in Eliot's fiction. Rather, the former position confuses will or desire with *choice*, which always is constrained and provisional; the latter position similarly confuses destiny or providence with *circumstance*, which increases rather than decreases individual responsibility. Both positions fail to account for the nature of the relationship between choice and circumstance. Both fail to balance self against other in the prescribed proportions. In the arena of the realist novel where individual choice is pitted against and tested by the constraints of circumstance, circumstance, as the embodiment of deterministic force, is vastly advantaged. It is this very condition, however, that places a greater rather than a lesser premium on the active exercise of moral choice.[6] Present choices can and (according to Eliot) should be informed by an understanding of one's past actions. This is in part because one's choices, or the consequences of them, become part of one's circumstances. Though never singularly determining or ever guaranteed to have a predictable effect, a choice or action becomes one among the large number of determinants that converge in each moment of each individual's life and that constitute one's circumstances. Every choice and action is overdetermined by a proliferation of probable causes, which is also to say that not one of them necessarily is determining.[7] No simple dichotomy such as that often attributed to freedom/necessity or will/destiny can be drawn between choice and circumstance.

Far from positing a one-dimensional linear model of causation, then, Eliot's model might be described in mathematical terms as the sum of the forces generated by the intersections of a potentially infinite number of vectors in an n-dimensional space. A less cumbersome name for this is "society," society as a quasi-natural or organic mutuality (which is to say, society as "culture" in the Arnoldian sense that I analyze in chapter four). One frequently commented figure that Eliot repeatedly uses to represent society or circumstance is the web of human relations and intersecting human lots.[8] As Eliot's narrator comments: "I at least have so much to do in unravelling certain human lots and seeing how they were woven and interwoven that all the light I can command must be concentrated on this particular web, and not dispersed over that tempting range of relevancies called the universe" (*MM* 140). This is the central claim of the realist novel: to report the convergence of a collection of lots as if they were sampled directly, even randomly, from the fabric of the (natural/social) universe. The implication is that the novel is a frame set upon reality and that the web of "relevancies" continues unpredictably but determinedly beyond that frame. Characters that meet within the frame become one another's web. Thus, it is not even sufficient to be an upright individual or to have an awareness as an individual of one's own past actions and current motives, as may be the case with Dr. Lydgate, for instance (and as the above quotation from Kavanagh might imply). One must be sensitive to one's context, adaptive to the changes that may occur at any time, because social context, like past actions, will take on determining force in one's life. Dr. Lydgate is the example of what happens to those who underestimate or fail to comprehend circumstance. He believes that he can impose rationalized reforms on Middlemarch's entrenched medical customs; he believes that his vote for the chaplaincy of the new hospital can be made independently; he believes that the loan (or bribe) of £1000 is between himself and Bulstrode, or himself and his conscience, even as it turns out to be between him and Middlemarch society. To his distress, he learns that gossip, like money, is a medium of circulation by which people are connected to one another in the web of society.[9] Bulstrode is caught in the inescapable connections traced first by money and then by gossip, and Lydgate narrowly escapes being similarly trapped between the two. To fail to heed social connectedness, then, is to gamble with one's lot.

Accordingly, chance meetings and coincidental events pose a particularly sticky problem, not only for Eliot's determinism but for realist novels in general (and perhaps for all narrative forms). On the one hand, if coincidences in daily life "really do happen," then a novel is only more "realistic" in portraying them, perhaps even more realistic for portraying utterly unexpected events, those said to have happened "by chance."[10] On the other hand, to admit chance and coincidence appears antithetical to the belief that, in order to be real or believable, events in general should conform to a commonsense logic of probability. As Kavanagh argues, however, the modern scientific discourse of probability arose in the eighteenth century alongside the formulation of the modern novel, and not without correlation: "Like probability theory, the novel imposed itself during the eighteenth century as a form privileging a representation of the present as the movement from a known past to an uncertain future. Like probability theory, the novel depended for its significance on an ability to solicit the reader's identification with its rationalized and causally integrated sequencing of events. Like probability theory, the novel promised a greater understanding and mastery of life's apparently random events" (117). In other words, the "unreality" of chance and coincidence was *produced* in the process of inventing what came to be recognized as "reality" within a worldview shared and propagated by the ethos of novelistic realism and the ethos of scientific rationality. (The widely noted impact of Comtean positivism on the thinking of George Henry Lewes and George Eliot, among others, is relevant in this regard.) What is more, any narrative form, but especially that of novelistic realism, *must* work against chance and coincidence to the extent that it stages the intersection of characters and events that appear causally related, if only because they are thus brought together. These characters and events then appear to progress (if only because time passes and the reader is still reading) through a series of incidents that generally follow a traditional narrative pattern and end unavoidably at some point in some form of closure.[11]

In this way, narrative forms operate by manipulating the ambiguous boundaries between the incredible, the too predictable, and, between these, the probable. Narratives do this to keep readers reading, which is to say that narratives rely heavily upon what Gillian Beer analyzes as the "reader's wager" on the outcome of events. The chance meetings and coincidental events that occur in Eliot's fictions therefore represent precarious moments for the maintenance of textual artifice. The highly improbable connections — such as the series of links that bring Bulstrode and Will Ladislaw together with the recognition that Bulstrode's first wife was Will's grandmother — are not to be read as the product of chance or coincidence alone. Certain conventions of nineteenth-century realism require, on the one hand, that these moments appear as "naturally" coincidental. At the same time, deterministic logic requires that they not be read as *purely* coincidental; they are to seem naturally determined. If their determined nature becomes too apparent, determinism risks appearing as providential order, realism verges on melodrama (as discussed at length in chapter three), and the figure of the author as the invisible God looms threateningly near the surface of the text. The smoothness or sophistication with which George Eliot typically handles this balancing act is a testament to her skill as a writer; nevertheless, chance and coincidence persist in her texts, as in all realist texts, as sites of potential contradiction and disruption.

For directly related formal and philosophical reasons, then, opposition to chance is at the heart of George Eliot's determinism. Gambling, as the paradigm example of surrendering to chance, cannot help but be made a scapegoat. Randomness and unpredictability undermine the necessary obligation of individuals to society and circumstance and, in the opposite direction, undercut the efficacy of choice and responsibility. Within Eliot's deterministic system, chance is the site of the amoral, which is *more* dangerous than the immoral by being outside moral reality all together. Chance raises the specter of the end of moral order in the universe. As D. M. Downes and coauthors observe in *Gambling, Work and Leisure*, traditional opposition to gambling in western societies consistently invokes this basic theme: "gambling rests on *chance*, and chance is a non-ethical (even *anti-ethical*) basis for the distribution of reward" (24). A universe modeled on random rewards and punishments offers no basis for merit or moral worth, or so it appeared to many bourgeois, liberal-intellectual Victorians for whom Darwin's theory of natural selection (1859) seemed to promise just such a universe. George Eliot's deterministic universe can be thought of as a stopgap measure in response to the perceived encroachment of a random universe, for which gambling served as the primary figure. Eliot's determinism therefore privileges a continuous model of time, a model of individual responsibility that demands active moral choice, a progressive model of personal development that depends in large part on individual striving, and, as a complement to individual choice, a model of society as a web of mutual sympathy and judgment.

Gambling is in every way antithetical to these qualities. It rests on a discontinuous model of time; past and future are severed from one another by a moment of suspension that relies on neither past nor future and claims the potential to alter both. Thus gambling is simultaneously escape from history and desire for sheer presence. Gambling surrenders the long-term for immediate gratification and sometimes is represented as a form of premature gratification (the same logic that underlies Freud's notion of gambling as masturbation). Individual responsibility is suspended, if only for the moment, and control over one's destiny is relinquished to chance. This sort of passivity is antithetical to the values of personal development and individual striving. Gambling replaces merit with chance, virtue with luck and a taste for risk. It attempts to escape and replace work as the means of producing value, which is consistent with one of the oldest criticisms of gambling: that it interferes with work, leads to or indicates sloth, and is only a means of trying to get something for nothing. By the same token, it dangerously reproduces itself, its own motion, for no other reasons than the perpetuation of excitement and, significantly, the circulation of money. This fetishization of that motion — circulation for circulation's sake — is stereotyped in the mechanical, repetitive motion of the rabidly addicted gambler.[12] Finally, gambling is isolating; when one gambles, one is alone with one's fate. It therefore destroys the image that is vital in Eliot's fiction of society as connectedness through circumstance.

If, as the preceding suggests, gambling "signifies a break in the moral closure of the dominant system" (Downes 26), it does so in part because in the nineteenth century it came to represent the indistinguishability of Providence and chance. Providence, as the ultimate determining force within the Christian tradition, became increasingly less tenable, while the apparent alternative, a belief in the sheer randomness of chance, was potentially terrifying. The response of George Eliot and other bourgeois liberal intellectuals was an appeal to scientific rationality on the one hand and to a social communality based on mutual sympathy on the other. Both positions required the domestication of chance, as Downes observes: "Chance events, which can only be incorporated in science as symptoms of inadequate knowledge, nevertheless pose problems of meaning which men resolve by resort to transcendental schemes, as in religion, magic and superstition. In our heavily rationalistic culture, gambling is the *only* area in which permissive attitudes towards such notions as luck and superstition prevail. Gambling thus encapsulates the area of mystery diffused throughout life in general but culturally 'silenced' in most institutional areas. It becomes, therefore, a laboratory for probing the meaning and grounds of the self's relationship to things and nature" (26). The very form of the nineteenth-century realist novel was an attempt to address these "problems of meaning" without resort to "transcendental schemes." The "area of mystery" for which gambling is a primary marker is perhaps the most pervasive and troubling issue within Victorian fiction. The moral perturbation that this issue elicited can be measured by the effort expended in rationalizing it. Eliot's determinism thus strains to demonstrate that what appears to be chance only appears so because of "inadequate knowledge." Given perfect foreknowledge of the manifold determinants impinging upon any given choice or action and a universalized perspective on the weblike spread of mutually determining ramifications of the choices made by all the actors within a social context, one presumably would be able to observe the systematic unfolding of the "lots" of all those actors. This description aptly fits the position prescribed by George Eliot's fiction for the ideal implied reader. The only world in which this sort of perspective appears to be available is the world provided by the realist novel, and the only positions to which this perspective can be available are those of the author and of the reader as constructed in and as the realist text.

Extraliterary Antigambling Discourse

The nineteenth-century realist novel, perhaps more than any preceding or subsequent broadly disseminated cultural form, functioned as a vehicle for antigambling discourse. In this, as in many other ways, novels both reflected and constructed broader cultural trends and societal concerns, which therefore also were represented through other forms of discourse. Gambling legislation was one form of discourse that took on particular significance in Georgian and Victorian society. In the 1820s, a series of acts of Parliament outlawed participation in lotteries, whether domestic or foreign, thereby ending a national lottery in England that had run with few interruptions since 1566.[13] While there had been antigambling legislation prior to this time, the acts of the 1820s were different in several ways. Lottery legislation traditionally had been enacted to maintain the state's monopoly over revenues that were important for supporting foreign wars and colonial exploits. British gambling legislation in general had been enacted primarily to protect aristocratic gamesters from the gamblers or "sharps," to protect aristocrats from themselves in the event of quarrels over gambling (which might lead to duels, for instance), and to limit the extent or rate of the redistribution of wealth that might occur through gambling (Brenner and Brenner 59–60). In contrast, in the later eighteenth and early nineteenth centuries legislation came to reflect a more explicit concern about the *morality* of gambling, as well as a new concern for protecting the poor from themselves. The banning of the lotteries in the 1820s was "the first predominantly *moral* opposition to a form of gambling to find legal expression" and signaled the point at which "the Puritan opposition to gambling on ethical grounds finally overcame the remnant of eighteenth-century licence" (Downes et al. 29, 35).

Rather than dampening gambling in England, however, legislation only produced new forms of gambling and altered the location and demographic mix of the gambling population. In the 1820s, gambling clubs or "hells" became the dominant institution of gambling in London.[14] What would become the most infamous of the "gentlemen's" gambling clubs of the 1830s and 1840s was opened in 1827 by a cockney fishmonger's son, William Crockford. The roster of the club included such members as the duke of Wellington and Benjamin Disraeli. In one evening at Crockford's Club, Lord Rivers, Lord Sefton, and Lord Grenville each lost the equivalent of more than $500,000 (Wykes 298). Ashton concludes, "One may safely say, without exaggeration, that Crockford won the whole of the ready money of the then existing generation" (*Gambling* 128). This phase of gambling intensified until the 1840s, when three major events curtailed it: a scandal erupted around the "fixing" of the 1844 Derby that would become a major topic of national gossip for decades; Crockford's Club was closed down; and a Select Committee of the House of Commons was appointed to look into the need for stricter gambling legislation.[15] The subsequent Gaming Act of 1845 tightened control of gambling establishments and rendered all gambling debts unenforceable by law. Nevertheless, between 1850 and 1853 an estimated four hundred betting shops continued to operate in London (Ashton, *Gambling* 210). This era was brought to an end by the 1853 Betting Houses Act, which closed down all the shops.[16] This Act, like the two before it, was designed with an explicit class bias: it was intended to squelch lower-class gambling, which was thought to contribute to a less productive workforce and to higher levels of crime (presumably in order to pay gambling debts), while leaving room for "the gentlemen's right to wager" to be exercised (Bailey, *Leisure* 24).

Far from putting a stop to gambling, legislation only drove a larger number of non-upper-class gamblers to the racetracks, which were the traditional preserve of the aristocracy and (therefore) were exempt from the 1853 Act by dent of being out of doors. The result was a greater confluence of lower- and upper-class gamblers, the institutionalization of the track as the stronghold of British gambling, and the professionalization of the bookmaker or, as some liked to call themselves, the "turf accountant" (Itzkowitz, "Bookmakers" 18). A pervasive illegal industry of street bookies arose, facilitated by technological developments such as the telegraph and the railway, which allowed easy communication between the city and the race courses. Off-course, lower- to middle-class betting soon greatly exceeded on-course, traditionally upper-class betting. In 1890, as a middle-class reaction against what was discussed in the media of the day as the "gambling craze" or "betting mania," the National Antigambling League was formed along the lines of temperance organizations. The League soon brought suit against the race courses in an attempt to apply the 1853 Act to them, which would have put a stop to all legal betting. The suit was defeated on technicalities by an aristocratically controlled court system that refused to allow that gambling was inherently immoral.[17] Gambling therefore continued to thrive in Britain through the third and fourth quarters of the century.

To summarize: between the 1820s and the 1890s, one can see a pattern of attempts to suppress or domesticate gambling with legislation followed by upsurges in new forms of gambling. The intensity of the historical struggle between suppression and adaptation seems to have intensified after the 1840s, the period of interest in this study. Nineteenth-century gambling legislation produced the net result of commercializing and professionalizing gambling. The institution of the gentlemanly wager gradually was replaced by a professionalized industry. The "underworld" of gambling among classes below the middle was at least in part brought into the light, transplanted from London neighborhoods to the suburban racetracks, and centralized around more clearly delineated institutions. This is the exercise of social control *via* incorporation. Gambling was policed and domesticated by being brought increasingly under the control of institutions that operated *within* — rather than outside — the dominant capitalist market system.

In this regard, gambling was only representative of a broader trend toward "rationalization" of recreation and leisure in the nineteenth century.[18] The population expansion, increase in urban population density, and growth of the lower-class industrial workforce that occurred in the early nineteenth century made lower-class recreation a major problem from the perspective of the middle class. Lower-class recreation in general, but gambling in particular, was linked to two other undesirable activities: disorder and idleness. This rhetoric from the report of the 1808 Select Committee on Lotteries is representative of a generalized judgment: "Idleness, poverty, and dissipation are increased [by playing the lottery] . . . truth betrayed, domestic comfort destroyed, madness often created, crimes are committed, and even suicide itself is produced" (qtd. in Downes et al. 30).[19] Disorder was a trope that linked any form of class-based social organization or protest with criminal activities. "Idleness" signified the notion that any activity that did not contribute to social production or personal development was a waste, indeed a crime against the related mandates of individual, societal, and moral improvement. Even when gambling was not in itself considered evil, it was considered wrong to the extent that it diverted energies that could and should be engaged in work. The class-based interests that these interdictions and the accompanying condemnation of gambling served are not difficult to recognize. This is not to say that many middle-class reformers (as represented, for instance, by Dorothea Brooke) were not concerned sincerely with the conditions under which the lower classes lived, only that nineteenth-century antigambling discourse must be read within the context of industrial and financial expansionism.

At the same time, however, that discourse, like the social order of which it was a part, contained telling contradictions. One of these was moral condemnation of lower-class gambling coupled with economic exploitation of it, as summarized by "the Wildean quip about newspapers fulminating against gambling on the front page whilst relying for their sales on the racing information given at the back" (Downes et al. 38). A related and broader contradiction is that the disorder/idleness mythology surrounding gambling may be logically reversed. There is a consensus among some twentieth-century sociologists that gambling, rather than producing social discontent and wasted labor, is produced by those factors: "Various commissions at the end of the nineteenth century could find no causal relationship between gambling and poverty or gambling and crime (other than the fact that gambling was illegal to start with). What they found was that poverty led people to gamble and to drink" (Brenner and Brenner 73).[20] This suggests that gambling does not generate the violence of disorder or a downward spiraling economic condition, as the novels studied here might suggest, but rather that the violence of poverty generates gambling. After all, if one has nothing to lose, everything to gain, and no other foreseeable means by which to attain prosperity, much less wealth, then why not gamble (or, for that matter, resort to violent crime)? Histories of the nineteenth and twentieth centuries suggest that advanced capitalist societies are adverse to the recognition or admission that structural inequalities contribute to social problems like poverty and crime. Gambling was such a troubling figure in part because it foregrounds questions about the structural inequalities in society, about the system of distribution of wealth, and about the contradictions inherent in the modern amalgam of Christian and capitalist ideologies that underlie antigambling discourse.

Finance, Panic, and Mode of Exchange

> When I was young, people called me a gambler. As the scale of my operations increased I became known as a speculator. Now I am called a banker. But I have been doing the same thing all the time.
>
> Sir Earnest Cassel, banker to Edward VII

Gambling is so pervasive in mid-Victorian novels in part because money is. As two recent studies put it, money is "perhaps the most common theme in nineteenth-century fiction" (Vernon 14), and "the universal, leveling power of money is a theme intrinsic to, perhaps even definitive of, the novel form itself" (Brantlinger 23). Gambling is one component of the discourse of money, which in turn is a component of the all-pervasive bundle of discourses within nineteenth-century Britain concerning the exchange of capital. The mid-Victorian decades in particular produced a relatively larger number of fictional texts engaged to a nearly obsessional degree with representing exchanges of capital (and so money, and so gambling) than any period before or since.[21] Why is this the case? Any attempt to answer this question must consider two broad historical events (or complex sets of interconnected events): the coming of age of finance capitalism and the resulting chain of financial crises that shook the mid-Victorian decades.

Finance capitalism, as distinguished from but linked to industrial capitalism and the economics of production and consumption, reached its modern institutional form in the first half of the nineteenth century. The instruments of finance capitalism are the signs of credit, which in the nineteenth century were all paper: bonds, stocks, promissory notes, and, most commonly, money as scrip. Finance capitalism's purview is the circulation of instruments that translate directly to and from money itself, money as the ultimate commodity.[22] I certainly am not claiming that paper money or finance did not exist before the nineteenth century. Rather, I am claiming that finance capitalism reached societywide dissemination in England in the first half of the nineteenth century and only then took on the institutional forms that still are in place in the late twentieth century.[23] I mark this event with the finalization in 1833 of the long transition from gold to paper — and thus from an economy of bartering to an economy based on capital exchange — signified by the standardization of currency on the Bank of England note. Only in 1844 were other British banks banned from issuing their own notes. As the standard, universal medium of exchange, money came into existence in Britain as recently as the Victorian period. Similarly, the central institutions of finance capitalism, the joint-stock company and the stock exchange, reached a critical stage with the full establishment of the London Stock Exchange in 1802 (Baskin 207). If, as James Thompson argues in *Models of Value*, the eighteenth century "witnesses the beginnings of the transformation from the older form of money as accumulated treasure or wealth to money in exchange as capital" (33), the early nineteenth century witnesses the culmination of that process in the coming of age of finance capitalism, signaled by the establishment of a societywide, abstract system of value. It seems more than appropriate that novels written in the decades following these events should concern themselves so thoroughly with money.

But the maturation of finance capitalism did not occur without the throes of puberty, which in a sense stretched from the 1820s to the climactic crash of the 1920s. Decades were required to establish relative stability (from the perspective of the interests of capital) between the extremes of an unchecked market and a restrictive government in areas like monetary policy, stock market regulation, and corporation law. Indicative of the period is that there were "eight million pounds more paper money in circulation in 1825 than in 1823, with no corresponding increase in trade and industry to justify it"; at the same time, "there had developed a vast extension of private credit — the 'new currency of the age' — and the market was flooded with bills of exchange, promissory notes, and similar paper" (Russell 45). Monetary crises occurred on a fairly regular ten-year cycle in 1824–25, 1837, 1839, 1847, 1857, 1866, and 1873.[24] The crises of 1825 and 1836 spanned the period in which *Middlemarch* is set, and those of 1866 and 1873 covered the period in which the novel was written and published. The latter crisis was followed by a sustained depression. If it was remarkable to people of the time that as many as ninety different banking companies were incorporated in England by 1810, it was shocking that in 1825–1826 alone sixty country banks, such as Bulstrode's in *Middlemarch*, failed. If it was a great boon to "the economy" that thousands of new corporations were formed in the initial decades of the nineteenth century, it was devastating for those affected by the 5,000 bankruptcies reported in the early 1830s. If the formation of the modern stock exchange — complete with brokers, rules of trade, and controlled membership — provided needed capital to companies and wealth to wise or lucky investors, speculation schemes such as the "Railway Mania" of 1845 brought ruin to thousands of investors, wiping out many family fortunes and names when the shares collapsed in 1847.[25] The combined frequency and intensity of these upheavals has not been matched in the twentieth century. It is little wonder, then, that many Victorians should have been deeply concerned with the origins and forms of wealth — particularly land versus bullion versus paper — and with the stability of value.

The question of value pointed to the issues of representation that money and realist novels share, which is a category of the issues of signification that money and language share. Much of the anxiety behind the financial crises of the early to mid-nineteenth century sprang from an awareness of the representational nature of money. A plethora of recent studies investigate these issues in relationship to eighteenth- and nineteenth-century British fiction, notably Patrick Brantlinger's *Fictions of State*, Mary Poovey's *Making a Social Body*, Marc Shell's *The Economy of Literature* and *Money, Language, and Thought*, James Thompson's *Models of Value*, and John Vernon's *Money and Fiction*. A number of these hinge their analyses on the simultaneous historical emergence in the eighteenth and early nineteenth centuries of two, major discourse domains or cultural forms (as I define that concept in chapter one). Those two cultural forms were political economy and the realist novel, each of which claimed the authority to explain the gap between representation and value. They participated integrally and mutually in the bourgeois revolution that produced the dominant order of middle-class civil society.[26] What is more, political economy and novelistic realism defined their domains, styles, and forms in direct reference to one another. Especially since Nancy Armstrong's *Desire and Domestic Fiction*, critics have tended to argue for a separation at this time between the domains of the novel and of political economy. While political economy claimed the right to speak for the public and economic concerns of civil society, novels claimed the right to speak for — or, some critics suggest, were limited to — the private, affective, and domestic realm. Without denying that the new "science" of political economy successfully shaped discourse about the financial superstructure of society or that the newly dominant cultural form of the realist novel reciprocally colonized the domains of individual subjectivity and "domestic economy," I challenge any strict separation of these concerns. Studies that maintain this separation run the risk of reproducing the Victorian notion of "separate spheres" and of underestimating the cultural work of realist novels. By contrast, I argue in this book that novelistic realism entered the nineteenth century engaged in historical competition with other forms for cultural dominance, which I define in terms of entertainment market share and access to definition of the subject in society. In other words, far from withdrawing from competition in the public sphere or abnegating responsibility to speak about economic matters, realist novels challenged political economy in these discursive arenas. The pervasiveness of the discourse on money in mid-Victorian novels evidences this, and the figure of gambling in particular serves as a site where novels engage these issues, and not simply to moralize against them.

These claims begin to gain support through the recognition that money is a constituent component of every relationship in mid-Victorian novels, even serving as a kind of taxonomy of types of relationships between characters. Almost every character in novels like *Middlemarch* and *The Duke's Children* is connected to other characters by specified and publicly observed monetary relations. In *Middlemarch*, for example, Fred Vincy's connection to Featherstone is inheritance; Lydgate's marriage to Rosamond Vincy comes to be defined by debt; Dorothea's relation to Lydgate, as to Farebrother, is one of charity; Bulstrode's link to Raffles, and to his own past deeds, is ill-gotten money and blackmail. While money is by no means the only determinant of relationships in Victorian fiction, it is the primary form that *social evaluations* of relationship assume. So while Dorothea's scandalous second marriage to Ladislaw is *not* about money, it is evaluated by Middlemarch society in those terms; much the same may be said of Tregear's marriage to Lady Mary in *The Duke's Children*. Similarly, while Lydgate's motive for twice standing by Bulstrode when the rest of Middlemarch has turned against him is not primarily pecuniary, it is evaluated socially in terms of money, specifically bribery. Money is the public yardstick of private relationship; part of the ideological work of the discourse of money was to make the private public.

The concomitant danger, however, is that it might rupture private loss or gain into the public domain of scandal. As the Duke of Omnium puts it, after his son Silverbridge tells him that his gambling is "nothing to speak of": "Nothing to speak of is so apt to grow into that which has to be spoken of" (*DC* 56). Major Tifto, with his Derby-fixing secret, and Bultrode, with his dirty money intrigues, are made to face the public through the combination of money and gossip. This function of money is facilitated by the nature of its form as a shared, universally translatable currency, which of course is why money is like language. Indeed, money provides the perfect medium of social connectedness underlying George Eliot's deterministic model; while Eliot strives to defend alternative modes of relationship, she makes use of money. She was not blind to the fact that "[b]oth the conventions of paper money and the conventions of realistic fiction constitute a code collectively shared" (Vernon 96).

But money as a basis of social connection comes with an even more threatening danger from the perspective of the middle-class liberal intellectual. Money is "external" to the intersubjective realm, and to the extent that individuals privilege it as a constituent of relations to others, they make the pubic private through an alienating internalization. Not only might this result in the objectification of others, but it threatens to alienate one from one's self. However, lest it appear that I too uncritically subscribe to the doctrine of "separate spheres," I reemphasize that Eliot's novels, like many others of the period, continuously entertain rather than evade the dangers of money. Far from portraying any strict boundary between public and private, internal and external, these novels portray a heterogeneous range of positions between these extremes, always revealing the interaction between the economic and the domestic. Marriage, the epitome of the domestic, is as much a publicly observed transaction as stock investment, and female and male characters take part in speculations of both kinds. Far from unequivocally privileging the private or denying the public, these novels continuously investigate the boundary between the two, focusing on the exchanges of both symbolic and economic capital across that boundary.

Therefore, the relationships between characters in nineteenth-century British realist novels typically are regulated by one or more of eight primary modes of exchange. By "mode of exchange" I mean the social channel and the type of the relationship between characters through which money and other forms of capital or sources of value are exchanged. Value is gained, earned, lost, or given in Victorian novels through these eight modes: (1) marriage; (2) inheritance or dispossession; (3) charity; (4) work, generally conceived as individual labor; (5) financial investment, usually represented as "speculation"; (6) credit and debt, especially bankruptcy; (7) foul play, particularly bribery and blackmail; and, not the least among these, (8) gambling. (A ninth might be direct purchase, which is the least thoroughly explored type of transaction.) Different modes of exchange come with different evaluations. Victorian texts typically assign a positive value to the first four and a negative value to the second four, though the valuations ultimately are more complex and ambivalent than these terms suggest.

If potentially reductionistic, it is not inaccurate to say that mid-Victorian novels are structured as a series of exchanges through different modes of exchange, which then serve as trials between "good" and "bad" sources or forms of value. However, this is not as simple as "marriage is always good" or "stock investment is always bad." Marriage *with* money is good, for example, while marriage *for* money is bad. Inheritance often is tied to the most

stable form of wealth, land, but it also is associated with traditional aristocratic ideology. Work always is appraised positively, though perhaps most
often by those who are not themselves compelled to work and who recommend it as a panacea for the discontents of the members of a lower class.
Work and/or marriage typically are the antidotes for bad forms of value
such as gambling. The channel through which one receives or pursues
money is taken as an indicator of one's character. This points to a problem
that is endemic to the nature of money: one of its defining characteristics is
its anonymity, and that in turn raises the familiar problem of origins. This
problem has two aspects: "origin" can refer to the distinction between "old
money" and *nouveau riche* or "city" money, with the attendant class bias, or it
can refer to the moral/legal distinction between ill-gotten and honestly acquired money (and Victorian novels love to cross the two). *The Duke's Children* exemplifies the former of these when the Duke impresses on his son
Gerald that money "is a commodity of which you are bound to see that the
source is not only clean but noble" (*DC* 517). The latter appears in *Middlemarch* when the crusade to save Farebrother from his one moral short-
coming — playing whist for money — is expressed as "a strong desire to rescue him from his chance-gotten money" (*MM* 481). In both cases, though
differently, questions of financial value become inextricably intertwined
with questions of personal worthiness, and it is at the particularly troubling
boundary between financial worth and worthiness that gambling serves as
a critical marker. Finally, the general point, which remains to be demonstrated, is that just as money is linked to every relationship within Victorian
novels in the form of the eight modes of exchange, so gambling is linked to
each of the other seven modes of exchange. Gambling is the problematizing
linchpin that links money and chance to every relationship portrayed in
Middlemarch and *The Duke's Children*.

Good Money and the Matrimonial Gamble

> Very good indeed, my Lord Duke; very good indeed! Ha, ha, ha! — all
> horses have heads and all have tails! Heads and Tails.
> Major Tifto in The Duke's Children

While the endings of Victorian novels typically suggest that marriage is an
unimpeachably "good" source of both value and values, many of those same
novels also represent matrimony as an extremely risky gamble. The eco-

nomics of marriage have never been absent from literature, but they begin
to take on the characteristically Victorian intensity from at least the time
that Marianne Dashwood insists that marriage not be a "commercial exchange" and her sister Elinor responds, "But wealth has much to do with it"
(Austen 32, 78). Indeed, marriage is never considered by characters in the
novels following Jane Austen without the issue of money being present.
One prevalent concern is with marrying up, or at least not marrying down,
though the romantic couple generally is required to denounce any such
considerations. Not all downward marriages are unacceptable, however;
downwardly mobile marriages *toward the middle* often prevail in Victorian
fiction, such as Lady Mary Palliser's marriage to Frank Tregear and Silverbridge's to Isabel Boncassen in *The Duke's Children* or Dorothea's to Will
Ladislaw in *Middlemarch*. A related, critical issue is whether the question of
up or down refers predominantly to money or to class. Seventy years after
Sense and Sensibility, *The Duke's Children* portrays marriage as an honor-
regulated, status and money-based economy in which some, such as Frank
Tregear, are long-shot winners and some, such as Lady Mabel Grex, are
ruined on the market.

References to gambling, speculation, and fate suffuse the discourse of
marriage in many novels of the period. While a "bad" marriage, such as
Lydgate's to Rosamond Vincy, may lead to gambling, drugs, and a generally
"narrowed lot," a "good" marriage operates within Victorian discourse as
that which can save one from such evils (*MM* 648, 775). The Duke's pressure on Silverbridge to marry is an attempt to redirect the son's passions
from hunting, clubs, and especially gambling to a more domestic outlet.
That is the very effect that even the contemplation of marriage to Isabel
Boncassen seems to have on Silverbridge: "When she had told him what she
would do for him to make his home happy [in addition to what he clearly
has imagined], it had seemed to him that all other delights must fade away
from him for ever. How odious were Tifto and his racehorses, how un-
meaning the noise of his club" (*DC* 543). The prospect of marriage to a
"good" woman, Mary Garth, has a similar effect on Fred Vincy; this prospect leads him — albeit with periodic backsliding — away from billiards and
gentlemanly pretensions. More generally, characters throughout Victorian
fiction discuss marriage in terms of an "unfortunate lot" or of "winning" a
"fortunate match" ("fortune" alternately meaning wealth and fate). Lady
Mabel's pursuit of Silverbridge, for instance, is cast in terms of a "sport" or
"game," paralleling the novel's horse racing and fox hunting themes. She
describes Silverbridge as her "prey," but in the course of the novel she

instead is figured as his horse, a "horse of another colour" (*DC* 367).
Though the "cup [of winning Silverbridge] had come within the reach of
her fingers," she, like Silverbridge's thoroughbred Prime Minister, failed to
place because she "craned at the first fence" (*DC* 432, 611). Similar imagery
appears in *Middlemarch* when Fred Vincy's "unlucky" horse, Diamond (as
in engagement ring), lames itself and, in the process, "just miss[es] killing
the groom" (*MM* 235). The reader is told that there "was no more redress
for this than for the discovery of bad temper after marriage." And it is the
potential for this very type of discovery — "bad temper after marriage" —
that makes marriage truly chancy. The role of chance in making marriages is
evidenced from the outset by the critical, fatelike role that chance meetings
play: for instance, Tregear and Lady Mary's meeting in Rome, or the repeated accidental meetings of Dorothea and Ladislaw in *Middlemarch*, the
second of which is also in Rome. But Dorothea, for one, is determined to
depend on neither fate nor custom. Concerning her prospects, the narrator
therefore comments with no small amount of bitter irony, "Certainly such
[unfeminine] elements of a marriageable girl tended to interfere with her
lot and hinder it from being decided according to custom, by good looks,
vanity, and merely canine affection" (*MM* 10).

In *The Duke's Children*, marriage and gambling are linked structurally
in the Silverbridge-Grex-Boncassen subplot. Silverbridge's shift in affection
from Lady Mabel to Isabel Boncassen is tied to his gambling. Both represent a weakness of character, as Silverbridge admits to himself: "After such a
misfortune [as his gambling loss] how would he be able to break that other
matter to the Duke, and say that he had changed his mind about marriage, — that he was going to abandon Lady Mabel Grex?" (*DC* 351). In the
Duke's mind, the second highest duty required of British aristocracy (after
that of "elevat[ing] those beneath them") is "to maintain their own position," and the prescribed method of doing this is to marry within one's class
and sire a son (*DC* 519). Having just lamented Silverbridge's gambling, the
Duke then laments his change from Mabel to Isabel in related terms: "And
now, having at first made a choice that was good, he had altered his mind
for simple freak, captivated by a pair of bright eyes and an arch smile; and
without a feeling in regard to his family, was anxious to take to his bosom
the granddaughter of an America day-labourer!" (*DC* 519). The Duke can
no more comprehend the "simple freak" by which love might occur irre-
spective of duty than he can understand gambling. The "theory of spontaneous love," as he conceives it, depends entirely too much on chance or
Providence (*DC* 271).

Indeed, to the extent that one's selection of a partner is determined in the first instance by whom one happens to meet rather than by design or duty, love is set in motion by nothing more than a roll of the dice. After all, Silverbridge meets Isabel by "the chances of society" that bring them into the same social setting at the same time (*DC* 380). In favoring the Silverbridge-Isabel match over the Silverbridge-Mabel match, the text appears to sanction the replacement of love-as-duty by love-as-gambling. This would mean that a form of gambling — marriage on the basis of spontaneous love — is offered as the antidote for gambling proper. It also suggests that *The Duke's Children* ultimately defines love as based on nothing more than "merely canine affection" (*MM* 10). Obviously, this basis would be no more acceptable within Victorian culture than is the notion of love-as-duty. A third term therefore is required, and that term, which is more familiar within George Eliot's deterministic doctrine, is choice. Silverbridge should be "entitled to his choice," and he claims that entitlement precisely through his willingness to give up what "fortune" has brought to him: "I will sooner lose all; — the rank I have; the rank that I am to have; all these lands that you [Lady Mabel] have been looking on; my father's wealth, my seat in Parliament, — everything that fortune has done for me, — I would give them all up, sooner than lose her" (*DC* 382, 475). In this way, the text attempts a partial replacement of fate by choice, although choice is also shown to be conditioned by chance (and, of course, Silverbridge holds on to the fruits of both). Love-as-duty and love-as-spontaneity must be mediated by or supplemented with love-as-choice. However, this can be achieved only by eliding the fact that what is treated as the choice to love can occur only *after* the dictates of duty or, more often, the spontaneity of feeling and desire. Novels like *Middlemarch* and *The Duke's Children* strain to accommodate a theory of love that in its essence is Romantic without fully admitting the gamble of spontaneous love. Love somehow must achieve a precarious balance between being too calculated (like Lady Mabel and Silverbridge's, or perhaps Dorothea's for Casaubon) and being too spontaneous, which implies an abandonment of responsibility. If love still is to be responsible, it is to be responsible not to rank, duty, or family but to one's "true" self.

What is it, then, that permits certain Victorian fictional romances to be true or real while others are shown to be false? One answer seems to be that love requires a disillusionment about romance itself, a surrendering of the belief that romance, like the fate or destiny of the gambler, magically will provide one with an ideal mate. This sort of debunking, which often occurs through humor, seems in turn to require a mutual understanding between partners of each other's individuality and, most important, of one's own limitations and desires. The "good" couplings in Victorian fiction — such as Mary Garth and Fred Vincy, but also Silverbridge and Isabel Boncassen — typically are matured to fruition through a trial, a passage of time, or as in the case of Fred and Silverbridge, a brush with gambling. After this, these couples are able to present themselves and to take each other at "face value," or, as Isabel repeatedly comments, "as good as gold" (as opposed to the questionable value of paper money) (*DC* 568).[27] Within the Victorian discourse of marriage, the falsity of romance, as in the case of Dorothea or Lydgate or Mabel Grex, arises, then, from a dual mis-valuation. It involves an over-valuing of the other, which is tantamount to a negation of the intended partner through self-projection, and an undervaluing or negation of one's self. Consider the way in which Lydgate's fall into gambling is described: "But just as he had tried opium, so his thoughts now began to turn upon gambling — not with appetite for its excitement, but with a sort of wistful inward gaze after that easy way of getting money which implied no asking and brought no responsibility" (*MM* 648). Lydgate is not the stereotypical figure of the rabidly addicted gambler; his "wistful inward gaze" is toward the self. He hungers to recapture the selfhood he has surrendered in marrying Rosamond, but he cannot do so within the discourse of the novel through gambling's "easy" abnegation of responsibility. Dorothea must go through the self-denial of Casaubon before she is finally able to discover "her passion to herself" in her desire for Will Ladislaw and thus reunite her severed subjectivity (*MM* 762–63). According to this conception, the risk of marriage is of not knowing one's own desires until it is too late. One cannot take the gamble out of marriage through either the romance of gambling or the gamble of romance, but only by being equal to one's self and, as a result, to one's partner.

What is required, then, in the discourse of marriage as in the discourse of money is a seeming *equality of value*. This question comes to the fore whenever class and money are crossed in a marriage prospect. Is Frank Tregear "worthy" of Lady Mary Palliser (emphasis on Lady)? Is Isabel Boncassen, a now wealthy American of working-class "stock," worthy of Lord Silverbridge? Tregear has the status, if somewhat equivocally, but not the money; Isabel has the money but not the status. Is money equal to status? Certainly not, according to Lady Mary's father, the Duke, for whom "maintenance of the aristocracy of the country was second only in importance to maintenance of the Crown" (*DC* 174). However, status without money will not do, either. When Isabel's father, Mr. Boncassen, points out that "men generally like to marry their equals," Silverbridge responds that, "People don't always know who are their equals" (*DC* 424). How, then, is an equality of value to be determined? The dilemma of cross-class marriage, and the related dilemma of birth versus money, is a definitive one for the nineteenth-century realist novel. While Victorian novels offer no single or easy solution, they ultimately portray worthiness as more valuable than economic worth. Critically, however, this is made possible only by the prior redefinition of "worthiness" in terms of a middle-class understanding of "character" as moral constitution, rather than the aristocratic conception of worthiness as an attribute of birth. At the same time, however, the shifting of worthiness toward the middle also unavoidably brings it into closer alignment with one of the primary means by which the rising middle classes acquired their worthiness, namely, economic worth. Worth is equal to worthiness if worthiness is equal to worth.

The brilliance of *The Duke's Children* — and one way in which the novel includes the subversion of its dominant discourses — is that the ongoing debate about worthiness for marriage is counterpointed by the debate, primarily in the Duke's mind, about social equality: "As by the spread of education and increase of general well-being every proletaire was brought nearer to a Duke, so by such action would the Duke be brought nearer to a proletaire. Such drawing-nearer of the classes was the object to which all this man's political action tended. And yet it was a dreadful thing to him that his own daughter should desire to marry a man so much beneath her own rank and fortune as Frank Tregear" (*DC* 175). The irony is that it is not the Duke but Tregear, the man who demands to be considered equal to the daughter of a nobleman who as a conservative politician fears social equality. Tregear fears that the Duke's liberal party will be swayed too far by its radical wing toward the dangers of equality still represented in British minds of the time by the French Revolution. Speaking of that subject to Silverbridge, Tregear says: "There were a lot of honest men who thought they could do a deal of good by making everybody equal. A good many were made equal by having their heads cut off. . . . [A]s he [Tregear's Liberal opponent running for Parliament] hasn't thought much about anything, he is quite willing to lend a hand to communism, radicalism, socialism, chopping people's heads off, or anything else" (*DC* 439). Two points are clear. First, social equality — like the illusion of an easy marriage that romance promises (or like the too easy social mobility that both gambling and stock speculation offer) — is dangerous and must be regulated. Second, a great deal of ambivalence and mystification about the origins of value are taking place here. The contradiction between the Duke's public policy and private practice (concerning his daughter's marriage) on worthiness and equality is mirrored, and therefore reversed, by the contradiction between Tregear's private practice (in thinking himself worthy of Lady Mary) and public policy on the same issue.

Dead Hand, Live Hand, Invisible Hand

Inheritance was an issue full of contradictions for the Victorian middle classes. It simultaneously was a sign of social and financial stability and a sign of an aristocratic order perpetuated by the system of primogeniture. Part of the stability promised by inheritance was its association with land. Landed value was part of an archaic understanding of value as "intrinsic" or materially embodied, which therefore posited a direct correspondence between a quantity of gold, for instance, and a value printed on the face of a pound note.[28] By the nineteenth century, that understanding was very rapidly being supplanted, through the institutionalization of finance capitalism, with an understanding of value as representational and relative, which in Marxist terms is to say by the replacement of use value by exchange value. But many Victorians never fully trusted the "fictitious value" of paper money; the issuing of money from banks appeared no less magical than a run of luck at cards. Thus the financial panics of the mid-1800s were characterized by flights away from paper value back to the "real" value of gold and land.[29] (Realist novels, of course, capitalized on this same distinction between real and paper value, though not without foregrounding the reliance of their own realness on paper.) At the same time, however, the power of the ascending middle classes issued increasingly from that same unpredictable financial market, and its laissez-faire ideology was antithetical to the system of primogeniture through which landed value traditionally had been preserved. Primogeniture, like the unified estate, restricted rather than freed capital for circulation and exchange, and for this reason it came under increasing legal pressure throughout the century, for example, the restriction on entail in 1882. On the other hand, one ambition of the upwardly mobile bourgeoisie was to step into the status and lifestyle of the landed gentry, to occupy the place of the very social order that it criticized. Part of this ambition was to replace "blood" with money or, as the middle classes were more likely to express it, to replace the randomness of inheritance (random because based on nothing more than the chances of birth) with the merit of industry and wise management. Thus inheritance too was linked with gambling.

This series of contradictions concerning inheritance produced, and was produced by, contradictory representations of it in Victorian novels. While the main characters in many novels are rescued by inheritance, they typically must demonstrate worthiness first, and texts often downplay the fact of the inheritance relative to the merit through which it supposedly was earned (Pip in *Great Expectations* is a prime example). In cases where part of the inheritance is a revelation of aristocratic origins, or at least origins from a class higher than the character's, the chiastic crossing of the four terms *blood*, *chance*, *merit*, and *choice* is redoubled. Especially in George Eliot's fiction, the hazard of inheritance is not only that it might substitute the randomness of blood for merit but that, in the process, it subjects characters to chance and thereby relieves them of the responsibility of choice. Eliot therefore requires some of her characters to demonstrate the primacy of choice by exercising it even to surrender claim to an inheritance, as Esther Lyon does in *Felix Holt*.

A related threat of inheritance arises when it subjects the responsibility (not right) of self-determination to the demands of a codicil to a will. Such is the case, for example, with Casaubon's inheritance to Dorothea, which he instructs her to accept, along with its restriction on her option for remarriage, as though it were consecrated by "providential arrangements" (*MM* 364). In contrast, Dorothea chooses to view inherited wealth not as a blessing that separates the individual from the mass of humanity, obligating her only to the familial lineage from which it came; rather, for her it throws the individual's connection to the web of society into relief, increasing her responsibility for the circumstances of others who are less fortunate by contrast. As Dorothea puts it: "But if one has too much in consequence of others being wronged, it seems to me that the Divine voice which tells us to set that wrong right must be obeyed" (*MM* 364). (The specific reference here is the inheritance that was kept from Casaubon's Aunt Julia, Ladislaw's grandmother, which is why Casaubon is suspicious of Dorothea's motives.) This same sympathetic view of society, and the zero-sum logic that accompanies it, is used in *Daniel Deronda* to characterize gambling as making one's gain "out of another's loss" (*DD* 500). Blind acceptance of inheritance is equated to gambling, and the foundation of value that inheritance otherwise represents is put in question. The fact that one apparently has no control over the conditions into which one is born should not be used as an excuse for a passive stance toward those conditions. In Eliot's fiction at least, circumstances do not obviate choice.

Dorothea's antidote for the passive, estate-preserving stance represented by inherited wealth is individual charity, which is an active attempt, as she says, "to make shares . . . even" (*MM* 744). Charity is the "live hand" that provides a solution to the "dead hand" of inheritance. The section of *Middlemarch* titled "The Dead Hand" portrays Casaubon's attempt through the codicil to his will to reach beyond the grave with the hand of mortmain and control Dorothea's live hand. Casaubon's desire to control the future through a projection of his character is analogous to Fred Vincy's gambler's attitude. It is telling in this regard that whist, which is the forerunner of bridge, can be played by three people and a fourth "dummy" or "dead" hand that is played face-up by the partner who sits opposite.[30] Casaubon is Dorothea's dead partner in the gambling game of inheritance, and Dorothea stands to lose her inheritance from Casaubon if she marries Will Ladislaw. As Ladislaw passionately confesses to Rosamond Lydgate, however, "I would rather touch her hand if it were dead than I would touch any other woman's living" (*MM* 755). Yet Ladislaw too must be taught by Dorothea about the active exercise of choice. At the penultimate moment, Ladislaw still suffers under the illusion that he will be prevented from marrying Dorothea by "petty accidents" and that his chances of success in life are "a mere toss-up" (*MM* 786). All hinges on Dorothea's choice of self-determination, which is analogous to Silverbridge's choosing of Isabel Boncassen in that Dorothea too opts for love (and passion) even at the loss of wealth. As with Silverbridge, however, this is a false choice. Dorothea's ability to choose Ladislaw is dependent on the fact that even without Casaubon's wealth the two of them can live more than comfortably on the £700 a year that she has inherited from her mother. Readers might miss this information, which the text gives in passing. The novel ends with the further suggestion that Dorothea's son will inherit Mr. Brooke's estate. The uncharitable reading, so to speak, is that the novel attempts to forward a message of choice and charity while disguising the basis for them in circumstance and inheritance. The charitable reading is that the novel represents a world in which the oscillation between choice and circumstance, charity and inheritance, or freedom and necessity is an endless process.

Charity, and the sympathy that inspires it, is the activity for which Dorothea's character is most known. Through financial charity, in combination with a prescription to work, Dorothea saves Lydgate from gambling, debt, and the tainted charity offered by Bulstrode. By the same means she reforms Farebrother from gambling, redirecting his energies toward more industrious religious practice. It is through "sympathy without check" that she puts aside all considerations of self in attempting to rescue Rosamond Lydgate from the selfishness that threatens to destroy her marriage (*MM* 774). Throughout *Middlemarch*, Dorothea is described in terms of an almost Christ-like martyrdom, but no matter how much Dorothea resembles Christ (or Saint Theresa) in her charity, she also resembles Fortuna, the patron saint of gamblers. After Dorothea grants the estate vicarage to Farebrother, his mother says to her: "They say Fortune is a woman and capricious. But sometimes she is a good woman and gives to those who merit, which has been the case with you, Mrs. Casaubon, who have given a living to my son" (*MM* 522). This passage perhaps inadvertently reveals the inherent similarity between charity as traditionally defined and gambling: the very individual selectivity that generally distinguishes such charity makes it no more predictable or effective in solving societywide inequalities than the random windfalls distributed by the state lottery.

Charity is a domesticated form of fortune or fate, then, one that supposedly takes care of the needy not on the basis of caprice but on the basis of merit. This is consistent with a traditional system of *noblesse oblige*, and Dorothea's charity initially appears to be a late example of that system, which survived as the dominant practice of charity roughly up until the time in which the novel is set, the 1830s.[31] The New Poor Law of 1834, its workhouses and severe penalties for vagrancy, came with (or produced) a pervasive change in social attitudes toward the poor. A shift took place from the traditional aristocratic view that it was the duty of the rich to look after the poor through personal husbandry and charity to the laissez-faire view that "poverty was the fault of the poor and that the middle and upper classes had no responsibility to relieve it" (Webb 48). Poverty became a sign of degradation that must be dealt with not on a personal basis but by state correction and the "invisible hand" of the market. Among other things, this shift served the need of a burgeoning manufacturing sector for a disciplined workforce. At the same time, and for the same reasons, working-class recreation, which was perceived as a threat to order, came under increased scrutiny. As Peter Bailey documents in *Leisure and Class in Victorian England*, the police force was enlarged, betting shops were prohibited and gambling codes strengthened, ordinances restricting mass meetings and street bazaars were enacted, liquor licensing was instituted after zealous campaigning by the Temperance League, blood sports like bear baiting were prohibited on humanitarian grounds (excluding the upper-class equivalents such as fox hunting), and fairs and race courses were required to buy licenses. These and other control mechanisms operated to regulate working-class (and sometimes upper-class) recreation. On the other hand, certain recreations were prescribed, specifically those that centered on the family unit rather than the ale house, those that encouraged solitary self-reflection (for example, fishing), those such as organized team athletics that aimed at wholesome fraternizing and physical improvement, and those that "instruct[ed] workingmen in the elementary accomplishments of social economy — time-budgeting and money management — and introduced them to the satisfactions of mental recreation" (Bailey, *Leisure* 170). In short, as Bailey concludes, a propaganda of rational recreation, in conjunction with a broad and diverse range of "re-socialisation" mechanisms in other spheres of daily life, contributed to "the house-training of the English proletariat" toward an industrial discipline (174). As in the practice of charity, these measures typically were represented by their middle-class proponents as the best way to help the poor.

This context recommends a reconsideration of Dorothea's most ambitious experiment in charity, her workers' cottages. From the first chapters, Dorothea proposes that her uncle, who is known for poor maintenance of his tenant farms, build such a set of cottages. The proposal is received sympathetically only by Sir James Chettam, and then because it coincides with his interest in "scientific farming," by which he hopes to set "a good pattern of farming among [his] tenants," and because he is romantically interested in Dorothea (*MM* 19, 33). Early in the novel, Dorothea conceives of her "plan" in an aristocratic combination of humanitarian and aesthetic terms: "Life in cottages might be happier than ours if they were real houses fit for human beings from whom we expect duties and affections" (*MM* 33). She reacts to her uncle's resistance to her plan and to the idyllic representation of rustic life portrayed in paintings which hang on his office wall as follows: "And those poor Dagleys, in their tumble-down farmhouse, where they live in the back kitchen and leave the other rooms to the rats! That is one reason why I did not like the pictures here, dear Uncle — which you think me stupid about. I used to come from the village with all that dirt and coarse ugliness like a pain within me" (*MM* 378). Here Dorothea's reaction is personal to the point of being internalized. Later, after her self-negating marriage to Casaubon, his death (the good fortune of which cannot be admitted), and her resulting financial independence, the "plan" begins to take on a new purpose: "I have a delightful plan. I should like to take a great deal of land,

and drain it, and make a little colony where everybody should work, and all the work should be done well" (*MM* 532). Finally, near the end of the novel when it seems Dorothea may have abandoned the "plan," she describes it as founding a "village which should be a school of industry" (*MM* 742). The progression in Dorothea's conception of her "plan" charts the *embourgeoisement* of aristocratic ideology toward the purpose of domesticating the working class. The end of the trajectory is what Peter Bailey describes as "the coercive power implicit in the semi-custodial institutions of factory villages or board schools" (*Leisure* 172). While one must read Dorothea's charity and sympathy as sincere, one also must recognize the way in which it operates to regulate play, whether as gambling specifically or as recreation in general. Charity is expressed through the discourses of money and work to meet ideological ends that Dorothea Brooke, and perhaps George Eliot, confused with more traditionally aristocratic humanitarian measures.

Bad Money and Class Mobility

Money is "bad" within the discourse shared by *Middlemarch* and *The Duke's Children* when it has too easy an origin, whether through gambling, market speculation, a speculative marriage, unmerited inheritance, debt, bribery, blackmail, or uncommitted work. Bad money breeds bad money, and it endangers good money. Fred Vincy's gambling therefore contributes to the loss of his inheritance and leads to debt, which endangers his marriage prospects with Mary Garth. Reversing this process, Lydgate's debt leads to gambling, and bankruptcy looms darkly at his door. Gambling, debt, and potential bankruptcy similarly are linked in the Grex subplot of *The Duke's Children*. Gambling and foul play are combined in the Bulstrode-Raffles subplot of *Middlemarch* and in the Tifto subplot of *The Duke's Children*. These examples are representative; it is not uncommon in Victorian novels for a character's circumstances to be determined by the bankruptcy that resulted from financial speculation, as is the case with Gwendolen Harleth in *Daniel Deronda*, Miss Mattie in *Cranford*, Mr. Melmotte in *The Way We Live Now*, and Amelia Sedley in *Vanity Fair*, to name only a few. A common cycle is for gambling, speculation, or foul play to lead to debt or bankruptcy, which then in turn drives the character to gambling, speculation, or foul play, and so on. Though typically only half of this cycle gets played out by a given character in the course of a novel, the pattern is potentially self-perpetuating. Moreover, these dangerous slips between sources of bad money are linked strategically to slips between classes. One of the chief dangers of gambling, which was commonly enough expressed in the seventeenth and eighteenth centuries but which became especially pointed for the middle ranks of Victorian society, is that it brought the classes into "unhealthy" proximity to one another, mixing upper and lower and exposing the middle to both. The figure of gambling was almost uniquely suited for certain interests of the middle classes because it applied bidirectionally. A primary ideological function of the figure of gambling was as part of nineteenth-century discourses aimed at the bidirectional *embourgeoisement* of those classes above and those below the middle. Bad forms of exchange and sources of value connected the upper and lower classes, and gambling was an indicator of that connection.

The Duke's Children works to drive these points home. After having been warned strongly by his father, the Duke, not to get entangled in the world of racing, Lord Silverbridge rationalizes to himself as follows: "He was sure that this [his father's warning] was exaggerated. Half the House of Lords and two-thirds of the House of Commons were to be seen at the Derby; but no doubt there were many rascals and fools, and he could not associate with the legislators without finding himself among the fools and rascals. He would, — as soon as he could, — separate himself from the Major [Tifto]. And he would not bet. It was on that side of the sport that the rascals and the fools showed themselves." However, it seems that Silverbridge, a would-be legislator himself, cannot avoid mixing with the fools and rascals and is unable to resist betting on the horse in which he owns a "share" with Major Tifto, eventually "plunging" for a loss of £70,000 (*DC* 147). Trollope did not invent this sort of tale, since not a few lords ended up in the tabloids after losing their fortunes either at gambling hells such as William Crockford's or at the track, whether fairly or as a result of Tifto's style of "fixing." Silverbridge's fraternization with Tifto, and Tifto's with a yet lower class of rascal, Captain Green, are portrayed as the primary cause for Silverbridge's fall. The critical question is whether Tifto is a gentleman, and the negative answer it eventually receives is central to the novel's message concerning worth, worthiness, and gambling.

The Grex subplot similarly illustrates the threat that gambling poses by bringing together the high and the low. The novel portrays Lady Mabel Grex as the victim of her father's gambling, and her own increasingly desperate speculations on marriage seem to be a response in kind to that gambling. With some bitter irony, then, Lady Mabel is made the primary vehicle of the novel's antigambling rhetoric, which she expresses again in relationship to the figure of the gentleman: "Of all things men do this is the worst. A man who would think himself disgraced for ever if he accepted a present of money will not scruple to use all his wits to rob his friend of everything that he has by studying the run of cards or by watching the paces of some brutes of horses! And they consider themselves to be fine gentlemen! A real gentleman should never want the money out of another man's pocket; — should never think of money at all" (*DC* 159).

Lady Mabel could have been a spokesperson for the movements that had been attempting to reform the track against unyielding aristocratic opposition since at least the end of the eighteenth century. As those predominantly middle-class movements portrayed gambling as the road to thievery for the losers and as little better than thievery for the winners, so a gentleman who games is represented as no better than a pickpocket. Indeed, the Duke uses the same simile in berating his second son, Gerald, for gambling: "On my word, Gerald, I think that the so-called gentleman who sits down with the deliberate intention of extracting money from the pockets of his antagonists, who lays out for himself that way of repairing the shortcomings of fortune, who looks to that resource as an aid to his means, — is worse, much worse, than the public robber" (*DC* 516–17). Perhaps even more threatening than the risk of the high being made low, however, was the risk of the low rising to "unnatural" heights. Gambling, like other forms of financial speculation, was seen as threatening "natural" social boundaries by facilitating rapid social mobility. As one eighteenth-century commentator put it, "The greatest scoundrel of the town, with his money in his pockets, shall take his turn before the best duke or peer in the land, if the cards are on his side" (qtd. in Brenner and Brenner 60). So in *The Duke's Children* Major Tifto, through horse-trading and track-betting canniness, can join the Beargarden, the preeminent private gentlemen's club.

In *Middlemarch*, Fred Vincy's pretensions to gentlemanly status similarly are linked with his gambling, and both are to be corrected in the course of the novel. Fred gambles on the expectations of stepping into the country gentlemen's life at Stone Court, which he bets he will inherit from his miserly Uncle Featherstone. Featherstone and Stone Court represent the "landed" interests of the old gentry, which are tied to a traditional aristocratic ideology that is threatened by and disdainful of the newly moneyed, middle-class townsfolk such as Bulstrode. Featherstone deprecates Bulstrode's means of getting money as "spekilations" (*MM* 134). It is perhaps telling that Bulstrode's downfall begins with Raffles's appearance at the very moment in the novel when he is poised to breach the barrier between the commercial middle class and the landed gentry by buying Stone Court after Featherstone's death. Fred Vincy is similarly thwarted from crossing the same barrier into the same estate and effectively for the same reason: Fred gambles, and he does so with the figure of the gentleman. When he accepts a gift of money from Featherstone with feigned diffidence, he is told, "You take money like a lord; I suppose you lose it like one" (*MM* 133). Indeed he does, and he needs Featherstone's money to pay the resulting debts. He is understood by Middlemarch society to be one of those young men who is "addicted to pleasure" (*MM* 223), and in this regard he is similar to the protagonist of Thackeray's *Pendennis* (analyzed in chapter four). He plays billiards for money, he makes a very "unlucky" horse trade, and he publicly "post-obits" (*MM* 106). And his speculations are contagious; out of trust and goodness, Caleb Garth "takes a chance" on Fred by co-signing a loan note on which Fred must default, thereby also endangering his hoped-for marriage to Mary Garth. Having not yet gotten the message, Fred believes that all of the unhappy outcomes were brought on "purely by the favour of Providence in the shape of an old gentleman's caprice" (*MM* 333). The text's message here concerns moral choice and responsibility, but also the importance of preserving certain forms of value, especially landed value instead of paper or "city" money, by regulating mobility across class boundaries.

"City money," as Madalina Demolines says in Trollope's *The Last Chronicle of Barset* (1867), "is always very chancy" (226). "City money" signifies the combination of the stock market and the middle-class social climber, for instance, the Broughtons in *The Last Chronicle* or, most famously, the Popsnaps in Dickens's *Our Mutual Friend*. A primary reason that gambling linked bad money to undesirable class mobility was because of its analogical relationship with stock speculation within a context of financial upheavals. After all, the modern institutions and discourses of gambling and stock trading developed during the same general period and inevitably in reference to one another. In the eighteenth century, "it was not only that stockbrokers sold lottery tickets along with shares; their whole business was regarded as a type of gambling" (Miers and Dixon 379).[32] The rhetoric used by John Ashton in 1898 to describe the stock market, whether accurate or not, is representative of a widespread nineteenth-century conception: "In conclusion, as a place of gambling, the Stock Exchange is of far greater extent than the Turf. . . . [T]heir advertisements and circulars, disseminate the unwholesome vice of gambling throughout the length and breadth of the land, enabling people to speculate without anyone being the wiser. It is needless to say, that, as on the Turf, they are the losers" (*Gambling* 274). Commenting on the "railway mania" of 1845, David Morier Evans similarly wrote: "Indeed, it is a common subject to remark among parties who have watched the career of events, that the gambling encouraged through the fictitious value which shares attained has done much to aggravate the existing evil—the looseness of principle and the sacrifice of probity to secure the golden prize, having been only too freely sanctioned in circles where a higher sense of moral rectitude should have prevailed" (52).

At the same time, however, Parliament apparently favored "fictitious value" over "the golden prize" and so saw the "existing evil" instead as an opportunity. Rather than moving to regulate a reckless market, it passed the Limited Liability Act in 1855, which broke one of the last barriers limiting corporate expansion and stock speculation. Stock trading, which previously had been reserved for those wealthy enough to afford the generally high price of entry and high risks, was suddenly opened to a new class of speculators. Dramatic economic growth indeed did follow. Hundreds of new companies were "floated," some of which sailed into prosperity, but a substantial number of which sank, taking investors down with them. As one critical member of Parliament went on record as saying, the new law "enable[d] persons to embark in trade with a limited chance of loss, but with an unlimited chance for gain. That was a direct encouragement to a system of vicious and improvident speculation" (qtd. in Weiss 138).

The "'disease' of speculation" became the century's most notorious cause of bankruptcy, and, as Barbara Weiss argues in *The Hell of the English: Bankruptcy and the Victorian Novel*, bankruptcy became the most fearful specter in mid-Victorian society of personal and national vulnerability to economic forces apparently beyond individual control. The cycle of "economic prosperity, loss, debt, and then final catastrophe" that Weiss identifies in many Victorian novels echoes "the old medieval parables of Fortune's wheel" (82). Indeed, to the extent that bankruptcy was interpreted as the result of Providence-like forces, then personal responsibility could be denied. The opposite alternative was to interpret bankruptcy as a sign of moral failure on the part of the individual, which is often how Victorian novels portray bankrupts. Victorian discourse tends to explain bankruptcy in reference either to the "invisible hand" of Providence *or* to the individual, but specifically *not* to the institutions within society that might have been more directly responsible. There is no doubt that quite specific interests and institutions, including the stock exchange and the Bank of England, not only contributed to the conditions that produced widespread speculation and bankruptcy but also gained immense wealth as a result. This same sort of omission of social reference appears in the fact that Victorian novels make relatively little mention of "investment" as opposed to the more sensational — one might say marketable — topic of "speculation." To characterize the stock market primarily in terms of "speculation" masks the majority of nineteenth-century investors who worked the market rationally for long-term returns by minimizing risk while maximizing potential gain (but who, of course, were not the majority of the population).[33] In many Victorian novels, investment is simply what the wisely wealthy characters are assumed to do, generally behind the scenes and without mention; speculation, whether in the market or at the track (and often in combination), is what the foolishly declining aristocrat or the avaricious social climber does, typically ending in bankruptcy on the front pages of newspapers and in novels alike. This omission of certain functions and effects of the stock market while emphasizing others represents a resistance to confusing the boundaries between the "play" of market speculation and the "seriousness" of work, which might apply even to investment. To confuse the two might suggest that the "fictitious value" produced by gambling or speculation is not so dissimilar from the value produced through means sanctioned by the dominant social order.

Work / Business

> It is not work itself, not even the excess of work, that is the mark of servitude, but the extreme antithesis of work and play. It is the mark of the free man that he does not differentiate between his work and his play.
> F. E. Sparshott, "Work — The Concept"

Work is the last best register of real value, the one "good" mode of exchange that might escape taint through association with gambling or speculation, the one left standing after all other sources of value have been found wanting. But work too is complicated by its relationship to questions of social structure, equality of value, and play. In the first place, the figure of work becomes tied to money whenever the question of remuneration arises, which it must or else become the sign of a forced omission. At the same time, the issue of class arises through the necessity to distinguish "work," understood as an individual endeavor in response to a moral imperative, from "labor," which is a shared activity and category *within* society. Perhaps recognizing these difficulties, Trollope made the spokesperson for work in *The Duke's Children* neither a working-class nor a middle-class character but the Duke himself. Having asked his son Gerald if he knows "what money is," and having received the timorous answer that it is "cheques, and sovereigns, and bank notes," the Duke explains the relationship between money and work: "Money is the reward of labour . . . or rather, in the shape it reaches you, it is your representation of that reward. You may earn it yourself, or, as is, I am afraid, more likely to be the case with you, you may possess it honestly as prepared for you by the labour of others who have stored it up for you. . . . There is nothing so comfortable as money, — but nothing so defiling if it be come by unworthily. . . . If a man have enough, let him spend it freely. If he wants it, let him earn it honestly. Let him do something for it, so that the man who pays it to him may get its value. But to think that it may be got by gambling, to hope to live by that fashion, to sit down with your fingers almost in your neighbour's pockets . . . — that I say is to have left far, far behind you, all nobility, all gentleness, all manhood!" (*DC* 517–18).

For the Duke, money is stored labor, but, unlike Karl Marx, he sees its value as belonging to the employer, not the laborer. Certainly labor must be defined very broadly to include the means by which the Duke's fictional forebears came to be one of the wealthiest families in England. Elsewhere, the Duke, who is known for his abstinence from the pleasures of eating, associates himself with what he calls the "power" of "the rural labourer who sits on the ditch-side with his bread and cheese and onion" (*DC* 194). He appears in contrast here to Gerald, who can only mildly remark, "Not to have money for your wants; — that must be troublesome," and Silverbridge, who observes, "I cannot bear to think that I should like to have a thing and that I cannot afford it" (*DC* 195). The Duke — like Lady Mabel Grex ("A real gentleman . . . should never think of money at all" [*DC* 159]) and like Dorothea Brooke ("I hate my wealth" [*MM* 787]) — can afford the luxury of viewing wealth as "a burden which [one] must carry to the end" (*DC* 197).[34] It is not with a little irony, then, that the reader must view the Duke's sincere comparison between himself and a fieldhand, or recognize that lack of money is more than "troublesome" to some people for whom "lik[ing] to have a thing" is overshadowed by genuine need. (Trollope should receive credit for being in on this irony, which comes clear with Gerald's final observation on the matter: "He says that a property is no better than a burden. But I'll try and bear it" [*DC* 198].) Nevertheless, the Duke is associated throughout the novel with the Carlylean "gospel of work," "the only pleasure in life which [he] has . . . enjoyed without alloy"

(*DC* 123). It is telling that this doctrine couples the Duke with the lower-middle-class Caleb Garth from *Middlemarch*, who values work even to the extent of working without concern for remuneration (*MM* 543). Thus the high and low once more are lumped together through a lesson derived most directly from middle-class doctrine. While the Duke recognizes that money is "the reward of labour," "the labour of others who have stored it up for you," he thinks of himself and his (male) forebearers as the "others" who have labored, denying his "rural labourer" and the generations of true laborers that he represents.[35]

A second, complicating aspect of work is indicated by the fact that the Victorians in particular defined it in opposition to play.[36] Play, especially the play of gambling, was the necessary Other to work (much as the play of mimesis is the necessary Other of nineteenth-century realism, which I argue in chapters one and four). As John Vernon observes, "If money's source of value is labor . . . then gambling gains its meaning and part of its attraction by subjecting money to an illicit condition, that of play" (124). The work/play problematic comes to the fore in the way that the discourses of money and work converge on the modern dichotomy between "business" and "pleasure." In *Middlemarch*, Mr. Farebrother's sin is less that he plays whist than that he plays for money. It is this feature of Farebrother's character — this "blot" of "money-winning business," as Lydgate describes it to Dorothea (*MM* 481) — that must be overcome in Dorothea's mind before she can offer him the vicar's position at the Lowick Manor chapel. She decides to do so specifically as a means of saving him from the financial need that she assumes drives him to gambling. After his conversion from gambling, Farebrother may still play for pleasure "a rubber to satisfy his mother," but not for money (*MM* 624). Like Mr. Farebrother, Silverbridge in *The Duke's Children* makes the mistake of confusing pleasure with business. The Duke comments as follows on Silverbridge's reasons for associating with Major Tifto: "If you associate with him, not for pleasure, then it surely must be for profit. That you should do the former would be to me . . . surprising. . . . That you should do the latter — is, I think, a reproach" (*DC* 213–14). Similarly, Silverbridge's more experienced colleague, Mr. Lupton, tells him: "A man in your position can hardly make money by it, but he may lose so much! If a man really likes the amusement, — as I do, — and risks no more than what he has in his pocket, that may be very well" (*DC* 356). But it is Lady Mabel Grex who sums up the novel's discourse on gambling: "I like a man to like pleasure. But I despise a man who makes a business of his pleasures. When I hear that this man is the best whist-player in London, and that man the best billiard-player, I always know that they can do nothing else, and then I despise them" (*DC* 78). (An irony of the text is that Lady Mabel does make a "business of her pleasure" in speculatively pursuing Silverbridge.) Caleb Garth, the discourse of work's leading proponent in *Middlemarch*, one also noted for his lack of interest and ability in finance, represents the prescribed attitude in these matters: "It must be remembered that by 'business' Caleb never meant money transactions, but the skillful application of labour" (*MM* 533).

Clearly, work, pleasure, and business must be kept separate, or, preferably, pleasure and business should be subsumed under work, erased *into* work. Only in this way can "work" be maintained as the only completely positive source of value. Once pleasure and business have been merged into work, it automatically becomes, as if by magic, an end in itself, free from questions of remuneration. Work thus conceived is its own goal and product, an aesthetic pursuit rather than an activity that produces capital in society. To admit the latter would be to recognize work as labor and labor as a primary source of value in society. In particular, business must be kept separate from work and pleasure and, optimally, should not be thought of at all: it should be forgotten, made invisible. Pleasure, on the other, hand is dangerous to the extent that it distracts from work and threatens to lead the weak to mix it with business. Therefore, while business disappears, pleasure must be regulated. Illicit play — whether as "bad" money, undesirable class mobility, recreation, or pleasure itself — is supplanted by work, though only by throwing the boundaries between work, business, and play into question.

Why is it that at this time in history when labor was being systematically devalued relative to exchange value and when inherited land, like precious metal, was being replaced as the basis of value by the magic of paper money, work and land still were represented as the sources of "real" value? Why is it that a rhetoric of the equality of value — whether between monetary media, marriage partners, or social classes — was launched at a time when the difference between "face value" and "fictitious value" appeared at every moment about to collapse, threatening to bring with it financial panic or class revolt? The rhetorical nature of these questions makes the answers — or my answers, at any rate — obvious. The separation of "work" from "business" and the implicit directive to concentrate on the former and avoid and ignore the latter is instructive here. Once labor has been erased and business has been mystified, what is left is work — "you can succeed on your own if you try hard enough" — and equality — "we are all in this together" or "your opportunity is as good as anybody's." Work then becomes a value in itself—work for work's sake—while business, meaning particularly finance capitalism itself, which increasingly *was* the source of value, is removed from attention. Thus social values are separated from value. "Equality" functions then to mystify the relation between values and value so that the former appears as the source of the latter when it is not, or in fact when financial value may have become the primary source of moral values. Between the fable of individual self-determination and the fable of social unity through a shared culture, the middle, which is society itself, the site of local practice and struggle, has been removed from consideration.

The Last Hand

> To deal with property on the principle of chance, which is non-moral, must be immoral because it involves the false proposition that property itself is non-moral.
>
> W. D. Mackenzie, *The Ethics of Gambling*

The figure of gambling was so troubling to the Victorians in part because it did raise questions about the moral reasoning that justified relations based increasingly on the rules of property. Gambling throws the ethics of property into question, which also is to say that it foregrounds the fact that property is not "non-moral," though for reasons opposite to those that W. D. Mackenzie assumed in 1895. The distribution of property, the decision about what justifies ownership and who deserves and does not deserve to own how much, is perhaps the most morally critical decision that any society makes, or it certainly became so in nineteenth-century England. Given the rise to dominance of bourgeois civil society, and the finance capitalism on which it depended, coupled with declining belief in a benevolent, controlling deity, Victorians were faced with having to form a basis of social judgment about issues of property and value, equity and equality. The "natural" basis for property relations founded on aristocratic hierarchy was beginning to lapse. As the familiar story goes, the "invisible hand" of "the market" emerged as the next best candidate to God as the adjudicator of value, worth, and finally worthiness. The naturalization of "the market" required that it be translated into discourse as an entity or force beyond human comprehension or control. As a result, a certain mysterious randomness was associated with the newly natural mechanisms of the market, and this was interpreted by some proponents of laissez-faire capitalism and utilitarianism as the best means of achieving social justice and the closest possible approximation of equality, conceived as equality of opportunity. Some early Victorians, Thomas Carlyle most notable among them, were disturbed by the omission of merit, choice, and responsibility from this model. The "gospel of work" was one response, though perhaps it ultimately served the interests of the very system at which it was aimed. Subsequent bourgeois liberal intellectuals, especially George Eliot, worked to define another register of value to the market, one based more on mutual sympathy and reciprocal responsibility. Gambling, as an analog to stock speculation and as a sign of any system that places chance above choice, became a common figure within Victorian discourse and, in midcentury realist novels in particular, for "the market." The pervasiveness of the figure of gambling in Victorian novels, its infiltration of all forms of value, good as well as bad, is only surprising until one considers it within this historical context, however condensed and simplified the preceding presentation of it may be.

By the nineteenth century the discourses surrounding gambling and finance capitalism had fully penetrated one another, and maintaining the boundary between the two therefore became increasingly critical in the mid-Victorian decades. The obvious similarities between stock trading and gambling and the conflation of the two in the people's minds only increased anxiety about the representational nature of money, individual financial survival, and national stability. As the speculative dangers of finance were demonstrated by events, the need increased to distance finance capitalism rhetorically from gambling. Gambling thus posed a paradoxical dilemma for the rising middle classes: it was analogous with the market system by which prosperity and upward mobility were effected, while it also represented a fearful specter of an economy careening out of control. Those in the commercial world concerned with respectability strove to maintain a precarious distinction. In America, for example, the Chicago Board of Trade mounted a campaign against gambling shops in the 1840s "because of the fear that they would bring into general disrepute the legitimate exchange, since trade in futures would be viewed as mere gambling" (Brenner and Brenner 92).[37] On both sides of the Atlantic, gambling legislation and a concerted effort to distinguish between gambling or speculation and investment facilitated the stock exchange's establishment as a pillar of society and an unquestioned source of real value. Gambling functioned in relationship to the stock market as what Stephen Marcus calls a "negative analogue": the necessarily evil Other toward which all critical attention is to be directed (*Other Victorians* 283).

Thus the London stockbroker and George Eliot similarly demonized gambling. One way to interpret this observation is the familiar ideological criticism of the Victorian novel, according to which it straightforwardly reproduces dominant bourgeois ideology. The situation is not that simple. In the first place, political economy and realist novels negatively represent gambling for opposite reasons: the former to create a distracting scapegoat, the latter as a foil against which to propose an alternative model of value and values. On the other hand, this sort of claim leads most frequently in recent criticisms to the "separate spheres" argument, articulated here by James Thompson: "Inverses of one another, political economy and the novel map, respectively, a zone of finance and a zone of affect, or money and feeling. . . . This zone of affect provides refuge from the competitive world of civil society as a place exempt from the laws and brutality of capitalist exchange" (23). As I have tried to show, however, the nineteenth-century realist novel's "zone of affect" is not only far from exempt from the brutality of the market but is as often as not expressed as itself a market. If, as Thompson argues, in eighteenth-century novels "finance and romance become dialectically related, so that the presence of one calls on the palpable absence of the other," in mid-ninteenth-century novels finance and romance are no longer defined by the absence of the other because they are both always simultaneously present (3). Money, the realm of political economy, and the world of finance are not the repressed plot (in the sense argued by Peter Brooks in *Reading for Plot*) of many Victorian novels; they *are* the plot, especially in novels like Dickens's *Dombey and Son* (1847) or Trollope's *The Way We Live Now* (1875), for instance. They are not below the surface or disguised; they are everywhere on the surface. But this might appear to return us to the standard ideological criticism and the claim that political economy and Victorian novels effectively reproduced the same discourse. In a limited sense this is accurate; political economy and the novel unavoidably participated in the culture and the society to which they mutually belonged. One cannot disregard, however, the ferocious critique of capitalist greed and middle-class self-satisfaction mounted by the novels of the nineteenth century. The figure of gambling was part of that critique.

Finally, gambling functions not simply as a figure representing "the market"; in the same instance it not only more generally indicates the philosophy of political economy but is a signifier for political economy itself as a cultural form. Political economy — in the form of treatises on the subject starting with Adam Smith's *Enquiry into the Nature and Causes of the Wealth of Nations* (1776) — and the realist novel entered the nineteenth century in competition with one another. That competition was in a literal sense over the number of books sold and read, but more significantly it was over which cultural form would disseminate most broadly and so have greatest influence on the definition of "value," the construction of the subject in society, and the understanding of representation itself. Eliot and Trollope were not naïve to this any more than they were blind to the analogous relationship between pound notes and manuscript pages, scrip and script. They build this very issue into their novels, thematically and formally. Novels of the period therefore stage discursive contests between the figure of political economy as "gambling" and generally privileged figures representing "real value" that the text associates with the form of its own realism. These claims will be developed more thoroughly in the two chapters that follow. Suffice it to say that novels published in the wake of the historical engagement between political economy and the realist novel respond to and construct that competition. Rather than limiting their domain to the domestic or the affective realms, relinquishing to political economy the right to define the economic rules of their society, they instead worked — successfully or not — to incorporate political economy, to remake political economy in their own image, and to *be* the political economy of their time.

3

Performing the Self

The line drawn between the two kinds of behavior, theatrical and un-
theatrical, depends on the selectivity of moral vision which is conditioned by the process of socialisation in a particular social milieu, at a
particular time.

Elizabeth Burns, *Theatricality*

When we alter our diversity for pleasure, when the body is made the
instrument of that pleasure, when the pleasure is available to anyone
who can pay for it, as with the actor, the activity turns into a form of
metaphysical prostitution for which no loathing can be too strong and
no repudiation too absolute.

Jonas Barish, *The Antitheatrical Prejudice*

Just Act Natural

Theatricality is play with identity, or that is one understanding of it suggested by a reading of Victorian texts. As such, theatricality haunts Victorian novels. Haunt can be taken literally if one considers the not uncommon
coincidence of theatrical and supernatural elements in novels like Charlotte
Brontë's *Villette*, in which the ghost-nun hauntings of Lucy Snowe are
revealed as the theatrical cross-dressing of Alfred de Hamal. But at the
moment I mean haunt in a broader sense: the figure of theatricality pervades mid-Victorian novels in particular and for particular historical reasons. These reasons largely have been overlooked in the past decade's flurry
of studies on theatricality, signaled by works such as Joseph Litvak's *Caught
in the Act*. Recent interest in theatricality is preceded by the important
groundwork laid by Nina Auerbach, Jonas Barish, Elizabeth Burns, and
David Marshall, among others.[1] A few novels have a history of analysis in
relation to the figure of the theater, especially Jane Austen's *Mansfield Park*
and George Eliot's *Daniel Deronda*.[2] But the mid-Victorian novelistic concern with theatricality was not limited to such conspicuously theatrical

novels as these. Indeed, the early to mid-Victorian period produced a relative spate of novels that persistently concern themselves with the theater, novels like *Villette*, *Vanity Fair*, and *Pendennis*, but also less explicitly theatrical novels like *Shirley*, *Jane Eyre*, *Alton Locke*, and *Felix Holt*. The pervasiveness of the figure of the theater in the 1840s to 1860s has unique historical significance in relationship to events in the formal development and commercialization of the novel. It expresses an historical contest that reached culmination in the first half of the nineteenth century between two, major, competing cultural forms: the realist novel and the popular theater.

This chapter concentrates on four novels, two by Charlotte Brontë, *Shirley* (1849) and *Villette* (1853), and two by George Eliot, *Felix Holt* (1866) and *Daniel Deronda* (1876).[3] *Villette* and *Daniel Deronda* are the obvious choices, being among the most patently theatrical Victorian novels. Both Brontë and Eliot were theater enthusiasts and, though writing nearly twenty years apart, they used the same famous Jewish actress of the time, Rachel Félix, whom they each had seen onstage, as a model for characters: Vashti in *Villette* and Leonora Halm-Eberstein in *Daniel Deronda* (Stokes 779). All of the critical events in *Villette* are Lucy Snowe's brushes with the theatrical: her forced performance in M. Paul's vaudeville; her ominous encounters with the ghostly Nun; her attendance at Vashti's inflammatory stage performance; her unwitting participation in the midnight masquerade in Villette's town square; and her juxtaposition throughout to the quintessentially theatrical Ginevra Fanshawe. In quite a different way, theatricality is ever-present on the surface of *Daniel Deronda*, particularly in the character of Gwendolen Harleth, who in effect acts out the stages of her own de-theatricalization, from her performance as the aristocratic gambler to her prophetic tableau vivant as Shakespeare's Hermione to her misguided aspirations to be a professional actress to her incarceration in the role of Mrs. Mallinger Grandcourt to her final renunciation of performance for a "new consciousness." Virtually all of the other characters in the novel are linked to the performing or plastic arts or otherwise are marked as theatrical. Only Deronda is supposedly free from the taint of theatricality — a supposition that I will dismantle. One question to be addressed is how Brontë's and Eliot's representations of theatricality coincide and differ, and why.

The choices of *Shirley* and *Felix Holt* are less obvious. These two novels, each considered minor within their respective author's *oeuvres*, generally would not be described in theatrical terms.[4] This is one reason why I chose them: to explore the potential representation of theatricality in novels that do not purport to and, in general, have not been read as representing theatricality. One point of commonality that proves relevant, however, is that both *Shirley* and *Felix Holt* are their author's one historical-political novel. *Shirley*—written at the end of the decade that witnessed the institutionalization of the first reform bill and the rise and fall of Chartism—is set in 1811–12 at the beginning of the Luddite rebellions. *Felix Holt*, written during a year of national debates that would end with the passage in the subsequent year of the second reform bill, is set in 1832 following the passage of the first reform bill. The two novels share similar Condition-of-England concerns, neatly spanning the period of the most dramatic (so to speak) social upheaval in Britain in modern times.

Victorian novels offer no single or simple definition of "theatricality." This is in part the case because the theatrical appears in a multiplicity of guises, most typically as discourse by narrators or characters about acting and the stage, representation of characters marked as "theatrical" and "nontheatrical," inclusion of theatrical scenes in which dramatic performances are witnessed or acted in by characters, the use of theatrical metaphors to characterize (and usually stigmatize) certain social groups or issues, the use in the novel of formal devices typically associated with drama, and the thematization (and textual enactment) of issues related to spectatorship and surveillance. But perhaps the most pervasive representation of theatricality is the figure of the theatrical woman, the female lead who makes selfhood a matter of performance. Indeed, the theatrical woman is the most consistent foil throughout Victorian fiction to the figure of the "angel in the house." Fanny Price has her Mary Crawford, Amelia Sedley her Becky Sharpe, Lizzie Hexam her Bella Wilfer, Dorothea Brooke her Rosamond Vincy, Mirah Lapodith her Gwendolen Harleth, Esther Summerson her Lady Dedlock, and so on. That this pairing of "domestic" and "theatrical" types is repeated throughout Victorian fiction evidences a general cultural struggle between two competing, highly gendered models of the subject. The mark of the theatrical model is externality and artifice—as opposed to internal authenticity—and association with the body, but the body coupled with a psychic mobility, which, though most often read as duplicitousness, also can be read as self-fashioning. What is more, the theatrical (like the supernatural) also sometimes serves as an empowering rite of passage for markedly "nontheatrical" female characters, such as Fanny Price in *Mansfield Park* or Lucy Snowe in *Villette*. While overtly stigmatizing one definition of femininity, then, theatricality also unavoidably foregrounds the performativeness of prescribed gender roles. In this way, it not only functions to police gender categories but simultaneously instigates a destabilization of those categories.

But the domestic/theatrical dichotomy, while critical, is only the most obvious, specific instance of a more diffuse dialectic. Theatricality signals the traditional, metaphysical dialectic of inner versus outer, the dilemma of identity split by self-consciousness. No wonder, then, that theatricality would be intriguing and troubling for a cultural form like the nineteenth-century realist novel that concerns itself so centrally with issues of self-reflexive subjecthood. For this reason, theatricality pervades the novels analyzed here in the form of a continual juxtaposition of two categories of characters and social issues: those marked as theatrical and characterized in terms of artificiality, falseness, and exteriority and, on the other hand, those marked as nontheatrical and characterized in terms of authenticity, realness, and interiority. As might be expected, the novels generally privilege the latter figures, and theatricality serves — at least at the first level of analysis — to stigmatize certain issues or groups opposed by the dominant discourses of the text, especially the following: decadent aristocracy, Romanticism, Catholicism, foreignness (especially Frenchness), "improvement" or social progress, class mobility, political activism in general and mob behavior in particular, and feminine vanity and desire. But the figure of the theater poses a much more complex problem for mid-Victorian realist novels than they can resolve simply by making it a scapegoating device.[5] In novels like *Pendennis* or *Felix Holt*, the repeated juxtaposition of nontheatrical and theatrical figures emerges as a dialogue within the text between the figure of the novel and the figure of the theater. This amounts to a dialogue about the novel's own formal assumptions. As such, it is extremely precarious, because it always threatens to reveal the artifice of realism and the performativeness of the subjective interiority in reference to which nineteenth-century realism defined its form. Moreover, the dialogue between the figure of the theater and the figure of the novel that appears especially in mid-Victorian novels was a response to and a construction of a quite material contest for entertainment market share in which publishing and staging, reading and theater-going, realism and melodrama, were engaged in the first half of the nineteenth century as in no previous or subsequent time.

Victorian Antitheatrical Rhetoric and the Novelization of the Theatrical

Shirley, *Villette*, *Felix Holt*, and *Daniel Deronda* share an antitheatrical rhetoric characteristic of the period, but also complicate that rhetoric beyond any simple antitheatrical conclusion. In *Shirley*, for example, Shirley's uncle, Mr. Sympson, fears that Shirley will bestow herself (and, what is worse, the family money) on what for him is the lowest of the low: "a low clerk, a play-actor, a play-writer, or — or. . . . Any literary scrub, or shabby, whining artist" (*S* 445). This might be taken as unmediated antitheatricality if not for the fact that Mr. Sympson is himself a buffoonish figure of an impotent patriarchy with whom Shirley parries in a series of dialogues that Charlotte Brontë styled after Shakespearean or Restoration comedy (*S* 515–17). Ironically, Mr. Sympson intends for Shirley to marry Sir Philip Nunnely, who is portrayed as an effete, effeminate, aristocratic aesthete whom Shirley feels is deserving of her uncle's epithet. Along similar lines, in *Felix Holt* the most egregiously theatrical alternative to the austere individualism and authenticity for which Felix is meant to stand is the aristocratic Romanticism of Byron: "His corsairs and renegades, his Alps and Manfreds, are the most paltry puppets that were ever pulled by the strings of lust and pride" (*FH* 59). The other two theatricalized alternatives represented in the novel are lower-class pretensions to gentility — which Felix equates with an arse-kissing, money-grubbing intention to "dress up swindling till it looks as well as honesty" — and displayed feminine beauty (*FH* 103). The novel charts Felix's instruction of Esther Lyon toward becoming "the woman whose beauty makes a great task easier to men instead of turning them away from it," much as *Daniel Deronda* charts the instruction of Gwendolen Harleth by Daniel (*FH* 222). But the most patently theatrical character in *Daniel Deronda* is Lapidoth (profligate father of Mirah and Mordecai), in whom a theatrical life is combined with oily deceptiveness, gambling, thievery, drinking, and, worst of all, prostitution of his own daughter, embodying all possible antitheatrical arguments in one. Finally, in *Villette*, the novel's anti-Catholic (anti-French) stance is expressed throughout in the theatrical terms that were common to the Protestant rhetoric of the time. That rhetoric characterized "popery" in terms of the ceremonial display and "costume" of Mass, the superstitious chanting and idolatry of Virgin worship, the moblike communality that threatens Protestant individualism, and the emphasis on external "works" rather than internal faith.[6] The most obvious reading that these novels offer of theatricality, then, is as a quality characterizing certain social or cultural elements that thereby are marked as undesirable.

This reading begins to complexify when one considers the narrator's address to the implied reader in the second paragraph of *Shirley*: "If you think, from this prelude, that anything like a romance is preparing for you, reader, you never were more mistaken. Do you anticipate sentiment, and poetry, and reverie? Do you expect passion, and stimulus, and melodrama? Calm your expectations; reduce them to a lowly standard. Something real, cool, and solid, lies before you" (*S* 39). Here, in a standard sort of opening disclaimer, Brontë's narrator uses theatrical terminology to distance the novel from a number of other genres or subgenres, particularly romance. This term (and, later, sensation) was used not only by subsequently canonized Victorian novelists to look down their noses at a less "literary" category of fiction, but also by some Victorians to characterize both Romantic poetry and melodramatic theater. Why, then, does a reading of this novel find no shortage of romance and a goodly share of sentiment, poetry (quoted and recited), reverie, passion, stimulus, and melodrama (for example, the two sickroom scenarios, the reunion of Caroline Helstone with her mother, the foretold death of Jessie Yorke, and the confessions in Louis Moore's diary of a supposedly doomed love for Shirley)? Nevertheless, the narrator aligns her story with the "real," establishing a scale with theatricality at the negative end, the real and the true at the positive end, and a text called *Shirley* resting squarely at the favored pole.

The narrator invokes this scale later in the novel when Caroline confronts the cruel realities of her apparently unrequited love for her cousin, Robert Moore: "Caroline Helstone was just eighteen years old; and at eighteen the true narrative of life is yet to be commenced. Before that time, we sit listening to a tale, a marvellous fiction; delightful sometimes, and sad sometimes; almost always unreal" (*S* 120). Real life is a "true narrative," not a "marvellous fiction," as romance or melodrama might mislead one to believe. *Shirley* offers itself as paradigmatic of "true narrative," and the text will go on to show not only Caroline but the reader what should be thought real. Real life is a realist novel; false life—delusion—is the theatrical. The traditional "theater metaphor"—that the world is a stage, that people perform their roles in life, that providential forces may save the day or sweep the stage without warning—is refigured as the novel metaphor.[7]

In the scene that culminates in the "true narrative" passage, Robert, under Caroline's tutelage, reads *Coriolanus* aloud. In terms that do justice to Thomas Carlyle's third lecture in *On Heroes, Hero-Worship, and the Heroic in History*, Caroline recommends Shakespeare as the "voice" of the wisdom of the past: "Let glorious William come near and touch [the lyre of your heart]; you will see how he will draw the English power and melody out of its chords. . . . You must have his spirit before you; you must hear his voice with your mind's ear; you must take some of his soul into yours" (*S* 114–

15). The reader knows that Caroline is quite interested in instructing Robert's heart toward a capacity for deeper feeling and that the practical-minded Robert, who would not woo a woman he could not financially support (or who could not financially support him), has willed his heart to silence on this topic where it most concerns Caroline. The figure of reading therefore operates in the first instance to domesticate the masculine.[8] It functions in the second place as a means of training Robert away from the French and Catholic influences of his Belgian upbringing back to a proper Englishness. Third, the text intends Robert to receive a lesson about feeling and politics: that Coriolanus's tragic flaw, and the reason for his death, is his unwillingness to show *sympathy* for "the people," just as Robert, a mill owner, is unwilling to sympathize with the plight of workers who have lost their jobs due to mechanization and market conditions (worsened by the war with Napoleon). He has said that he is an "alien" to such "English clowns" as the workers, concluding, "I might act the benevolent with them, but acting is not my *forte*" (*S* 100). *Shirley* is set on showing that acting is in any case not the route to learning sympathy. Though Robert's characteristic tendency is to "sympathize with that proud patrician who does not sympathize with his famished fellow-men," not even he can resist the truth and reality of reading *Coriolanus*: "As he advanced, he forgot to criticise; it was evident he appreciated the power, the truth of each portion; and, stepping out of the narrow line of private prejudices, began to revel in the large picture of human nature, to feel the reality stamped upon the characters who were speaking from that page before him" (*S* 116). Though Robert does not yet learn the lesson, the novel will trace his uneven evolution toward sympathy at every level: for Caroline, for the workers, and for England. But the real point concerns the role of reading, and this is where a potential contradiction arises. Here is Caroline, age eighteen, sitting and listening to a theatrical tale; however, the text presents this tale not as "unreal" but as "true narrative." Therefore, according to the logic of the text, it should be a novel—indeed, like *Shirley*—when, in fact, it is a play, a theatrical form.

This contradiction, if a small one, nevertheless is symptomatic of the wider dilemma that theatricality poses for Victorian novels by engaging them repeatedly in a revealing dialogue about their own formal assumptions. The surface antitheatricalism is turned on its head when confronted by certain representations of the theatrical, in this case Shakespeare. On the other hand, the text's response to such a theatrical emblem of the greatness of Britain and the redeeming power of Art is, in effect, to *novelize the theatrical*. *Shirley* co-opts Shakespeare, placing the dramatic text within the novelistic text, and saying, in effect, "This is like the novel, not like what passes for drama these days." George Eliot does the same thing in her many allusions to Shakespeare and her frequent use of Shakespeare in the epigraphs to her chapters. Realist novels of this period textualize "high" drama as a means of enlisting the authority of a mythologized racial and national history. Shakespeare, Victorian novels repeatedly suggest, is to be read, not performed.[9] Performance is taken out of it. This discursive contest between reading and performance, realism and theatricality, represents a historical contest for cultural dominance between the novel as commodity and commercial theater. At stake was which model of the subject would hold moral sway in society, the melodramatic subject of performance or the interiorized reading subject.

The Novel Versus Melodrama

Four dates are especially relevant to an understanding of Victorian theatricality and antitheatricalism: 1737, the Theater Licensing Act; 1789, the advent of the French Revolution; 1802, the opening of Thomas Holcroft's *A Tale of Mystery* at Covent Garden; and 1843, the rescinding by Parliament of the 1737 Licensing Act. The specific dates are less significant than the social and cultural shifts that they indicate.

The Licensing Act of 1737, which in a sense is the reassertion of the state control of public media that had been initiated in 1642 by the Puritans and curtailed by the Restoration, limited the performance in London of spoken or "legitimate" drama to two patent theaters, Drury Lane and Covent Garden.[10] The impact of the Act on the development in England of dramatic form — and, significantly, the formulation of the novel — can hardly be overestimated; it "killed the free theater and drove its most gifted writer, Fielding, from the stage altogether" (Barish 235). It represents the beginning of a modern cycle of antitheatricalism in Britain that comes to an end only with the rescinding of the Act nearly a century later.[11] Further, the Act generated a distinction that was carried into the nineteenth century between "legitimate" theater — meaning primarily the "literary" drama of classical tragedy and Shakespeare — and "illegitimate" theater, which came to mean "melodrama, pantomime, spectacle, burlesque and anything . . . with some musical accompaniment and a few songs" (Booth et al. 42). The Act hinged, then, on a distinction between the theater of "pure spoken drama" (Kent 98) or, as it was called, spoken "prose" (Donohue, *Kean* 49), and the theater of music and spectacle. The developing eighteenth-century novel represents one response to this edict: a movement into *written* prose. The other response was, in effect, the invention of British melodrama, which takes its origins in part from the efforts of eighteenth-century "illegitimate" theater owners to circumvent the law by creating theater that included everything *except* spoken prose. The 1737 Act contributed to the spawning of two extremely important cultural forms, the novel and melodrama, which would come to represent opposed aesthetics and competing entertainment markets.

The French Revolution theatricalized History on a scale comparable in the minds of Georgians and Victorians only to Classical mythology and Arthurian legend. It also fueled antitheatrical sentiment and intensified the class-specific aspects of antitheatrical rhetoric, which carried into the nineteenth century. In *Masquerade and Civilization: The Carnivalesque in Eighteenth-Century English Culture and Fiction*, Terry Castle argues that masquerade as a carnivalesque social event was the "exemplary" phenomenon of the eighteenth century (5). Near the end of the century, however, masquerade became threatening to the increasingly dominant middle-class social order in two ways: by destabilizing gender boundaries and by blurring class boundaries. A threat to either of these foundational categories ultimately was a metaphysical threat, as Castle describes it: "The pleasure of the masquerade attended on the experience of double-ness, the alienation of inner from outer, a fantasy of two bodies simultaneously and thrillingly present, self and other together" (4–5). It is little wonder, then, that masquerade should become emblematic of a certain Victorian nightmare, and the terms used by Castle to describe eighteenth-century masquerade are consonant with nineteenth-century antitheatrical rhetoric. What is both surprising and appropriate is the precipitousness of the decline in the practice of masquerade after the Revolution began. Castle writes, "The deinstitutionalization of the masquerade and the relegation of 'costume parties' to the periphery of collective life were so rapid as to suggest a kind of cultural amnesia. The masquerade's duplicitous fantasia were disavowed; its utopian spectacle was exorcised. . . . Somewhere between epochs a break occurred: all sense of the masquerade's cultural significance was mislaid" (99).[12] This claim is further supported by a similar pattern in the practice of private theatricals, which were the rage in England until the 1780s, when a decline began in the direction that is aptly captured in *Mansfield Park*.[13] The general point is twofold: First, the French Revolution, and then the cultural and industrial revolutions of the late eighteenth century, were accompanied by a class-based antitheatrical sentiment. Second, at least by the nineteenth century the figure of the theater became part of discourses aimed at the bidirectional *embourgeoisement* of British society. As my readings of *Felix Holt* and *Shirley* illustrate, theatricality took on connotations in one direction of upper-class debauchery (masquerade, private theatricals) and the "corrupt ruling class" (the French monarchy, the British Regency) *and*, simultaneously in the other direction, of "the mob" and any form of populist communality (carnival, "seditious meetings," unionization).

I take 1802 and the opening at Covent Garden of *A Tale of Mystery* as a milestone because it signals the coming of age in Britain of melodrama. Thomas Holcroft's play was billed as "'a New Melo-Drame'" (*Playbill* qtd. in Donohue, *Kean* 106). But the specificity of the date is irrelevant, since my use of it is to mark the entry into England of a cultural form that already was so latent in the culture of the time — or for which the culture already was so primed — that it came to dominate the London stage within the few years between the opening of *A Tale of Mystery* and the infamous "Old Price" theater riots of 1809.[14] Melodrama dominated London theater for the first half of the century, and its influence on popular forms certainly did not end there. It came to represent aesthetic and moral values antithetical to those that liberal-intellectual critics of the day defended as the purview of realism: realism in painting, realism on the stage, but especially realism in the novel. According to critics like George Henry Lewes and Edward Bulwer-Lytton, melodrama was too "popular" in the pejorative sense (though they did not use that particular term). Melodrama gave audiences all they wanted: "sensation, spectacle, violence, true love, romantic fantasy, strong narrative, fine sentiment, rhetoric, courage, low comedy, domestic realism, home and family, eccentric characters, patriotic spirit and a happy ending" (Booth et al. 35).[15]

Melodrama exhibited four salient characteristics: nonambivalence, externality, effect, and providentiality. It provided audiences with an "unmixed clarity of expectations" (Donohue, *Kean* 125). In the world of melodrama, everyday life is pervaded by a profound ethical struggle between the forces of good and the forces of evil, which are distinctly represented by recognizable characters and figures. Melodramas also exteriorized emotions and intentions in the form of costuming and music (the villain's black hat, minor-key music) as well as a "flattened" but expressive style of acting consisting of large, easily readable gestures and poses designed to spark stock audience responses.[16] This also partially describes "effect," which Victorians understood as "a direct appeal to emotion through unmediated sensation" (Meisel 71). Effect was realized visually through the use of "situation," the opposite of narrative, which was presented as moments of timeless significance rendered onstage as striking, pictorial compositions (for example, "the villain seizes the maiden and raises his arm"). Thus Lewes lamented the "*theatrical* effect" (as opposed to "*dramatic* art") of the "spectacle and sensation pieces" that dominated the popular stage of his day (*On Actors* 137, 142).[17] Earlier in the century, Walter Scott had written scathingly of the "art of effect" in fiction, claiming that "[p]robability and perspicuity of narrative are sacrificed with the utmost indifference to the desire of producing effect; and provided the author can but contrive to 'surprise and elevate,' he appears to think that he has done his duty to the public."[18] This criticism also points to the providentiality of melodrama, according to which Providence beneficently guarantees a happy ending for the good and a not-so-happy one for the bad. Redemption is demonstrated all the more strongly the *more* improbable the coincidence of the happy ending, since its providential nature and the organic connectedness of all things thereby are considered to be proved.[19] Melodrama generates effects regardless of what might be seen as rational causes.

In contrast, the conventions of nineteenth-century realism typically demand that effects (appear to) have a logic of commonsense probability, indeed that actions are likely to produce like effects and that it is wise for people to govern their lives with this in mind, as Mr. Jermyn finds in *Felix Holt*: "Here, in fact, was the inconvenience; he had sinned for the sake of particular concrete things, and particular concrete consequences were likely to follow" (*FH* 99). The admission of coincidence, chance, luck, fate, Providence, or the supernatural threatens an order in which history is expected to be juridical, individual responsibility is given precedence, and rational progress is thought possible. In short, the formal qualities of melodrama were — at least in the most obvious sense — the opposite of the moral ambiguity, interiorized subjectivity, narrative development, and logical probability that novelists like George Eliot claimed to practice.

Perhaps it is not surprising, then, that highbrow critics traditionally have typified the theater of the first half of the nineteenth century with the epithet "the decline." The term was used first by critics of the time, such as Lewes, who in 1875 wrote, "That our drama is extinct as literature, and our stage is in a deplorable condition of decline, no one ventures to dispute" (*On Actors* 113).[20] This common criticism represented a pointed resurrection of the "legitimate"/"illegitimate" distinction and a longing among such critics for a return to more "literary" drama. But "the decline" was not a critical invention; it occurred quite materially in terms of audience demographics and economic conditions for theaters and playwrights. In the first quarter of the nineteenth century, classes below the middle came to dominate London theater for the first time since the Renaissance, and the theaters failed to be sufficiently profitable.[21] Attendance by middle- to upper-class theater patrons declined as the theaters produced fewer "literary" dramas and more melodramas. Between 1808 and 1812, the two patent theaters each burned and were rebuilt on a grander scale. Larger audiences were needed to fill the theaters, which in turn provided greater access to patrons of the pit. At the same time, however, more private boxes and private entrances were introduced to cater to upper-class desires for privacy and exclusivity. Not only did this steepen the status hierarchy within the audience (as well as fueling middle-class anxiety about the already existing presence of prostitution in theater boxes),[22] but it raised the issue of equal access to "the national theater," which became a moral theme in the "Old Price" (OP) theater riots of 1809.

The OP riots were sparked by a rise in ticket prices that occurred after the rebuilding of the burned Covent Garden. They were carried on every night for sixty-seven consecutive days and consisted mainly of organized performance disruption by the audience in the pit. Marc Baer's *Theater and Disorder in Late Georgian London* argues that they were about much more than ticket prices; in addition to being an enactment of class-based political unrest, they were a conservative lower-class effort to preserve and maintain control of a "traditional theatre dynamic" (185). That tradition included a certain communal and interactive theater ethos, not only among audience members but also between audience members and actors, which was threatened by changes in the form of the theater related to the advent of melodrama and to the architectural expansion of the theaters. Baer interprets the eventual success of the riots in relowering theater prices as a victory, however temporary, of the "custom and moral economy" of "cultural property" over the private property of the theater owners and managers (76).[23] Despite—or perhaps because of—the eventual capitulation of theater management in dropping ticket prices to former levels, the main theaters continued to suffer financially for decades. Finally, then, the coming of age of melodrama in England, the "decline" in British theater, and the OP theater riots were not unrelated events but part of the same larger event: the early-nineteenth-century crisis in British theater.

And this leads to the fourth and final date: 1843 and the rescinding of the 1737 Theater Licensing Act. Concern among both middle and upper classes (though for different reasons, perhaps) generated a Parliamentary Inquiry in 1832 into theater patent legislation and the causes of "the decline." At issue was whether the government should continue to try to regulate such an influential cultural form as the theater or allow it to operate on a laissez-faire basis (Donohue, *Kean* 177). After the Act was rescinded, Victorian theater did revive economically. The middle and upper classes began to return to London theaters, with the music halls and football matches perhaps absorbing some of the "less desirable" audience elements. Queen Victoria became the visible champion and sponsor of the British stage. A new, perhaps characteristically Victorian sobriety came to typify the dominant dramatic style, one "perfectly suited to overcoming the antitheatrical prejudice of the respectable middle class." It was "the underplayed, nonchalant, drawing-room style which became the orthodoxy for nearly a century and perhaps created as much as reflected the middle-class conception of gentility for a succession of generations" (Kent 103, 104). Changes in copyright laws in the 1860s and 1870s afforded greater protection for playwrights; successful authors, such as Dion Boucicault, were able finally to draw an income comparable to that of a successful novelist.[24] By the 1880s, large London theaters were dominated by middle-class attendance and a bourgeois aesthetic and were thriving once again. The cycle that started with the Licensing Act of 1737 had come full circle.

What remains to be added to this narrative is the realist novel. My claim is an apparently simple one: the so-called rise of the novel was materially related to the decline of drama, and the decline of the theater was in part a result of the cultural and commercial success of the form of novelistic realism.[25] If this claim appears obvious, then it is all the more surprising — given its profound significance to both the novel and the theater — that important histories of the novel such as Ian Watts's *Rise of the Novel* and Michael McKeon's *Origins of the English Novel* make almost no mention of it. The claim is more specific than the general observation that the period between the Theater Licensing Act of 1737 and its repeal in 1843 roughly marks *both* a decline in British theater and the development of the realist novel from its earlier picaresque and epistolary forms. Rather, my claim is that during this period each of these two cultural forms determined (through the combined choices of individual authors and institutions, obviously) their formal properties and thematic territories *in direct reference to the other*. By the turn of the century, in part through innovations in printing technology, the spread of literacy, and the popularization of Gothic and historical novels, "the novel" reached what D. A. Miller calls "literary hegemony" at roughly the same time that British theater experienced a crisis. The two are causally related. As the circulation of the novel increased through the first half of the nineteenth century, theater attendance declined; Michael Booth observes, "It was frequently argued that the lateness of the dinner hour in the best society and the comforts of a good book by the domestic fireside kept these [upper] classes away from the theatre. . . . [T]his argument was popular: Macready [the famous actor] propounded it to the Select Committee on Dramatic Literature in 1832, and in 1863 Henry Morely [the drama critic] was of the same opinion" (Booth *et al.* 10).

While playwrights as yet lacked any copyright protection and so eked out a living as the hostages of theater managers, successful novelists were beginning to command large royalties. No self-respecting and pound-wise mid-Victorian novelist would think seriously of abandoning the novel to pursue greatness as a playwright in the line of Shakespeare. As melodrama came to dominate London theaters, liberal-intellectual critics and realist novelists colonized the high ground of "literature," and George Eliot, for one, recognized the novelist as its new guardian and the heir, in particular, to Shakespeare, though necessarily in a new form. As the modern decline cycle in British theater came to an end around midcentury, the market penetration and cultural dominance of novels was achieved. It is no coincidence, then, that novels produced around this time concern themselves especially with the figure of the theater, staging within their pages a dialogue between the figure of the theater and the figure of the novel in which the latter prevails.

Theatricalization of the Social / Socialization of the Theatrical

The most theatrical events in *Felix Holt* and in *Shirley* are the scenes of lower-class social protest. Two such "mob" scenes appear in *Shirley*, and the first of these is the capture of Mr. Barraclough, a leader of the workers who opposes the mechanization of Robert Moore's mill and who was seen hijacking Moore's first order of new machines. Mr. Barraclough and his comrades are expected at the mill, and the possibility exists for a violent exchange. For no better reason than the drama of it, it seems, Moore stages the capture. Affecting a debonair manner, he goes out alone to face the twelve workers. The exchange progresses in a way that Hollywood westerns (if not Elizabethan drama before them) have made a cliché: the two lead men swap feigned pleasantries, which progress in stages of increasing tension toward out-and-out insults, at which point the bad guy's bluff is called, and he is summarily put in his place. Yet, despite Moore's stage-direction of the event, it is Barraclough who bears the brunt of the theatrical discourse. At a midpoint, Barraclough is described as a mugging showman who "uplift[s] the palms of his hands and the whites of his eyes, evincing in the gesture a mere burlesque of hypocrisy" (*S* 154). Moore responds by "cooly and drily" calling him a "double-dyed hypocrite," then saying, "You expect indeed to make me laugh at the cleverness with which you play your coarsely farcical part, while at the same time you think you are deceiving the men behind you." Moore characterizes Barraclough using theatrical rhet-oric in a way that will become the standard in many Condition-of-England novels: the leader of the mob is a two-faced scoundrel who does not really care about the workers (as the middle class does, it is implied) and is not really representative of those who, after all, are just honest, hard-working blokes who need us, the middle-class readers constructed by the text, to guide them. Then Barraclough's second-in-command is shown preening in his supporting performance, "enunciating each word very slowly, as if with a view to giving his audience time to appreciate fully the uncommon ele-gance of the phraseology" (a joke on the part of the narrative about his lower-class dialect and pretensions beyond it). This receives an ironic "Brayvo" (also in dialect) from Joe Scott, Moore's assistant, who thereby adopts the role of theater critic. Moore's performance is, of course, more impressive, but it is not described in theatrical terms, because it is "sincere" and "natural." He gives Barraclough (and the reader) a short lecture on the evils of protest organizers and the rights of small-business men, calls his bluff by throwing a challenge back in his face, then beckons the bailiff, who has been awaiting his cue backstage (inside the mill). The workers, who have the advantage in number, must be impressed with the performance, because they allow a single bailiff to lead Barraclough away.

The second mob scene is equally theatricalized. It is the battle that takes place at the mill. Caroline and Shirley have rushed to the mill at night to warn Moore that an armed mob is on the way, but by the time they arrive on foot the battle is under way, for which, as it turns out, Moore was well prepared with red coats and rifles. Caroline and Shirley (and, therefore, the implied reader) are positioned as the audience to what the text describes as a "theater of war," which is intended to reproduce on a local scale the battles that the Duke of Wellington, a proclaimed hero of Shirley's, is fighting on the Continent at that time against Napoleon. But Caroline and Shirley are two different types of audience members: Caroline wants to rush onstage to be with her Robert, but Shirley knows that this would itself be too theatrical and damaging not only to his chances in the battle but to Caroline's chances of realizing her love for Robert, which, as Shirley seems to understand better than Caroline, depends on Caroline continuing to play the role of the undemonstrative, submissively waiting woman. Further, Caroline's position is analogous to the OP theater rioters of 1809; she expects direct audience-actor contact in the tradition of the more communal eighteenth-century theater. Shirley is positioned as the new, more respectable audience that keeps its place apart from the stage, indeed enjoys that aesthetic distance, as Shirley does: "I am glad I came: we shall see what transpires with our own eyes: we are here on the spot, and none know it. Instead of amazing the curate, the clothier, and the corn-dealer with a romantic rush on the stage, we stand along with the friendly night, its mute stars, and these whispering trees, whose report our friends will not come to gather" (*S* 335). What follows is presented as a piece of dramatic dialogue, with the guns outside of the mill speaking as the workers (and Napoleon, and Dissenters) and the guns inside the mill speaking as Robert (and Wellington, and the Church). After the workers' first "comment," the guns inside the mill reply, and Shirley exults: "Moore speaks at last!" (*S* 336). A great commotion ensues, but the dramatic-dialogue form continues:

> They heard the rebel leader cry, "To the back, lads!"
> They heard a voice [Moore's] retort, "Come round, we will meet you!"
> "To the counting-house!" was the order again.
> "Welcome! — We shall have you there!" was the response.

The narrator casts this exchange in the most melodramatic and allegorical terms, summoning the national mascot: "You never heard that sound, perhaps, reader? So much the better for you ears — perhaps for you heart. . . . Wrath wakens to the cry of Hate: the Lion shakes his mane, and rises to the howl of the Hyena: Caste stands up, ireful against Caste; and the indignant, wronged spirit of the Middle Rank bears down in zeal and scorn on the famished and furious mass of the Operative Class. It is difficult to be tolerant — difficult to be just — in such moments" (*S* 335). Part of the text's general ideological position is fairly clear. The theatricalization of such scenes operates within the discourses of the time to brand any lower-class movement — violent or no — as moblike, incendiary, and foolish. A potential contradiction arises, however, because at the same time that theatricality stigmatizes class-based violence it simultaneously glorifies Britain's Tory-supported,

Whig-opposed war against Napoleon (in retrospect, since Brontë is writing decades later, though as an Old Tory still). In this regard, *Shirley* may only be reflecting the fact that theatricality has functioned historically to glorify war, as in the case of review and victory parades and memorial celebrations. The contradiction demonstrates a flexibility by which the figure of the theater can carry a negative value in relation to one class's war and, simultaneously, a positive value in relation to another's.

Felix Holt similarly portrays mob scenes, including a working-class election-day riot, the theatricality of which sweeps up even the antitheatrical protagonist. But the first use of the figure of the theater in this novel, as in *Daniel Deronda*, is to characterize the opposite end of the social spectrum, the aristocracy. The initial chapters of *Daniel Deronda*, for instance, are dedicated largely to the portrayal of a series of aristocratic diversions and recreations: gambling, travel, private theatricals, musical performance, equestrian sports, archery, ballroom dance, and formalized courtship. These will come back to haunt the primary targets of the antitheatrical discourse in the novel, Gwendolyn Harleth and especially Mallinger Grandcourt. In *Felix Holt*, the figure of the decadent aristocracy appears through a history of overbred idiocy, gambling, corrupt legal dealings, and adultery. All of these are embodied in the Transome-Durfey plot with which the novel opens and, in particular, in the character of Mrs. Transome. Her incarceration in a self-fashioned but patriarchally conditioned world of mocking portraits and mirrors is the tragic aspect of the story. At the same time, however, there is something melodramatic about the allegorization of Transome Court as a haunted gallery of ruined aristocracy in which the paintings' eyes watch accusingly. Mrs. Transome becomes the stylized specter of grandeurs past, pacing the dark, drafty corridors in a white shroud with "the melodramatic convention of the ghost story" (Coveney 40). The Transome-Durfey subplot, like the Grandcourt plot in *Daniel Deronda*, is the means by which the text exhibits the inherent theatricality of a decaying aristocratic order.

It is this order that poses a threat to the novel's heroine, Esther Lyon, who, like Gwendolen Harleth, is endangered by theatricality. From Felix's perspective, Esther is a "nice-stepping, long-necked peacock" (*FH* 59). He says, "I should like to come and scold her every day, and make her cry and cut her fine hair off" (*FH* 62). There is nothing subtle, then, about his patriarchal objective: to correct Esther's theatricality and train her toward what the text will describe as an "inward vocation" (*FH* 223). Esther, it seems, is too much concerned with "fashion," an essentially theatrical term for "exteriority" in this novel, which is applied both to the aristocracy — "gentlemen of

unspeakable woes, who employ a hairdresser, and look seriously at themselves in the glass" (61) — and, in the opposite direction, to lower-class social climbers, whom it is Felix's mission in life to oppose: "I'll take no em-
ployment that obliges me to prop up my chin with a high cravat, and wear
straps, and pass the livelong day with a set of fellows who spend their spare
money on shirt-pins. That sort of work is really lower than many handicrafts;
it only happens to be paid out of proportion. . . . I mean to stick to the class I
belong to — people who don't follow the fashions" (*FH* 54–55). "Fashion,"
then, is a theatrical vehicle — a disguising costume — for the central ideological message that Felix speaks with regularity: "Stick to your class."

Most of the other main characters in the novel also are theatricalized,
especially Mr. Jermyn, Mr. Christian (aka Henry Scaddon), and Harold
Transome. These three are linked literally or figuratively by blood (Jermyn
is Harold's illegitimate father, Christian is the double for Esther's father,
and Esther is the cousin to Harold), as well as by a characterization in terms
of the playing of games and gambling. Jermyn's duplicity and *nouveau riche*
gentility are mocked throughout by his theatrically pompous manner of
speaking, and Christian's entire life is a put-on identity, a role he stole from
Esther's father (Maurice Christian Bycliffe, the heir, as it turns out, to the
Transome estate). Harold is more complex and is portrayed not unsympathetically, but he is in competition with Felix, both as "representative" of
the working man and in the contest to shape and claim Esther. Harold,
portrayed largely as a egotist, is tied to the model of identity and society
represented by his mother, Transome Court, and radical Toryism. He therefore finds himself in dialogues with Esther that apparently bear too much
resemblance to Restoration drama, in contrast to the Classical dialogues she
expects with Felix:

"Well, I am conscious of not having those severe virtues that you have been
praising [in Felix]."
"That is true. You are quite in another *genre*."
"A woman would not find me a tragic hero."
"O, no! She must dress for genteel comedy — such as your mother once described
to me — where the most thrilling event is the drawing of a handsome cheque."
(*FH* 351)

Harold is not simply theatrical; he is even the wrong sort of theatrical.

What is most damning about Harold within the discourse of the novel,
however, is that he represents the threat of working-man suffrage. This ties
him to a yet more damaging variety of theatricality. A metonymic chain

runs from the pretensions of working men who think they should have the vote, to the theatrics and drunkenness of the election riot, to the electioneering of Mr. Johnson, to Johnson's boss, Mr. Jermyn, and straight to the candidate who hired Jermyn, Harold Transome (who therefore bears the sins of his father, Jermyn, in more ways than one). Mr. Johnson is the linchpin. It is he with whom Felix has two theatrical duels, the first of which is at Mr. Chubb's pub, where Mr. Johnson has come to stir up grassroots support for Transome. Mr. Johnson is portrayed as a canny manipulator of the working man, because he has had "large experience in the effect of uncomprehended words" (*FH* 114). Johnson entertains with jokes and flattery; Felix bores with issues and earnestness. Johnson is superficial theatricality; Felix is depth and authentic concern. The working men themselves are portrayed as those who are unable to tell the difference, who can understand Reform only as "'sport' and drink, and keeping away from work for several days in the week" (*FH* 115). Johnson accuses Felix of "stuffing" the workers only with words, and indeed Felix is the representative of the novel's own prose (*FH* 116). Johnson, the representative of dramatic form and of "politics," knows to stuff the workers with "the King's likenesses" and beer, which Felix condemns as bribing the men to appear as a heckling mob in support of Transome on election day. In fact, Johnson is using what was the time-honored Tory approach to maintaining a feudal order: "The Liberals were the party of education and respectability, the Tories were associated with drink, violence and what may be termed the politics of bonhomie, of the good time" (Joyce 35–36). In the course of the novel, this equation is established: *Reform = drink = riot* (and there is a further implication that Reform is a ruse by Old Tories to regain power that had been lost to the Whigs in recent years). Of course, the men from Chubb's, under the influence of more beer, are named in the riot. In motives and methods, Johnson is given the same sort of character as is Barraclough in *Shirley*. To support working-class rights is to be steeped in the theatricality of the mob.

It would seem, then, that about everyone in *Felix Holt* is theatricalized in one or more ways except Felix himself. He is intended to represent a nontheatrical middle ground between the archaic, aristocratic theatricality represented by Transome Court and the theatricality of the riots, which is tied to the too-rapid progress of steam-engine trains and working-man suffrage. Even Felix, however, is forced by events into a theatrical role. As the riot intensifies and it appears that lives may be in danger, Felix can no longer stand to be the appropriately distanced audience member that Shirley enjoys being in *Shirley*: "Even some vain effort would satisfy him

better than mere gazing" (*S* 265). So, "assuming the tone of a mob-leader,"
Felix takes command and, by a series of improvised moves and melodramat-
ically stylized postures, he nearly succeeds in stemming disaster. Eliot writes
the stages of Felix's performance with a meticulousness characteristic of
crime or thriller writing, showing at each juncture how Felix is perceived by
his "audience," which consists of various middle-class, sideline witnesses
and the implied reader. Felix with arm raised to draw the mob, Felix with
saber clinched above his head, Felix throwing Tucker the constable to the
ground, Felix binding Spratt to a pole: these sorts of "situational" poses (in
the melodramatic sense defined by Meisel) make Felix appear "to the un-
discerning eye, like a leading spirit of the mob" (*FH* 265). *And he is*. He *does*
lead the mob. Tucker, along with others (most importantly Tommy Trounsem), *is* killed. Felix is shot. What is the difference between acting the part
of leading a mob that kills someone and leading a mob that kills someone?
How much do intentions matter next to material consequences? This is the
question put to the jury in Felix's trial: can one, should one, differentiate
between what is acted and what is real, the social mask and the authentic
self? In short, the novel itself and the form of interiority that its form
represents is put on trial. The central concern of *Felix Holt* is making a
distinction between the theatrical and the nontheatrical. The novel works to
represent this distinction as a difference between justice and violence, yet it
ultimately reveals the inherent violence of justice, undercutting the difference between the two.

Something else is on trial as well: the extent to which humans are
or should be subject to contingency, chance, coincidence, or Providence,
which are linked to theatricality (as to gambling) and are handled differently in melodrama than in realism. Before Felix's trial, Harold Transome
and Esther are talking about what Harold might do to help Felix if or when
he is set free. Esther scoffs at Harold's assumption that he *could* help Felix,
and the two have the following exchange.

"What would you offer Felix Holt? a place in the Excise? You might as well think
of offering it to John the Baptist. Felix has chosen his lot. He means always to be a
poor man."

"Means? Yes . . . but what a man means usually depends on what happens. I
mean to be a commoner, but a peerage might present itself under acceptable
circumstances."

"O there is no sum in proportion to be done there. . . . As you are to a peerage,
so is *not* Felix Holt to any offer of advantage that you could imagine for him."
(*FH* 350–51)

Harold is aligned with contingency, with changing one's "meaning" in relation to circumstance. Felix's meaning is nonnegotiable, constant, fixed. It also is chosen. Harold's "lot" is not chosen. In the first place, in contrast to Felix, Harold is portrayed as performing his self nonreflexively, from which it follows that he is subject to performing a social role without knowing it. In the second place, the novel demonstrates that Harold, unbeknownst to himself, is not in control of his lot: the web of family sin, which must be expiated, and the almost unbelievable coincidence that places him, Esther, Christian, and Tommy Trounsem in one small village at the same time combine to determine first that he shall lose his whole inheritance, then that he shall get it all back again (with the important loss of his legitimacy). More tellingly, it is Felix's choosing of his own lot, which becomes Esther's choosing, that determines Harold's lot: Esther refuses to take the Transome estate. Harold is subject to birth and circumstance; Felix is the subject he chooses.

This is a central part of Felix's lesson to Esther: choose your subjection. The narrator comments that "the first religious experience of her life, the first self-questioning, the first voluntary subjection, the first longing to acquire the strength of greater motives and obey the more strenuous rule — had come to her through Felix Holt" (*FH* 225). What most distinguishes Felix Holt from other working-class people in the novel is that he *chooses* "to withdraw [him]self from the push and the scramble for money and position" and instead to go "shares with the unlucky" (*FH* 220). If Felix won the lottery, he would turn the money down, and so Esther must do that very thing, must take the Cinderella slipper from her foot and toss it back to the prince (Harold). She comes to her "inward revolution" by learning thus to refuse Providence: "It was difficult by any theory of Providence, or consideration of results, to see a course which she could call duty" (340). Felix is her example here as well: "As long as a man sees and believes in some great good, he'll prefer working towards that in the way he's best fit for, come what may. I put effects at their minimum, but I'd rather have the minimum of effect, if it's of the sort I care for, than the maximum of effect I don't care for" (*FH* 363). The sort of "effect" for which Felix does not care is any material change in social conditions, but in another sense it also is the providential "effect" of melodrama. Eschewing all such effects, Felix's "great good" is what? It is nothing other than to choose to be the cause of himself, rather than the effect of society. Only thus can he be an example to other poor men to choose to remain in their class, to maintain the heritage of their "handicrafts" against the progressive pressures of the time. Judith

Butler's observation in reference to gender identity is applicable here: "If the 'cause' of desire, gesture, and act can be localized within the 'self' of the actor, then the political regulations and disciplinary practices which produce that ostensibly coherent gender are effectively displaced from view" (136). Felix's "inward vocation" is to internalize, and therefore displace from view, the social as chosen self (*FH* 223). This is the martyr's power to say, "You do not make me poor; I make me poor! You do not make me a subject; I make me the subject that you would have made me if I had not beaten you to it!"

Thus what is on trial at Felix's trial is the efficacy of interiority, the form of the novel itself. One might expect then that the novel would find itself innocent. But unlike Jem Wilson in Elizabeth Gaskell's *Mary Barton*, Felix *is* guilty of something. It would threaten the credibility of the novel to free him outright; it would smack of a providential hand and render the novel a melodrama. This would be to duplicate the crime that Felix has committed, not the crime against Tucker, about whom text and readers care little, but the crime against the code for which the novel itself stands.

In the riot, Felix surrenders the aesthetic distance, or distanciation, of the proper audience member and, in effect, rushes the stage. [26] In doing so he surrenders his control over his "lot," allowing for a moment circumstance and contingency to determine his meaning (as Harold Transome has said any man might do). One way of reading the resulting events is that they prove all the more Felix's doctrine, because they illustrate the very dangers of theatricality that the dominant discourse in the novel intends to demonstrate and validate Felix's authentic interiority, which indeed is shown to prevail over that theatricality in the ending of the novel. In the process, however, *theatricalization of the social*, which operates to stigmatize and reduce the issue of class struggle, has come precariously close to revealing its own mechanism and, therefore, through a sort of reversal of figure and ground, to pop up as *socialization of the theatrical*. The means used to illustrate the difference between the authentic self and the assumed role risk showing the "authentic self" to be a social effect, a construction of context, nothing more or less than a role. This would invalidate the primary moral of the novel, because it leads to questions about the interests behind the construction of social roles and raises the possibility that responsibility lies not in accepting "the nature of things," as Felix puts it, but in attempting to participate in the construction of them (*FH* 248). If this were the case, then Felix would be the one who blindly follows the herd of the mob by subscribing unquestioningly to what is dictated to him. In assuming the role of the mob leader, Felix treads too near the boundary that separates theatricality from authenticity, rendering it too visible, too liable to reveal its constructedness.

Felix Holt responds to this dilemma in the first instance in a direct if apparently contradictory way: by staging an inherently theatrical situation, a trial, as the means of demonstrating the efficacy of interiority. At the penultimate moment, it falls upon Esther — the very character whose soul hangs in the balance between Harold and Felix, theatricality and authenticity — to testify one way or the other. Here again, as with the riot scene, the text precariously balances, on the one hand, insistent claims for purity of motive and trueness of feeling against, on the other hand, the theatrical effect of the scene itself: the last-moment impulse to take the stand, the "vibration, quick as light" that passed through the crowd, the plea that brings tears to the eyes of many, most importantly Sir Maximus Debarry (*FH* 374). Esther's movement from deep "sympathy" and "feelings" toward "a necessity for action" and the resulting "acting out of that strong impulse" effectively reenacts — for the benefit of the jury / audience — the similarly impulsive but well-meant acting out for which Felix is on trial (*FH* 373, 375). If Esther is found innocent, then perhaps Felix can be, too. If Esther can show convincingly how one can "act one's self," then maybe Felix can be forgiven for *not* having acted himself when he played the mob leader. But, no, apparently the two are not commensurate. If, as I would argue, this scene effects the ultimate detheatricalization of Esther (even — or perhaps especially — if by theatrical means), it fails to reauthenticate Felix enough to excuse him within the world of George Eliot's fiction, where real actions must have real consequences, not melodramatic, last-minute reprieves. If "half a year before, Esther's dread of being ridiculous spread over the surface of her life; but the depth below was sleeping," now depth has awakened and moved to fill the role that surface played (*FH* 375). At the same time, it seems, Felix must be held accountable for moving — even appearing to move — in the opposite direction. While this makes a potentially important distinction, it fails in the same instant to redress the indiscretion of having foregrounded the boundary between the theatrical and the authentic, which Esther's reenactment after all has only duplicated. In order for the novel to recuperate from this awkward position — or in order to reassert the form of realism, which is the same thing — Felix must be found guilty and sentenced for manslaughter. Felix — the novel itself — must be punished in order to save realism from melodrama.

As it turns out, however, there is a deus ex machina waiting in the wings in the form of a royal pardon. Having recovered from the threat of theatricalization, the novel can allow for a bit of providentiality (coupled appropriately with aristocratic, backstage string-pulling by Sir Maximus), though it may be a sign of discomfort that the pardon is mentioned only briefly and then suppressed. The text skips to the happy ending, assuming that the reader will *assume* the pardon. Why can the reader assume this so easily? Because, after all, there was an invisible member of the jury: the implied reader. Indeed, the text relies very heavily upon the reader's presence, because it is the reader who is the necessary witness to Felix's interiority. Only the implied reader can testify that Felix's intentions were in the right place, that he is not the "red-hot Radical demagogue" that he appears to be, that he is in fact not a radical but a middle-class subject just like you and me, so constructed (*FH* 250).[27] And so Felix and Esther live happily ever after in the model nuclear family, and the reader, if successfully constructed, loves it. The social is theatricalized and the theatrical is novelized.

The result is to domesticate Felix, and the reader, in a way summarized by Nancy Armstrong as "social redemption through the domestication of desire" (185).[28] Once married, Felix has no further need as far as the text is concerned for social consciousness-raising beyond the confines of the home. Indeed, he *has* fulfilled the object of his "great good," which, it turns out, was to *be* a George Eliot novel entitled *Felix Holt*, a text intended to live within us all. The royal pardon that sends Felix home to Esther represents the use of an archaic juridical power to sanction and mask a more interiorized form of power, self-surveillance, the Felix Holt that *Felix Holt* would lodge inside each reader.[29] The reader is positioned to "assume" the granting of that pardon in a double sense, then: both as "to take for granted" and as "to take upon oneself," as in the form of a role. The pardon is a bit of melodramatic reward that the reader grants to the reader.

The Theatrical Subversion of Gender Roles

The brilliance of *Shirley* lies in the tension it sustains for most of its length by balancing a configuration of gender roles that potentially is unresolvable. As in most Victorian novels (one important exception being *Villette*), the expected resolution does come in the end. Shirley Keeldar, a financially independent, land-owning businesswoman who is able to act like and be treated as the equal of a man, ultimately is domesticated in marriage with Louis Moore. Caroline Helstone, who shows early signs of succumbing to what the text portrays as Romantic fancies and theatrical displays of desire, finally is rewarded with marriage to Robert Moore by sticking to Mrs. Yorke's maxim that "discretion and reserve is a girl's best wisdom" (*S* 176). Indeed, as in *Felix Holt*, the social is domesticated in its entirety by the end of the novel; international politics, national markets, class conflict, and financial debt are telescopically collapsed to the domestic level as problems at each of these levels appear to be solved by the imminence of marriage. Much as in *Felix Holt*, a providential hand sweeps down at the end, lifting the Orders of Council, which kept British trading ports blockaded, magically solving all of Robert's financial problems and paving the way for marriage. Therefore, it might be easy to discount the most potentially subversive aspects of the text.

The aspects to which I refer are not those that can be read as the explicitly feminist discourse of the novel, which in itself may be remarkable for its time. Examples of this discourse include Shirley's radical rewriting of the figure of Eve as a "woman-Titan" or "Woman God" on par with the patriarchal counterpart (*S* 315, 458), her directly stated claims of equality to any gentleman (*S* 222), and her discussions with Caroline about the shortcomings of the masculine conception of woman, which presage Virginia Woolf's *Room of One's Own*:

> If men could see us as we really are, they would be a little amazed; but the cleverest, the acutest men are often under an illusion about women: they do not read them in a true light: . . . their good woman is a queer thing, half doll, half angel; their bad woman almost always a fiend. Then to hear them fall into ecstasies with each other's creations, worshipping the heroine of such a poem — novel — drama, thinking it fine — divine! Fine and divine it may be, but often quite artificial — false as the rose in my best bonnet there. If I spoke all I think on this point; if I gave my real opinion of some first-rate female characters in first-rate works, where should I be? Dead under a cairn of avenging stones in half an hour. (*S* 343).

But it is the characterization of Shirley in relation to masculine role-types — her nickname is "Captain Keeldar" — that is potentially more subversive, particularly when one considers the positionings of her character with those of the other three. Shirley is given a role that is marked as masculine; she has the power to refuse, at least in part, to play the female roles prescribed by the society of the text. Louis is a mere tutor, and for reasons of class, as well as of financial disparity between his position and Shirley's, he is unable to fulfill the prescribed masculine role of the pursuer in courtship. Because class codes are in direct conflict with gender codes, he must maintain the "role" of "keeping up the professor" (*S* 472–73). Shirley, despite her masculinized position, refuses to reveal her affections for Louis before Louis reveals his to her. This amounts to a tacit demand that Louis "be man enough" to act the prescribed masculine role, regardless of class barriers. "Feeling" and "sympathy," the end of the novel hopes to demonstrate, should surmount class and financial boundaries. Shirley plays cat-and-mouse with Louis until, in the penultimate move, when it appears that Louis cannot rise to the occasion, she throws down the gauntlet by turning to leave him. Here is Louis's perspective (a point of view awkwardly adopted by the text to perpetuate the tension over Shirley's real intentions): "She turned to leave me. Could I now let her part as she had always parted from me? No: I had gone too far not to finish. I had come too near the end not to drive home to it. All the encumbrance of doubt, all the rubbish of indecision must be removed at once, and the plain truth must be ascertained. She must take her part, and tell me what it was. I must take mine, and adhere to it" (*S* 576). The "part" Shirley must play is that of the woman, the courted woman who has the female power of acceptance or refusal. Louis must assume the prescribed male power that can bear refusal or, on acceptance, rule thereafter. However, not only must Shirley teach Louis to take the man's risk; she also must soon after teach herself to relinquish the masculinized position so that Louis is provided with an appropriately gendered position into which to move: "In all this, Miss Keeldar partly yielded to her disposition; but a remark she made a year afterwards proved that she partly also acted on system. 'Louis,' she said, 'would never have learned to rule, if she had not ceased to govern: the incapacity of the sovereign had developed the powers of the premier'" (*S* 592). An archaic system of power must give way to a more domestic, internalized, and normalized system of power, though significantly in *Shirley* it is the lead woman who must domesticate herself.

The Shirley-Louis configuration is replicated by Caroline and Robert. Because of the stigma of debt (linked, as might be expected, to "disastrous speculations" and the French Revolution [60]), Robert too is constrained from fulfilling the prescribed gender role of romantic pursuer, though not by the class code, since he and Caroline are of the same class, but by another tenet of the gender code: a man may not burden a woman with a proposal unless he can support her in the manner to which she is accustomed. Robert must feminize his position, according to the discourses of the time, by suppressing his desires for Caroline and, in addition, discouraging hers for him, because to do otherwise would be dishonorable given the circumstances (though Robert's honor does not escape question later in regards to his intentions toward Shirley). Not until Robert—incapacitated by a Luddite sniper — is sequestered in the generally feminine domain of the sick-room can Caroline take the offensive and pursue him.[30] Therefore, all four characters at different times are shown to be "acting" a mandated part that nevertheless is incommensurable with a socially prescribed role. To a degree perhaps unprecedented in Victorian fiction, the dynamic of the novel depends on this uneasy suspension of roles and codes. By creating a sustained separation within each character between his or her socially prescribed gender role and the "part" he or she is constrained to play, the text not only foregrounds the social-constructedness of gender codes but the performativeness of identity itself.[31]

The dilemma created by incommensurable subject positions is illustrated best by the scene in which Caroline finds herself locked in conversation with Mrs. Yorke. The scene begins with a telling debate between Mrs. Yorke and her daughter, Rose, about the appropriate activities and aspirations of a girl. Caroline becomes aligned with Rose's radical claims for a girl's right to seek her own fortunes and, in effect, to have her own desires. Mrs. Yorke accuses Caroline of being led by romantic sentiment and "feelings," a position "better suited to a novel-heroine than to a woman who is to make her way in the real world, by dint of common sense" (*S* 387). Caroline vehemently defends feelings — "Whom my feelings teach me to love, I *must* and *shall* love" — in terms replicated later by Shirley — "Before I marry, I am resolved to esteem — to admire — to *love*" (*S* 444) — and supported by the outcome of the novel. Mrs. Yorke then makes the antitheatrical nature of her charges explicit: "Do n't waste your dramatic effects [on me]. . . . There should have been a disengaged gentleman present. Is Mr. Robert nowhere hid behind the curtains [as of a stage]?" (*S* 388). This certainly lets the cat out of the bag. Caroline is forced into a position of denying her love for Robert, into dramatics proper. Mrs. Yorke accuses Caroline of "intrigue" and "plotting to win a husband." Caroline's only defense is the theatrics of moral indignity and feigned naiveté: when Mrs. Yorke asks her directly if she is fond of her cousin's company, she replies, "Which cousin's?" (389). Mrs. Yorke is a bully, and her charge against Caroline of "craft" may or may not be substantiated, but the charge of "false sentiment" certainly is, if it means denying sentiments one has and acting those one does not have. Caroline is forced to use theatrics to defend herself against the charge of being theatrical. Feelings — which Mrs. Yorke views in theatrical terms, but which Caroline, who is representative of the text's dominant position, feels are the highest reality — are defended at first by Caroline, then denied by Caroline in herself, and done so using the very tool, theatrics, that *proves* Mrs. Yorke's original charge of theatricality.

What is the text doing? It is placing Caroline in a double bind, and foregrounding that double bind, precisely to demonstrate the incommensurability of gender role requirements placed on women and therefore on the text. The text itself becomes "hysterisized" at this point, which is not to say that Caroline is an hysterical woman character but rather that a radical instability at the level of content concerning gender or sexuality threatens to manifest *on the surface of the text* itself (in the way that an hysteric's repressed memories manifest as symptoms on the surface of the body, according to psychoanalytic theory).[32] Geoffrey Nowell-Smith describes this in terms of an "ideological failure" that occurs when a text "cannot accommodate its problem" (194). *Shirley* cannot accommodate the problems of gender roles and feminine desire without disruption. The most telling symptom of hysterisization in a realist text is the foregrouding of textual artifice. This occurs in *Shirley* when the narrator launches into an obsessive definition of the gender role that Caroline is expected to fulfill, then, in a surprising reversal, flatly denies that the definition applies to Caroline, because, we are told, Caroline's condition is her own fault. The narrative embodies on the surface of the text the denial and self-recrimination that the character is expected to undergo. It would seem that the narrator identifies with this gender role, which is one that the text prescribes for Caroline, whether as the recommended means of catching a husband *or* of preparing the appropriate posture for the role of the old maid, a role explored extensively in the novel. Here is the first portion of the narrator's statement:

A lover masculine so disappointed can speak and urge explanation; a lover feminine can say nothing: if she did, the result would be shame and anguish, inward remorse and self-treachery. Nature would brand such demonstration as a rebellion against her instincts, and would vindictively repay it afterwards by the thunderbolt of self-contempt smiting suddenly in secret. Take the matter as you find it: ask no questions; utter no remonstrances: it is your best wisdom. You expected bread, and you have got a stone; break your teeth on it, and don't shriek because the nerves are martyrized: do not doubt that your mental stomach — if you have such a thing — is strong as an ostrich's — the stone will digest. You held out your hand for an egg, and fate put into it a scorpion. Show no consternation: close your fingers firmly upon the gift; let it sting through your palm. Never mind: in time, after your hand and arm have swelled and quivered long with torture, the squeezed scorpion will die, and you will have learned the great lesson how to endure without a sob. (*S* 128)

The heavily freighted symbolism here is difficult to overlook. What else is an egg but an embryo, a baby, or the figure of the mother, and what might a scorpion's stinger be but a phallus, an impotent, injuring, absent phallus in this case? The text seems to invite a reading along the lines of Jacques

Lacan's theory of woman as "lack" or "*objet a*," the Other of patriarchal desire. In more practical terms, one certainly can read *Shirley*'s narrator as expressing-while-repressing a cry of outrage against being situated as a silenced reflector of male power. Her desire is that which cannot be represented within the "symbolic order."

The role that *Shirley* reserves for Caroline's character can be understood best as a form of "masquerade" in the sense developed by Luce Irigaray: "what women do in order to recuperate some element of desire, to participate in man's desire, but at the price of renouncing their own" (133). The nature of Caroline's masquerade is described in the passage that follows the one above: "Nature, however, as has been intimated, is an excellent friend in such cases; sealing the lips, interdicting utterance, commanding a placid dissimulation: a dissimulation often wearing an easy and gay mien at first, settling down to sorrow and paleness in time, then passing away and leaving a convenient stoicism [the old maid's], not the less fortifying because it is half-bitter" (*S* 128). Caroline's "placid dissimulation" — the making of an image of a self that she is not — is a largely internalized, and therefore "martyrized," form of masquerade. It therefore manifests hysterically on the character's body as a slight, gradual wasting, which is remarked upon frequently thereafter. It is a form of masquerade that is "part of the incorporative strategy of melancholy, the taking on of attributes of the object/Other that is lost, where loss is the consequence of a refusal of love" (Butler 48). But the type of masquerade that Caroline's character takes on has a low "degree of ostensiveness"; it does not call attention to itself as performance or standout from its context as unnatural and so passes well for normalcy (Naremore 22). Thus Caroline is able to act the model of the "domestic" woman once she has suppressed her impulse to express her desire. In other words, Caroline's masquerade demonstrates that the figure of the domestic woman, the figure that dominant mid-Victorian discourse naturalized as what "woman" should be, is no less a role, no less a theatrical contrivance of society, than the figure of the "theatrical" woman. This has the potential — even if recuperated in the ending of *Shirley* — of radically destabilizing basic Victorian tenets of morality and gender identity.

Leonora Halm-Eberstein, Daniel's mother in *Daniel Deronda*, represents masquerade of a very different sort, one with a very high degree of ostensiveness. Her character is one of the most theatrical in Victorian fiction, and perhaps least for having been, in her words, "the greatest lyric actress in Europe" (*DD* 703). The scene in which Deronda first visits Leonora is one of the most melodramatic in the novel, rife with unresolvable "situation" and emotive "effect," full of stylized gestures and poses (on Deronda's part as much as or more than Leonora's), and indicated by such hyperbolic lines as "Mother! take us all into your heart—the living and the dead" (*DD* 697). Leonora's character is aristocratically stylized in every respect—dress, carriage, accent. She is the very antithesis of the "domestic" model of femininity. She is the figure of a mother who can say to her son, "I did not wish you to be born. I parted with you willingly" (*DD* 697). She is the figure of a woman who recognizes her proximity to society's monstrous woman: "Every woman is supposed to have the same set of motives, or else to be a monster. I am not a monster, but I have not felt exactly what other women feel—or say they feel, for fear of being thought unlike others" (*DD* 691). She is the figure of a woman who demands to fulfill her desires and ambitions and who acknowledges the subterfuge necessary to do so: "And when a woman's will is as strong as the man's who wants to govern her, half her strength must be concealment" (*DD* 695). In other words, Leonora is the figure of the not-mother, the not-woman, who thus is marked through and through with theatricality. She represents the theatricalized life that Mirah has escaped, the escaping of which and the distance from which allows Mirah to be portrayed as an "angel" figure, despite her drawing-room singing, which is carefully distinguished from both Gwendolen's private theatricals and Leonora's stage acting. Surely, then, the text and the reader must condemn Leonora, and indeed some readers of the novel have read it as condemning her.

But Leonora's character is used by George Eliot for purposes more complex than antitheatrical propaganda. In the first place, she is one of Victorian fiction's most outspoken representatives of women (and in particular of George Eliot), as here in an often-quoted passage: "You [Daniel] are not a woman. You may try but you can never imagine what it is to have a man's force of genius in you, and yet to suffer the slavery of being a girl. To have a pattern cut out—'this is the Jewish woman; this is what you must be; this is what you are wanted for; a woman's heart must be of such a size and no larger, else it must be pressed small, like Chinese feet'" (*DD* 694). Leonora is shown to be engaged in a deadly struggle with the figure of the father, having rebelled against her father's "pattern" for her by becoming an actress. She set out, under the threat of a curse for doing so, to overthrow the order for which her father stands. She refuses to perform the role of "the Jewish woman," and she keeps Daniel's Jewish heritage from him by having him raised as a typical English gentleman. She alone is the voice of opposition to the providential dream at the heart of the novel, the dream of reclaiming a national heritage that can become "the ultimate unity of mankind" (*DD* 802).

The nature of Leonora's masquerade empowers her to speak. Not only does she speak directly, but she also more subtlety undermines authoritative voices by reversing the direction of the charge of theatricality. For example, when Daniel asks if his grandfather was a learned man, Leonora answers, "A man to be admired in a play — grand, with an iron will. Like the old Foscari before he pardons" (*DD* 694). Foscari is from Byron's play *The Two Foscari*, and George Eliot's attitude toward Byron as expressed through *Felix Holt* seems clear. But Leonora's subversive potential is most in play when she speaks (as in the above quotation) *in the voice of patriarchy* in order to mimic it. As Luce Irigaray writes, "To play with mimesis is thus, for a woman, to try to recover the place of her exploitation by discourse, without allowing herself to be simply reduced to it . . . to make 'visible,' by an effect of playful repetition, what was supposed to remain invisible: the cover-up of a possible operation of the feminine in language" (76). A similar understanding of mimicry informs the creation of Leonora as a woman who plays herself, plays her femininity as a doubleness, as the narrator describes her here: "The speech was in fact a piece of what may be called sincere acting: this woman's nature was one in which all feeling — and all the more when it was tragic as well as real — immediately became a matter of conscious representation: experience immediately passed into drama, and she acted her own emotions" (*DD* 691). Leonora is the figure of a woman who attempts to enter into the patriarchal symbolic order, not directly (which would mean to become somehow male, perhaps like Shirley Keeldar in *Shirley*), but by being a conscious and conspicuous sign of femininity. The intention of this type of "masquerade of femininity," as Joan Riviere originally formulated it, is to mask a castrating desire for masculinity. While such a desire undeniably is present in Leonora's character, as it is in Caroline Helstone's in *Shirley*, the ostensiveness and reflexiveness of Leonora's masquerade makes it a parodic masquerade, one designed as a "subversive repetition" that reveals the performativeness of gendered identity (Butler 136, 146). In reversing the direction of the charge of theatricality and in using theatricality as mimicry, George Eliot opens a space of ambiguity, a space of play, that deflates the most sincerely held moral convictions of her novels. Through her consummate performance in the form of Leonora's consummate performance, George Eliot is able to play both sides of the line that supposedly distinguishes domesticity from theatricality.

In contrast to Leonora's style of masquerade, Gwendolen Harleth's masquerade has little subversive potential. Her character nonreflexively identifies with the patriarchally generated spectacle of herself. It is this lack of self-consciousness that Deronda sets out to correct in Gwendolen, and it is for this reason that the theatricality that she represents is negatively marked. Leonora, on the other hand, is aware of the mask of femininity she wears, and she wears it with a vengeance. This awareness produces a "gap" between the mask and something else, and this "visibility" (in the sense discussed by Irigaray) is the source of parody. Thus it would be possible to read Leonora's masquerade also as demonstrating a depth beneath the mask, which is precisely how Gwendolen's theatricality is used by the text, to demonstrate an authentic interiority. But it should be remembered that Leonora's masquerade represents an oxymoron, an unrepresentable, within the discourse of the novel, namely, "sincere acting." The text's primary dichotomies—inner/outer, authentic/theatrical, depth/surface, private/public—here are deconstructed in a stroke. In the character of Leonora, theatricality *is* authenticity, which would represent an impossibility for a Felix Holt, for example. Behind Leonora's mask is a similar mask, and so on. The parody her character offers does not testify to some "original" or authentic femininity that is being parodied, but to the impossibility of being a woman.

For this reason, Daniel Deronda has nothing to teach Leonora, though this does not stop him trying. When he attempts to impress on her the "obligation" that she should feel toward the Jewish patriarchy, she admits defeat to the extent that she has been the instrument of perpetuating that order in the form of her son. More importantly, however, she again offers a parody. Putting on the voice of her father, Daniel's grandfather, she "narrowed her eyes, waved her head up and down, and spoke slowly with a new kind of chest-voice, as if she were quoting unwillingly" (*DD* 726). Perhaps this "unwillingly" indicates George Eliot's wish to suggest that Leonora is being ventriloquized by patriarchal discourse. But Eliot also has Leonora respond to Deronda's History talk about the weighty import of Jewish heritage by saying, "You speak as men do—as if you felt yourself wise." Leonora's character is used with great subtlety to foreground the fact that Daniel, too, is imitating the voice of a man, speaking "as men do." The central reference for "man" is always a form of mimicry, the very theatricality of culpable femininity that it denies.

As Mary Ann Evans masquerading as a man, George Eliot felt wise and exercised the right to speak "truth" like a man and at length. However, rather than thinking that Eliot was ventriloquized entirely, I prefer to credit her for creating a character that saw through the act of patriarchal authority, even while recognizing the inevitability of her own recuperation. Charlotte Brontë masquerading as Currer Bell was perhaps less convinced of her/his own wisdom than was George Eliot. Brontë therefore uses the figure of theatricality more flexibly and less to make a moral point. The theatrical, coupled with the supernatural, therefore empowers Brontë's lead female characters, particularly Jane Eyre and Lucy Snowe. However, that power is dangerous not because, as generally in Eliot's novels, it threatens to invalidate or obscure some authentic self, but precisely for the opposite reason. For Lucy Snowe in *Villette*, theatricality threatens to allow the expression of a repressed self in such a powerful way that it might destroy the personality and its ability to continue to exist within the social order by which it is repressed.

One example of this is the scene in which Lucy is enlisted by M. Paul for the vaudeville performance. There are numerous aspects of this scene that deserve analysis, such as the incarceration of Lucy by M. Paul in the attic to learn her lines, which invites comparison with Bertha Mason in *Jane Eyre* and with the figure of the monstrous woman. I will make only two points here about the scene. First, despite the manhandling Lucy receives from M. Paul, it is her choice to undertake the role. Each time someone attempts to assign a role to Lucy, it is always she who makes the choice. She decides to accept Madame Beck's challenge to become a teacher (her first performance) and M. Paul's to act in the play, but she refuses M. Paul's attempt to foist upon her the roles for "a woman's life" represented by the four paintings in the museum (*V* 277). She refuses to play the role of go-between for Dr. John, as shown in this passage: "With now welcome force, I realized his entire misapprehension of my character and nature. He wanted always to give me a rôle not mine. Nature and I opposed him. He did not at all guess what I felt. . . . [H]e said, softly, '*Do* content me, Lucy?' And I would have contented, or, at least, I would clearly have enlightened him, and taught him well never again to expect of me the part of officious soubrette in a love drama" (*V* 404). Here Lucy's refusal is less an antitheatrical statement than an assertion of self-determination. Lucy does not perform roles not of her choosing. Though she is a character who well understands the constraints placed upon her by being an orphan, poor, untrained, female, and unbeautiful, she refuses as far as her social condition will allow to play patriarchally constructed roles, which means that her character refuses to fulfill either the "domestic" or the "theatrical" models of femininity.

There is one role that Lucy claims but never performs, and it is telling that the passage in which she claims it follows immediately from that quoted above. Just as Dr. John is inveigling her to play the role she refuses, M. Paul, unexpectedly fired with jealousy, "hisses" something in her ear in French, which translates as "You alluring little coquette! . . . You seem sad, submissive, dreamy, but you aren't really: it is I that says this to you: Savage! with a blazing soul and light in your eyes!" Lucy impulsively answers him in French before he dashes away: "Yes, I have a blazing soul, and the right to have one!" (V 404/613). This is the boldest claim that Lucy makes for herself in the novel, and not, tellingly, in her native tongue. The allusion here to Vashti's stage performance in the Villette theater is obvious. Lucy's sensibilities are so enflamed by the attendance of that performance that, the novel suggests, they find a corollary in the literal flames that prematurely end the play at its climax. Vashti is the figure in the novel who simultaneously attracts and repulses Lucy most, as indicated by her divided and dividing reaction to the performance: "It was a marvellous sight: a mighty revelation. It was a spectacle low, horrible, immoral" (V 339). Vashti's character is able to elicit such a reaction in part because it escapes gender definition, as Lucy notes: "I found upon her something neither of woman nor of man" (V 340). What is more, Vashti is presented as transcending the body itself, as being the essence of "spirit," the antithesis to the corporeality of Cleopatra (the portrait in the Villette gallery), "or any other slug" (V 340). But Vashti ultimately represents a form of power. The performance, "instead of merely irritating imagination with the thought of what *might* be done, at the same time fevering the nerves because it was *not* done, disclosed power like a deep, swollen, winter river, thundering in the cataract, and bearing the soul, like a leaf, on the steep and steely sweep of its descent" (V 341). Vashti's power is the ability to fully embody one's emotions and desires at the moment that they occur regardless of the consequences to one's psyche or to surrounding society. In this regard she is more extreme than Leonora Halm-Eberstein.

In however mild and masked a form, it is this power that Lucy tastes in her vaudeville performance. Like Vashti, she escapes, or doubles, gender. She refuses to be costumed male, adding only "a little vest, a collar and cravat, and a paletôt of small dimensions" to her normal attire, and so goes on half woman, half man, or neither (V 209). Suddenly she is able, as she has never done before, to parody gender, as here she comments on the impudent and mocking girl Zélie: "If she were not a lady and I a gentleman, I should feel disposed to call her out" (V 209). Beginning to act, Lucy feels

"the right power come — the spring . . . gush and rise inwardly," the spring
that would widen into Vashti's river (*V* 210). Lucy *becomes* the role, though
it is intended to be that of a silly fop courting a lady. She does not surrender herself to the role, as does Ginevra (on and off the stage); she shapes
it *to her*. "Retaining the letter," she claims, "I recklessly altered the spirit
of the role." She adds, "I acted to please myself" (*V* 210, 211). Lucy's
onstage character takes on the new dimensions that Lucy has given him/
her and becomes a serious rival in courtship for Ginevra's hand (while
Ginevra effectively plays herself): "I put my idea into the part I performed;
I threw it into my wooing of Ginevra. In the 'Ours,' or sincere lover [the
rival], I saw Dr. John. Did I pity him as erst? No, I hardened my heart,
rivalled and out-rivalled him. I knew myself but a fop, but where *he* was
outcast *I* could please" (*V* 210). At the same time, Dr. John, who is in the
audience, also becomes the object of Lucy's wooing. Therefore, Lucy, as
woman *and* man, is able to make love to a woman, to outrival the man
whom it happens she loves, and to make love to that same man, all in the
same instant. While this sort of parodic multiplication of gender — both
hilarious and extremely pointed — might be common in Shakespeare, it is
scarce in Victorian fiction (and generally foreign to George Eliot). It represents a radical statement about gender in its time and a radical deconstruction of the boundary between authenticity and theatricality. Lucy's character carries a bit of this power to parody patriarchal figures offstage. After the
performance she parodies Dr. John's insensitivity in praising Ginevra to her
by pretending to overly admire Alfred de Hamal. Cruelly and deliciously,
Dr. John is shown as not even reading Lucy's mockery, despite her overplay-
ing of the role.

The second point to be made about this scene, then, is twofold: Lucy's
character is empowered by contact with theatricality, but she recognizes the
impracticability of her trying to realize that power in everyday existence.
After the play, Lucy states, "Though glad that I had obliged M. Paul, and
tried my own strength for once, I took a firm resolution never to be drawn
into a similar affair. A keen relish for dramatic expression had revealed itself
as part of my nature; to cherish and exercise this new-found faculty might
gift me with a world of delight, but it would not do for a mere looker-on at
life: the strength and longing must be put by; and I put them by, and
fastened them in with the lock of a resolution which neither Time nor
Temptation has since picked" (*V* 211). This is neither antitheatrical rhetoric
nor self-pity, but rather a recognition of the conditions in Victorian society
for a working woman. Theatricality is dangerous not because it confuses

identity or permits duplicity and illicit desires, as in Jane Austen or George Eliot, but because it releases desire that is destabilizing because there is no social outlet for it. That desire, female desire, is not judged to be "bad," but is conversely itself the "authentic." Therefore, Charlotte Brontë, like George Eliot, perpetuates a Cartesian inner/outer metaphysics, but the authentic inner self in Brontë's writing is in one sense opposite to that in Eliot's writing. If there is an antitheatrical message in *Villette*, it is that the theatrical provides a taste of power so sweet that it will make the subsequent, unavoidable necessity of going without it all the more unbearable. The implication is that if a woman—like Leonora Halm-Eberstein, like George Eliot—should find herself in conditions that allow her to sustain this act of power, all the more power to her.

Antitheatrical Discourse/Theatrical Form

> The [actors] are the only honest hypocrites. Their life is a voluntary dream; a studied madness. The height of their ambition is to be *beside themselves*. To-day kings, to-morrow beggars, it is only when they are themselves, that they are nothing.
>
> William Hazlitt, "On Actors and Acting"

Near the end of *Villette*, Lucy Snowe is sent on a fallacious errand to the house of Madame Walravens, who is the ancient grandmother of Justine Marie, the dead nun who once was betrothed to M. Paul Emanuel and who it seems has been haunting Lucy at the school at Rue Fossette. Lucy is sent there vindictively by the jealous schoolmistress, Madame Beck, to find all this out and to find that M. Paul can never marry her, because he has given his heart and soul to Justine Marie and given all of the money with which he might support a wife to support Madame Walravens and the Catholic Church (represented by Father Père Silas). As soon as Lucy steps into the Walravens house, she enters a Gothic melodrama. She finds herself in a darkened antechamber before a large painting, through which Mrs. Walravens makes her entrance: "Bye-and-bye the picture seemed to give way: to my bewilderment, it shook, it sunk, it rolled back into nothing; its vanishing left an opening arched, leading into an arched passage, with a mystic winding stair. . . . Down this donjon stair descended a tap, tap, like a stick; soon, there fell on the steps a shadow, and last of all, I was aware of a substance" (*V* 481). The staginess of this is obvious. Indeed it appears that Brontë self-consciously is deploying what had come to characterize the

"low" theater of her day, melodramatic "effect." Brontë has Madame Walravens enter and fade away with appropriately timed lightening flashes
through the windows, and Father Silas appears on cue in order to tell Lucy
the melodramatic tale of M. Paul and Justine Marie. Lucy then delivers this
aside to the reader: "I got, in reply, quite a little romantic narrative, told not
unimpressively with the accompaniment of the now subsiding storm. I am
bound to say it might have been made much more truly impressive, if there
had been less French, Rousseau-like sentimentalizing and wire-drawing;
and rather more healthful carelessness of effect" (*V* 484).

The layers of irony and narrational myopia are indistinguishable at this
point. Is Brontë's narrator making fun of Brontë's own writing? The novel
has just finished using the same "wire-drawing" effect on its readers. To
argue that Brontë intends to include the reader in an ironic send-up of theatricality in the Walravens scene does not explain the apparent contradiction,
because the novel unabashedly has been using such techniques throughout
in the form of the "voices" that address Lucy and in the form of the ghost-
Nun visitations, during which the implied reader is situated roughly in the
same, uninformed position as is Lucy (and may or may not be as much
thrilled by the sensational "effects"). To argue, as I imagine that Charlotte
Brontë would, that the novel as a whole debunks the supernatural (along
with Catholicism) by revealing the ghost-Nun to have been nothing more
than the theatrics of Ginevra Fanshawe and Alfred de Hamal still does not
do away with the contradiction between the antitheatrical discourse and the
use of theatrical "effect."

In the first place, the text already has made ample use of the theatrical
"effects," much in the way that Terry Castle argues that eighteenth-century
fictions that include masquerade scenes draw on the "plot-engendering"
and entertainment functions of those scenes: "By its very comic agency,
the carnivalesque episode contradicts its superficial negative inscription
within the eighteenth-century text, and reveals itself instead as part of the
hidden, life-giving machinery of narrative pleasure" (118, 123). In the second place, the ghost-Nun *is* haunting Lucy Snowe in two ways that are very
real to her and to the emotional struggle that it is one of the novel's chief
goals to convey. The dead Justine Marie very much determines the conditions within which Lucy's character must struggle to establish a relationship
with M. Paul. Also, the ghost-Nun functions as an externalized symboliza-
tion of Lucy's internal state. The Nun just happens to make her appearances
at moments of emotional crisis or excitation when Lucy's romantic passions
for Dr. John Bretton and then M. Paul threaten to show themselves. The

Nun also must be read, however, as one of the many figures of womanhood that the novel offers to Lucy as a model. While Lucy could not (physically, financially) be a Cleopatra (as Gwendolen in *Daniel Deronda* could be), and will not be a Vashti, though Vashti is closest to representing Lucy's psyche, she could well end up like a nun. It is the model of womanhood represented by the ghost-Nun that threatens to bury Lucy alive in denial of her passionate self, just as Lucy buries her love for Dr. John in a little "casket" in the garden, the Nun's known haunting grounds. The ghost-Nun ultimately becomes the very emblem of theatrical "effect" in *Villette*. It comes to function as the central, sliding signifier in the following, internally contradictory chain of signifiers: Justine Marie = M. Paul's devotion = Lucy Snowe = buried passion = M. Paul's niece = Alfred de Hamal, cross-dressing = aristocratic theatricality. At the very same time, however, the ghost-Nun is more "real" to characters and readers alike than she would be if *Villette* were a Gothic novel and the ghost were a ghost (not that a ghost is always a ghost in Gothic novels). The ghost-Nun figure embodies the contradictory combination of antitheatrical discourse coupled with theatrical form.

The same type of contradiction can be found in the other novels under consideration. *Daniel Deronda* is particularly interesting in this regard. Not only does it present a heavily antitheatrical message while using some of the techniques of melodrama but it also reveals a discomfort or self-consciousness in doing so. One of the most melodramatic "effects" in *Daniel Deronda* is produced by the coincidence that occurs during the oft-cited theatrical scene in which Gwendolen demonstrates her talents in the tableau vivant of Hermione from *Winter's Tale*. Gwendolen — at least until Daniel teaches her to see a larger arena than "the small drama of personal desires" — is very much interested in the effect she generates, whether at the gaming table, at the archery contest, or through "the pleasure of producing an effect by her appearance in society" (*DD* 483–484). However, she does not intend the effect produced when, during the tableau vivant, the panel that covers the painting of the "dead face and the fleeing figure" flies open. Gwendolen then performs a bit of "sincere acting" as the figure of Terror, and Herr Klesmer tries to save her face, so to speak, by responding, "A magnificent bit of *plastik* that!" (*DD* 92). In itself this is very interesting; it raises a question about the boundary between acting and authenticity that particularly arises later in the character of Leonora Halm-Eberstein, and it shows the text using a melodramatic effect as a means of making an antitheatrical criticism of Gwendolen's desire to have an effect. But the "coincidental" nature of this event is its most interesting aspect, because it eventually proves to be more of a providential sign of Grandcourt's "accidental" drowning than a coincidence.[33]

In *Daniel Deronda*, George Eliot has difficulty squaring the antitheatrical discourse, which initially damns Gwendolen and utterly damns Lapidoth, with the text's reliance on coincidence, which Eliot recognized as a melodramatic formal device antithetical to realism. The plot of *Daniel Deronda*, like that of most novels, depends on certain coincidences, such as Daniel's happening by Mirah on the riverbank, or his finding of Mordecai through the name Cohen, and Mordecai's turning out to be Mirah's brother, or Daniel's running into Joseph Kalonymos (his father's friend and executor) in Frankfurt. It is not these coincidences that seem to worry Eliot, however, but the one that lands Daniel and Gwendolen in Genoa at the same time: Daniel has come to meet his mother for the first time, and Gwendolen and Grandcourt have been sailing the coast of Italy (a trip planned by Grandcourt to get Gwendolen away from Daniel) when a storm happens to cause the yacht to need repairs in none other than Genoa. The text twice offers what amounts to an excuse for this coincidence, serving no other purpose and creating instances of extreme awkwardness in the text. One of these comes from Daniel's surrogate uncle, Sir Hugo Mallinger, who tries to rationalize the coincidence on behalf of the text by explaining that he too once ran into "an early flame" of his in unexpected circumstances in a foreign hotel but that, after all, the meeting had "nothing to do with knight-errantry, any more than [Daniel's] coming to Genoa had to do with the Grandcourts" (*DD* 784). The question is not why Eliot would use the coincidence of the meeting in Genoa, nor whether it is realistic and believable, but why she would risk emphasizing textual artifice by displaying what appears to be discomfort. For that matter, the coincidence itself is not so far-fetched as to stretch the reader's credulity beyond recovery, nor does it too greatly overstep the conventions of use of coincidence among realist novelists. Indeed, it does not bear the handprint of Providence nearly as much as do the other "coincidences" in the text, all of which have to do with Daniel's Jewishness and his ultimate union with his "people" through union with Mordecai and Mirah.

And this is precisely the point. The big, providential "effect" in *Daniel Deronda* is the "spiritual destiny" (*DD* 555) behind Daniel's Jewishness and the saga of the Jewish "nation," which Eliot intends as a model for the type of redemption required by the British nation. The novel's understanding of the Jews is encapsulated in a passage from nineteenth-century Jewish nationalist Leopold Zunz, who is quoted in German in a chapter epigraph and translated in the body of the text: "If there are ranks in suffering, Israel takes precedence of all the nations — if the duration of sorrows and the patience with which they are borne ennoble, the Jews are among the aristocracy of every land — if a literature is called rich in the possession of a few classic tragedies, what shall we say to a National Tragedy lasting for fifteen hundred years, in which the poets and the actors were also the heroes?" (*DD* 575). George Eliot, a novelist intent on remaking society in the image of her novels, would be such a poet-actor-hero (if not actually a Jew, and not quite an actor of the ilk of either Gwendolen or Leonora).[34] Eliot meant to produce a form of novel that could rise to the occasion of "a National Tragedy," that would be to literature what the Jews were, in Zunz's understanding, to nations. The figure on which she relied to fulfill this theatrical ambition within an ostensively antitheatrical form, solving the dilemmas of coincidence and Jewish destiny, was the figure of sympathy.

A familiar term throughout Eliot's fiction, sympathy in *Daniel Deronda* takes the special form of "historic sympathy" and the selfless self that sympathy engenders, the "self-abhorrence that stings us into better striving" (*DD* 412, 764). Thus Daniel instructs a disillusioned Gwendolen toward the path of sympathy in terms that have the unmistakable ring of the proselytizer: "The refuge you are needing from personal trouble is the higher, the religious life, which holds an enthusiasm for something more than our own appetites and vanities. The few may find themselves in it simply by an elevation of feeling; but for us who have to struggle for our wisdom, the higher life must be a region in which the affections are clad with knowledge" (*DD* 508). The novel charts what comes more and more to seem like a fated path for Daniel, followed by Gwendolen, toward this "higher life." It suggests that Eliot wanted to generalize Daniel's struggle to humankind (or at least to the British), and needed a vehicle now that the Christian God no longer served that purpose. That vehicle was Jewishness understood as "nation," as distinguished from Judaism as a monotheistic faith. As a result, Daniel's personal struggle to find his parentage and heritage and the historical struggles of the Jewish nation become emblematic of one another. Daniel's progress toward the "sympathy" and "maternal transference of self," which he is to effect with Mordecai (though only after contact with his biological mother), becomes of a part with Old Testament predictions, as in turn does Gwendolen's "awakening of a new life" (*DD* 553, 762). However, the coincidences through which Daniel is guided toward Mirah, Mordecai, and his "people" threaten at every moment to reveal the providential nature that they share with the teleology of the Jewish people. That teleology balloons to embrace all peoples in a universalized sympathy, as Mordecai summarizes it: "Seest thou, Mirah . . . the *Shemah*, wherein we briefly confess the divine Unity, is the chief devotional exercise of the Hebrew; and this made our religion the fundamental religion for the whole world; for the divine Unity embraced as its consequence the ultimate unity of mankind" (*DD* 802). As the novel progresses toward providential fulfillment, Mordecai increasingly uses the archaic thou and shalt. He becomes not tragic but melodramatic. Likewise, as Daniel's story increasingly acts out the part of Jewish History, the form of *Daniel Deronda* increasingly risks theatricalization by its reliance on an archaic providential ethos. The reader witnesses a sort of inverted masquerade in which the text increasingly threatens to let its melodramatic formal elements show through the costume of the realism that it presents as novelistic normalcy.

Finally, then, the excuses that the text offers for the *other* coincidence—the meeting at Genoa—are a sign of a larger sense of concern over the more providential coincidences of Jewish destiny and, at the same time, a baffle or diversion away from those coincidences. The pervasive antitheatrical discourse of the novel, particularly as applied to Gwendolen and to Leonora, functions in part as a straw woman. This is not to say that the Gwendolen-Grandcourt plot, for instance, does not illustrate the evils of aristocratic theatricality, the danger that one may lose one's authentic self in a social role, and the risk that one takes of being trapped in an assumed role. It is to say that, in addition to such first-level purposes, the theatrical figures function as the necessarily evil Other and scapegoat for the use of theatrical form—melodrama—which is necessitated by the ambition of the novel to produce a modern, secular, humanist mythology.

Sympathy / Theatricality

The figure of sympathy can be understood both as a reaction against the Romantic doctrine of feeling and as the culmination of that very discourse within the Victorian context.[35] Sympathy, or one permutation of it, is defined by demoting feeling to "mere feelings," stripping away the Romantic connotations, and heightening the altruistic aspects by tying the justification of the need for sympathy to a recognition of that which is taken to establish a common humanity, namely, suffering. Eliot in particular attributes the quality of sympathy to those characters that her novels show to be engaged in a form of personal growth that expands their ability to imagine the suffering of others and, as a result, to imagine a universal, unifying culture that embraces and erases social difference. Thus Deronda's character is epitomized by "sympathy, an activity of imagination on behalf of others" (*DD* 218). Several aspects of this sympathy deserve noting. First, it is defined in opposition to theatricality, being founded on authenticity of feeling and an identity between inward makeup and outward appearance. Second, it typically is gendered feminine. Deronda, for instance, is "moved by an affectionateness such as we are apt to call feminine," and "all the woman lacking in [Leonora] was present in him" (*DD* 367, 723). Third, it operates through an effective splitting of the self that occurs as the prerequisite of the ability to identify with the suffering of another. The self is split between a spectating, self-identified part and a vicarious, performing, other-identified part. Fourth, it therefore introduces a danger of diluting or emasculating the self and of undercutting morality with relativity, since all positions become deserving of sympathy. The narrator of *Daniel Deronda* worries about Daniel on this score: "A too reflective and diffusive sympathy was in danger of paralysing in him that indignation against wrong and that selectness of fellowship which are the conditions of moral force" (*DD* 413).[36] Fifth, as may be obvious by now, sympathy thus constructed is itself inherently and thoroughly theatrical.

Those familiar with Adam Smith's *Theory of Moral Sentiments* (1759) will recognize a precedent for Eliot's model of sympathy and, indeed, for the understanding of that concept which pervades Victorian culture. Smith defines "sympathy" in terms of the notion of a universal, internalized "impartial spectator," "the great inmate of the breast" (*TMS* 134). Far from skirting the theatrical nature of sympathy, Smith purposefully uses it as the foundation for an essentially theatrical morality. According to this morality, the subject is doubly split: *externally* between the self as simultaneous spectator of others' actions and performer before society, and *internally* between a monitoring gaze or voice and the part of the self that is aware of performing its motives and feelings before this gaze or voice. Smith writes, for example: "When I endeavour to examine my own conduct, when I endeavour to pass sentence upon it, and either to approve or condemn it, it is evident, in all such cases, I divide myself, as it were, into two persons; and that I, the examiner and judge, represent a different character from that other I, the person whose conduct is examined into and judged of" (*TMS* 113). The same structure of *dédoublement* is replicated in sympathizing with and judging someone else. Thus, at the same time that the subject is cut off and isolated from all others in society, it is distanced internally from itself. By the same token, it is linked dependently to every other person in society *via* the representation of all others — and of the self as Other — in the figure of the internalized impartial spectator.

The moral economy of sympathy balances *distanciation* against *identification*. Social harmony becomes a function of an internally borne representation of the connectedness of all members of society. The similarities to Friedrich von Schiller's "play drive" and to Matthew Arnold's "culture," as I analyze it in chapter four, are obvious. Also obvious is the disciplinary function of sympathy in a sense similar to Michel Foucault's analysis of Jeremy Bentham's panopticon (Foucault's book, like Smith's, opens with a scene of torture), as well as in the sense of self-surveillance suggested by George Eliot in *Theophrastus Such* (1879), which describes "the spiritual police of sentiments or ideal feelings" (*Selected* 441). There are other parallels as well, one being the internalized, all-seeing God of Protestantism, which it might be argued George Eliot strove to convert into a secularized, internal moral regulator called sympathy. It is with good reason, therefore, that David Marshall argues that *Daniel Deronda* "acts as a dramatization of Smith's *Theory of Moral Sentiments*" (194). Marshall also observes, "The dream of sympathy, the fiction of sympathy, is that an interplay and interchange of places, positions, persons, sentiments, and points of view could cancel out the theatricality of the most theatrical of situations" (192). This applies aptly to the balancing act that George Eliot performs in her novels between sympathy (or authenticity) and theatricality. For Eliot as for Smith, the "most theatrical situation" is being a moral subject in everyday society.

But the figure of sympathy is deeply problematized by its incestuous relationship with theatricality. Deronda's sympathy is dangerous to the extent that it threatens to reveal the theatricality underlying the text's antitheatrical premises, to reveal that *sympathy is internalized theatricality*. Theatricality, and all that it came in the nineteenth century to represent — duplicity, superficiality, physicality, illicit sexuality, communality, violence, purposeless pleasure, play — is the essential proof of interiority. Interiority is that which is not theatrical, according to the dominant discourse of the novels read here. Theatricality produces interiority, and that distinction is both maintained by and deconstructed in the figure of sympathy. Thus the first-order function of the figure of the theater is as the necessarily evil Other; as long as the finger is seen to be pointing at theatricality, it will not be seen to be working the strings of the puppet sympathy. It is no wonder, then, that the narrator of *Daniel Deronda* is uneasy about Daniel's too-sympathetic nature.

Daniel, at once the primary representative of authenticity and sympathy in the novel, is the most thoroughly theatricalized character by dint of that very sympathy, more so than either Gwendolen or Leonora. Thus it is not that Gwendolen "acts" her self and that Daniel does not, but that Daniel simply is the better actor, the more "sincere" actor. After all, who is the greater actor, she whose acting ostensively calls attention to itself, or he whose acting passes itself off for "real life"? The difference between Daniel and Gwendolen becomes an aesthetic distinction between styles or genres. Gwendolen is the melodramatic actor, while Daniel embodies "naturalism" (which will come to be associated in the twentieth century with the psychological interiority of Konstantin Stanislavsky's "method" acting). Gwendolen is melodrama; Daniel is realism. The more realistic actor, the novel attempts to demonstrate, is the one whose ideology wins in the end.

Reader Identification and Audience Form

There is a final characteristic of sympathy that has significant ramifications for understanding theatricality and its relationship to the nineteenth-century realist novel's formal strategies. The structure of sympathy bears marked similarity to the structure of the acts of writing and reading or, indeed, to the structure of representation itself. Adam Smith's theorization of sympathy makes it clear that one has access to the suffering of another only through the representation of that suffering within the imagination. Smith describes a scene in which one witnesses the torture of one's own brother: "It is the impressions of our own senses only, not those of his, which our imaginations copy. By our imagination we place ourselves in his situation, . . . we enter as it were into his body, and become in some measure the same person with him" (*TMS* 9). Implicit in this statement, and in *The Theory of Moral Sentiments* generally, is the further claim that one only has access to an understanding of one's own suffering by imagining how one appears to others or to the "impartial spectator," which are roughly the same thing. One's access to the world always is through the copying of the imagination, as in the Platonic conception of mimesis. Sympathy is identification not with a real object or referent external to the self, but with a representation within the self of that object that is generated by the imagination. At the theoretical level, there is no difference between this process and the experience of what might be defined very generally as a "sympathetic reader," a reader who is engaged with a text to the point of sympathetically identifying with one or more of the characters. Smith implies this very point: "When we read in history concerning actions of proper and beneficent greatness of mind, how eagerly do we enter into such designs? . . . In imagination we become the very person whose actions are represented to us: we transport ourselves in fancy to the scenes of those distant and forgotten adventures, and imagine ourselves acting the part" (*TMS* 74–75). Reading is an act of sympathy and, therefore, inherently theatrical.

Nineteenth-century realist novels position their implied readers to identify with those characters whom the text intends to be the moral heroes. The result, however, may be to double *dédoublement*: identification with such characters often is identification with the act of identification itself, since what they typically exemplify is sympathy or some other form of reflexivity that allows them to identify with the plights of other characters and, more important, to be their own interior spectators. The implied reader, then, is positioned as the spectator of the internal spectator, the conscience of conscience. As suggested above in relation to Felix Holt's trial, the implied reader is positioned by the form of the realist novel as the necessary witness to the interiority of the characters. The reader is not outside of the text but is centrally implicated in the text's formal strategies. What is more, readers engaged in "sympathetic" readings are being trained or are training themselves in that very form of interiorization by replicating the act of identification that the character is shown to be performing (and, no doubt, a reading in a study such as this one constitutes the next level of reproduction). Since this method for cultivating nontheatricality is by definition theatrical, realist novels appear to recommend a form of interiority that can only be generated by a theatrical act. As both preparation for and fulfillment of identification with interiority itself, reading is a highly theatrical act.

But there may be another level at which readers are positioned for identification. Identification with the interiorizing character, and so with interiority itself, and so with the act of reading, may be understood as synecdocheal stepping-stones that prepare for identification with the textual apparatus itself. Jean-Louis Baudry's "Ideological Effects of the Basic Cinematographic Apparatus" provides a model for this sort of identification. In discussing the nature of "primary identification," which he distinguishes from "secondary identification" with characters, Baudry writes: "Thus the spectator identifies less with what is represented, the spectacle itself, than with what stages the spectacle, makes it seen, obliging him to see what it sees; this is exactly the function taken over by the camera as a sort of relay. . . . Ultimately, the forms of narrative adopted, the 'contents' of the image, are of little importance so long as an identification remains possible. What emerges here (in outline) is the specific function fulfilled by the cinema as support and instrument of ideology. It constitutes the 'subject' by the illusory delimitation of a central location—whether this be that of a god or of any other substitute" (540).[37] Reading—whether of a film or a novel—can be understood as identification with the apparent continuity and omniscience of the world-generating subject-position that the text invites a reader to assume. This is the reader's "sympathy" with the text. One does not need to subscribe to Baudry's theory (which can be criticized for idealizing "the reader," among other things) in order to observe that the character of Felix Holt, with which the text intends the implied reader to identify, functions as a metonymic stand-in for *Felix Holt* and, therefore, that the reader is intended to identify with the form of the novel itself. This type of transfer of identification arguably operates in all of the novels read in this study, perhaps in all realist novels. Nor does one have to subscribe to a monolithic definition of "the realist novel," or deny the particularity of individual texts and the specificity of individual readings, in order to argue that nineteenth-century realist novels generally reproduce a certain privileged subject-position, which might be described best as the *subject of reading*, the reading subject.

In order to understand fully the impact of the form of the reading subject in the Victorian period, it is necessary to recall the historical changes that took place in British theater starting in the early part of the century. Architecturally, the main London theaters were rebuilt in the 1810s on a larger scale and in a significantly altered form: stages were expanded, but the apron was reduced; seating was removed from the stage; tiers of seating, and thus levels of pricing, were sometimes added; the use of proscenium doors was gradually discontinued; the proscenium arch itself became more of a separating frame; and by midcentury the pit was abolished in the more reputable theaters.[38] As the architectural structure of the theaters changed, the audience-actor dynamic was, as Joseph Donohue argues, "significantly altered"; there was a "withdrawal" of the actor from the audience (*Kean* 179, 180). At the same time, changes in social conditions, such as the ballooning London population and the increasing interclass tension (reflected in the OP theater riots of 1809), contributed to greater segregation of audiences along class lines. The advent of melodrama in the same period heightened segregation of the audience along lines of taste, which unavoidably were linked to class differences. Melodrama also introduced a dramatic form and a style of acting that, if anything, contributed to the distancing of the audience from the performance. These factors, taken collectively, can be interpreted as producing a series of related effects:

- they curtailed audience-actor interaction, which had been part of the traditional dynamic in English theaters since the Renaissance and which was considered all but a right by the OP rioters;
- they changed the style of acting from an intimate and familiar style to the more externalized and formally semiotic style characteristic of melodrama;
- they ushered in the music of melodrama and the dance of vaudeville along with a theater of spectacle and effect, lights, mirrors, and deus ex machinae, the "realism" of which was enhanced by greater authenticity of props, costumes, and sets and by advances in stage technology;
- they therefore contributed to the illusion that the actions onstage were part of a separate reality, a realm to be witnessed, to be either alienated from or identified with, but certainly *not* to be interacted with physically; and
- as a result of these factors, they constructed theater audiences in a subtle but profoundly different way, changing the role of the audience from a communal and participatory one to a more passive and receptive one.

The confluence of social, economic, and artistic developments operated to separate class from class, audience from actor, and, ultimately, the audience within itself. The net effect was to reconstruct the audience into a form not unlike that of the "sympathetic" reader, held in check between the imperatives of distanciation from performance and identification with it.

In other words, as realistic fiction gained cultural dominance over melodramatic theater, the *subject of reading* supplanted the *subject of performance* as the more widely disseminated, culturally reproduced subject position. This effect was not limited to novel readers; it manifested in the form of the theater, too. Even melodrama evolved through the first half of the century toward what is now called "domestic realism," moving from historical and gothic melodramas to nautical and patriotic melodramas to melodramas in which all political and psychic struggles were played out within the confines of the drawing room and the (behind-the-scenes) bedroom.[39] These changes in dramatic form accompanied a general *embourgeoisement* of both acting style and audience demographics around midcentury. As Michael Booth summarizes, "The general movement of nineteenth-century dramatic taste was from the romantic to the realistic, from the illusionist to the solidly physical, from the poetic to the prosaic, these tendencies applying to all aspects of theater: acting, costuming, scenery, staging and the content of the drama" (Booth et al. 33). The point, then, is that what might be described as a *novelization of the theater* took place in nineteenth-century British culture.[40] This is not to assign the "rise of the novel" with causal force in changing theater, only to see it as perhaps particularly representative of cultural trends of which it was a part.

Another way of making this claim is to say that the subject of reading proved more socially acceptable than the subject of performance as a model for the ideal spectator and the ideal citizen. After all, the reading subject is isolated, inwardly directed, socially deactivated, and engaged in the cultivation of the capacity for identification. The *reading audience* is perhaps the ultimate nineteenth-century form of a certain historically specific, socially prescribed "proper" audience. In this book, I have identified what appears to be a trend of development throughout the first half of the century away from the sort of subject-position and audience form represented by the doubly theatrical theater audience of the 1809 OP riots — or by a Felix Holt who might impulsively rush the stage and join a mob — toward an audience form that is more discrete, civil, and ideally distanced, not only from the action on the stage but from social and political action as well.

Finale

A more pervasive engagement with the figure of theatricality and with a dialectic of novel-versus-theater or reading-versus-performance existed in mid-Victorian society and its literature than generally has been recognized. This claim receives support in the first place from the fact that the two "nontheatrical" novels, *Shirley* and *Felix Holt*, are as thoroughly engaged with issues of theatricality as their more overtly theatrical counterparts, *Villette* and *Daniel Deronda*. These novels are representative of a cluster of theatrical novels that appeared in England around midcentury. The relative spate of theatrical novels at that time is no coincidence in that it *is* coincident with the end of the modern decline cycle in British theater. It might be interpreted as an expression of the assimilation of a culturewide paradigm shift, or simply as a celebration by and in the cultural form that represents itself — accurately or not — as winning the campaign against theatricality. At the grossest level of analysis, I too have dramatized history, sketching an Oedipal contest between a rising cultural form, the realist novel, and one that the novel came to supersede in the mid-nineteenth century (if only briefly, and only until superseded by other cultural forms — the photographic image and cinema spring to mind). This contest is represented in these novels in the form of a self-conscious dialogue between the figure of the novel and the figure of the theater. This chapter has outlined the strategies by which these novels use this dialogue to represent the claim to victory of a particular form of narrative realism and the subject position that accompanied it, or for which it was a vehicle. Those strategies include:

- the demonization of theatricality by association of it with the activities and subject-positions of unsympathetically represented characters, social groups, and ideologies;
- the novelization of the theatrical, according to which the novel is represented as the heir and successor to one sort of theatricality, the "legitimate" or "literary" drama of Greek tragedy and of Shakespeare, and as the necessary moral replacement for another sort of theatricality, specifically melodrama;
- the theatricalization of the social, which operates to trivialize certain segments of society and, in general, to demote all engagement with social issues, particularly those concerning class equality, as beneath consideration, thereby facilitating a general process of domestication; and
- the novelization of the subject by disseminating a form of subjectivity that is represented in the text by its character-type and, more important, is reproduced directly in the reader in two ways: through identification with the text and through the act of reading itself.

The figure of theatricality, as one manifestation of the more pervasive discourse(s) of play, is absolutely central to the formal strategies of nineteenth-century novelistic realism. It served as that against which realist novels defined their form. However, this is in no way to settle for the simplistic conclusions that a less critical reading of Victorian discourses might imply: theatricality is bad, authenticity is good, and moral rectitude comes to those who avoid the former and cultivate the latter. This study shows the representations of theatricality to be far more complex and conflicted than this.

In the first place, the relationship between theatricality and gender is more complex than can be explained by a simple dichotomy between a theatrical and a domestic model of femininity. Theatricality both empowers and disempowers female characters in Victorian novels. Illustrating this, I have used the concept of masquerade to identify four levels of theatricalized femininity, ranging from most recuperative to most subversive. Exemplifying the first level, Gwendolen Harleth performs a masquerade of femininity that reproduces patriarchal desire nonreflexively as pure *display*, which the text therefore suggests must be corrected by patriarchal instruction. At a second level, Caroline Helstone's character, while still almost completely subject to male desire, nevertheless instigates a subversion of socially prescribed gender roles by implying that the domestic model of woman is as theatrical as the theatrical model. At the third level, the character of Leonora Halm-Eberstein masquerades ostensively, wearing the dissonance between prescribed gender roles on and as her face. The form of masquerade thus represented is, in Judith Butler's formulation, "a failure to repeat, a deformity, or a parodic repetition that exposes the phantasmatic effect of abiding identity as a politically tenuous construction" (141). Finally, Lucy Snowe is a character who refuses — or is given a social condition that necessitates the refusal of — the masquerade of femininity. In *Villette*, theatricality empowers female characters, but at the cost not only of becoming disembodied but of becoming unrepresentable, a "sex which is not one." Always on the verge of this condition, Lucy's character wears her refusal to be subjugated — which *is* her subjugation — like a vacancy, a "signifying lack" that points to the subjugation as to the refusal.

In the second place, the historical contest between realist fiction and melodramatic theater is, of course, less categorical and more complex than the reading here at times might suggest. No impermeable boundary exists between cultural forms within the same society. Realist novels always have shared formal and thematic strategies with melodrama. Nineteenth-century melodramas, like nineteenth-century realist novels, embodied "the working out in popular culture of the conflict between the family and its values and the economic and social assault of industrialization" (Vincinus 128). Victorian novelists, like Victorian melodramatists, saw their fictions not as mirroring social reality in any simple, mimetic sense, but as providing an image of what would be a truer, more rational, or more sympathetic social reality. In this regard, nineteenth-century realism shared with melodrama (and probably all art forms) the goal of "reorder[ing] the material world so that it mirrors inherent truths" (Donohue, *Kean* 112). Melodramas no less than novels "image the spiritual in a world voided of its traditional Sacred, where the body of the ethical has become a sort of *deus absconditus* which must be sought for, postulated, brought into man's existence through the play of the spiritual imagination" (Brooks 11). Melodrama was less the opposite of realist fiction than a competitive twin vying within a specific society's cultural market for the claim to represent that society to itself.

In the third place, the scapegoating of theatricality that has been highlighted in this chapter cannot be interpreted simply as a naïve evasive strategy on the part of realist texts. Rather, I hope that I have suggested that these texts can only be understood if one gives them credit for using this strategy as only one among an array of strategies that combine to form something called "realism." No small number of textual attributes renders a text mimetic. Nineteenth-century realism can no more be comprehended by a reductive definition of "bourgeois realism" than nineteenth-century British society can be summed up with the overworked phrase "bourgeois ideology." Any account that portrays novelistic texts as merely trying to hide artifice while failing to successfully put on a false front is a projection of the critic's own limitations. The novels read in this study not only make use of their antitheatrical claim to realism but also construct in advance the potential recognition by readers of the inherent theatricality of that claim. Scapegoating, and appearing to scapegoat, and appearing to try to hide scapegoating, are all textual strategies.

And the same sort of argument applies to readers and readings. Readers do not simply surrender themselves to the phantasmatic world of a realist text. The subject-position constructed in the text-reader nexus that novels make available is not a position of essentialized presence but is multiply divided, if not ultimately indeterminate. Identification with sympathy-divided characters splits the reader; further levels of identification with narrational positions or with the centralized perceptivity of the world-generating locus of the text continue the splitting process. The splitting is compounded and embodied in the physical act of reading. Readers perform the split. At the simplest level, this means that readers know that the world of the text is not "real" *and* participate in it as if it were. More complexly, readers read at multiple levels and in multiple ways, including reading narrational tactics and "double-voiced" words on the surface of the text (to use Bakhtin's term). Hysterisized textual elements, intrusive narrators, foregrounding of textuality, and other elements that might be thought to threaten the continuity of the spectacle of realism can enlist readers all the more thoroughly (witness the appeal of postmodern fictions).

At the same time, textual verisimilitude — through successful elision of the authorial position, for instance — may only compel readers to work harder, as it were, in shifting back and forth between "inside" and "outside" the text, which occurs in all reading but perhaps especially in reading fiction. It is precisely this type of movement that the figure of sympathy both represents and forces the reader to enact. If "authenticity" represents an identity between inward state and outward appearance and "theatricality" represents the absence of this identity (or the denial of the inward and the multiplication of the outward), then "sympathy," as the third term, is the absorption of the external by the internal. The figure of sympathy and the realist novels for which it is a figure therefore generate a geometric increase in theatrical multiplicity toward the infinity of identification with all others. It is not, then, that George Eliot's fiction opposes theatricality but that it opposes anything short of total theatricality. Universal "sympathy" is a type of hypertheatricalized omniscience. The production of the split reader — regardless of how that split is generated — is the production of a stronger identification on the part of a reader who is not simply "sympathetic" or "critical" but who is identified with the act of textual production in the moment of reading.

Finally, and the previous caveats notwithstanding, it is inevitable that the figure of the theater should come to function as the Other within realist novels, since realism is theatrical at the level of its primary, antitheatrical claim. Realism is inherently performative. It constitutes the reality that it claims to report; it manufactures the "natural" in its own image. The figure of theatricality is therefore absolutely central to the nineteenth-century project of realism. It is the necessary foil against which the mid-Victorian novel defines its form, which after all is nothing more or less than a performance as a life-world. On the other hand, in order to produce subjects of reading (as opposed to subjects of performance), realist novels first had to produce subjects who read. To the extent that the dissemination and consumption of novels indeed has contributed to the social reproduction of the reading audience, the novel does participate in the manufacture of social materialities, proving its realism after the (f)act.

4

Theorizing the
Aesthetic Citizen

The idea that the true purpose of art was to express personality could
only gain ground when art had lost every other purpose.
                                         E. H. Gombrich, *The Story of Art*

In other words, we should finally work out the consequences of the
realization that art and play are not a subversion of or an alternative to
power, but an older, more immediate form of it.
                                         Mihai I. Spariosu, *Dionysus Reborn*

Aesthetic Play

Aesthetics is the theorization of specific categories of pleasure. Aesthetic
pleasure issues forth in the course of a conjunction between a subject,
whether producer or consumer of the aesthetic object, and that object,
whether theorized as internal or external to the subject. The quality of this
linkage and the status of the subject and of the object thus engaged have
been the central concerns of modern aesthetic theory. The subject-object
nexus, which is the defining issue of western epistemology generally, is the
site within aesthetic theory of the figure of play. Philosophers from Immanuel Kant to Jacques Derrida have conceived play as occupying the gap that
occurs between the subject and the object (or the subject and its objectified
self) in the act of taking aesthetic pleasure. As such, play is pleasure's most
specialized form. The pleasure is *in* the gap; play is that gap.

   Play as an explicit philosophical concept predates Plato, but it is not
until the eighteenth-century revolution in aesthetic theory that play again
becomes a central, if generally undertheorized, concept in modern aesthetic
theory.[1] As the culmination of that aesthetic revolution, Kant's *Critique of
Judgment* (1790) attributes to play the explanatory power that it thereafter

will be given variously in a long line of philosophical texts including, for instance, Friedrich von Schiller's *On the Aesthetic Education of Man*, Friedrich Nietzsche's *Philosophy during the Tragic Age of the Greeks*, Martin Heidegger's *Principle of Reason*, Karl Groos's *Play of Man*, Eugene Fink's *Play as Symbol of the World*, Hans-Georg Gadamer's *Truth and Method*, Theodor Adorno's *Aesthetic Theory*, Roland Barthes's *Pleasure of the Text*, and Derrida's *Writing and Difference*. Play is perhaps the single most pivotal concept in Kant's aesthetics, in Nietzsche's philosophy, and in all of Derrida's writings.[2] Nevertheless, other concepts — such as "the beautiful," "the sublime," "judgment," and "taste" — receive more explicit attention in the aesthetics of the eighteenth century. Perhaps logically enough, then, the same is true for the twentieth century. The sublime has received a great deal of critical attention in the past decade, while play as a concept in aesthetics has received relatively little.[3] While many of the terms of postmodern philosophy, such as aporia or simulacra, which themselves are derived from play concepts, long have passed into (and perhaps out of) common usage, play has remained largely unacknowledged, perhaps especially by those who use it most freely, certain postmodern theorists. These are the signs of play's foundational status. They evidence the extent to which theorists — intentionally and unintentionally — have worked for centuries, and from vastly differing theoretical orientations, to protect play's status as the magic of aesthetic pleasure: the free, disinterested, spontaneous, and universal experience of the subsumption of subject and object, the merging of self and other.

And there are some very good reasons for wanting to protect this experience, not the least of which is the potentially liberatory nature of aesthetic experience on an affective level and, precariously aligned with that experience, the potential of art as a force within society for critiquing and subverting dominant discourses and institutions. Nineteenth-century realist novels are centrally concerned with this potential, both with controlling it *and* with instigating it. This last statement puts me somewhat at odds with the trend in recent criticism, which became notable with D. A. Miller's *The Novel and the Police* and Nancy Armstrong's *Desire and Domestic Fiction*, that focuses largely on the ways that nineteenth-century realism recuperates dominant ideologies. While contributing to that trend, I also am in partial agreement with George Levine's corrective to it in his introduction to *Aesthetics and Ideology*. Levine laments what he sees as a critical environment in which the "appropriation of the aesthetic by politics is almost a given of much contemporary theory" (12). He argues that, "however thoroughly absorbed into dominant ideological formations the aesthetic has been, it has always served also as a potentially disruptive force, one that opens up possibilities of value resistant to any dominant political power" (15). While I analyze aesthetic play precisely as the "potentially disruptive force" that novelistic realism instigates and embodies, I also acknowledge the ideological appropriation of the aesthetic that occurred at the end of the eighteenth century. Doing so is necessary, because it is impossible to ignore the imbrication of aesthetics and dominant ideology while writing about either eighteenth-century theory or the advent of the realist novel.

It is no chance coincidence that roughly during the same decades in the eighteenth century both aesthetic theory and the theoretical underpinning for the already thriving practice of laissez-faire capitalism cemented their discursive formations, most particularly in the writings of Kant (followed by Schiller and the Romantics) and of Adam Smith. The most frequently forwarded explanation for the explosion of interest in the aesthetic in the eighteenth century is that the theorization of art came to serve the rise to dominance in Britain of a bourgeois civil society, its accompanying political economy, and the internalized form of subjectivity upon which it depended.[4] As Howard Caygill puts it, somewhat modestly, "The change in the conception of the civil society at the beginning of the eighteenth century was accompanied by a change in the understanding of the pleasures of art" (41). Stated more strongly, British civil society and the individual internalized bourgeois subject of which it is constituted emerge at the end of the eighteenth century through a process in which the theorization of art and the institutionalization of laissez-faire economic practice become, at least in part, mutually defining. Mary Poovey reverses, or redoubles, the critical trend in this area by "complicat[ing] the assumption of many literary critics that economic theory is the repressed truth of aesthetics by demonstrating that the reverse is also true" ("Aesthetics and Political Economy" 80). She analyzes the origins of Adam Smith's economic theory in eighteenth-century aesthetic theory, arguing generally that "each discourse continues to make visible issues and formulations that are still active but no longer definitive in what was once its other half" (82). This latter point is important for its recognition that the mutual construction of the discourse of political economy and the discourse of aesthetics marks at the same time the violent separation of those two spheres of human experience, the sphere of art and the sphere of economics, the sensuous particular and the communal ideal. It is not until the nineteenth century that the violence of this separation finds full expression in the form of realist novels, which struggle to reconcile the aesthetic and the economic. This is perhaps the central dilemma of bourgeois ideology.

That dilemma, and the violence underlying it, is the subject of two influential studies, Terry Eagleton's *The Ideology of the Aesthetic* and Howard Caygill's *Art of Judgment*. Eagleton's book is at heart a historical treatise on the parallel structuring of the object of aesthetics, the bourgeois subject, and the commodity form. Noting the range of issues that typically are associated with the aesthetic subject-object nexus — "freedom and legality, spontaneity and necessity, self-determination, autonomy, particularity and universality" — Eagleton argues that "the category of the aesthetic assumes the importance it does in modern Europe because in speaking of art it speaks of these other matters too, which are at the heart of the middle class's struggle for political hegemony." He concludes, "The construction of the modern notion of the aesthetic artefact is thus inseparable from the construction of the dominant ideological forms of modern class-society, and indeed from a whole new form of human subjectivity appropriate to that social order" (*IA* 3).

By contrast, Caygill's book begins with a comparative analysis of two distinct eighteenth-century social orders, the German political state and the British (and French) civil society, and the divergent but complementary theories of art that those social differences produced. In short (and to oversimplify a long and erudite book), the German police state of Frederick the Great generated the discourse of aesthetic theory, as exemplified by Samuel Pufendorf's *De Jure Naturae et Gentium Libri Octo* (1672), and thereby juridically forced the particular to bow to the universal, diversity to give way to unity. In contrast, British civil society, which Caygill traces from the social theories of Thomas Hobbes and the aesthetics of Richard Cumberland's *Treatise of the Laws of Nature* (1672), produces a discourse of taste, which makes the universal bow to the particular. The discourse of taste is complemented, however, in being coupled with a discourse of the *je ne sais quoi* — "the inexplicability of the workings of taste" — which disembodies taste and turns it back into a providential regulative (39). The outcome, Caygill concludes, "justifies a moral civil society through a natural law which is prior to the state and which manifests divine providence through sentiments of benevolence, private property in things and labour, and commerce. . . . For [the British] reason could not be legislative, because this granted excessive power to the state; but nor could sensibility, since this valorized activities perceived as base. The civil society which this theory justified is like a work of art in being regular without being legislated or produced. The hand which both made and apportioned the fruits of its making was invisible" (33–34).

Caygill—surprisingly similar to Eagleton, given their very different theoretical orientations—writes here about power and about the violence it takes to make the providential hand invisible. His approach is to analyze the convergence of the discourses of taste and manners, which helped shape the bourgeois subject of civil society, with the institutions of public credit and contractual obligation, which in effect produced refinement and enforcement of the rights of things.[5] In this regard Caygill follows the historian J. G. A. Pocock, who in *Virtue, Commerce, and History* argues that as part of the cultural paradigm shift that occurred at the end of the eighteenth century "a right to things became a way to the practice of virtue, so long as virtue could be defined as the practice and refinement of manners" (50). Pocock distinguishes between a prior dominant order represented by the discourses of civic duty, virtue, and stable property and an emerging order represented by the discourses of civility, manners, and mobile property. One might say that, according to Pocock's telling, duties became rights, propriety became property, virtue became commerce, and (in terms more Marxian than Pocock would allow) relations between people increasingly became relations between things. The figure of culture, as I will analyze it in Matthew Arnold's *Culture and Anarchy,* for instance, operated to efface the differences between these pairs of terms, making relations between things appear to be relations between people through the mediating discourses of manners, taste, and cultivation. Thus culture became the vehicle for social order and for the exercise of power in an effaced and internalized form, which of course is one definition of "ideology." Pocock makes the connections between aesthetics and authority explicit when he concludes, "Without belief in the progress of the arts, the investing mercantile society literally could not maintain itself" (98).

Eagleton argues along related lines: "The ultimate binding force of the bourgeois social order, in contrast to the coercive apparatus of absolutism, will be habits, pieties, sentiments and affections." Thus the exercise of power is abstracted from the state apparatus and posited as the markers of customary practice and culture identity that each individualized citizen carries inside him / herself. Social order is "inscribed in the minutiae of subjective experience, and the fissure between abstract duty and pleasurable inclination is accordingly healed." Through this process the new bourgeois subject, "which bestows on itself self-referentially a law at one with its immediate experience, finding its freedom in its necessity, is modelled on the aesthetic artefact" (*IA* 20). Thus Eagleton, like Pocock and Caygill, though from very different perspectives, identifies a process whereby *social power is aestheticized*. The form of the autotelic subject emerges in conjunction with the form of the autonomous object of art, as with the form of the universally communicable (and therefore alienated) commodity. These forms are emblematized on a culturewide basis by the providential hand of the *je ne sais quoi*, which underwrites the value of the artifact, and likewise by the "invisible hand" of the market, which becomes the central mystified source of efficacy for laissez-faire capitalism.

However, the "fissure between abstract duty and pleasurable inclination" is not so easily healed as the passage from Eagleton might imply. Aesthetic theory — like political economy — arises as a response to the problem produced by the necessity to suppress the difference between the universal and the particular, unity and diversity. As Caygill puts it, "The establishment of the civility of a commercial society on moral sense demanded the violent repression of the difference between sense and idea, and their analogues, private interest and public good" (53). Public good, the harmonious wholeness of society as designated by Providence, requires the submission of the particular to the universal. In the realm of aesthetics, this occurs through the supposed spontaneity, universality, and disinterestedness of aesthetic pleasure, which indeed will become the tenets of Kant's aesthetics. In the realm of the market, the same "invisible hand" is taken as the guarantor of orderly and equitable circulation. But the institutions of market circulation cannot deny their dependence on production, however hard they may try, and here aesthetic theorists and political economists alike confront a problem that cannot be subsumed easily: no pleasing, providentially underwritten proportionality elicits a willingness for labor (unless one is an Adam Bede or a Caleb Garth). As a result, the industry that sustains commodity circulation is always "the subject of rational direction and violence" (Caygill 61), but this direction and violence cannot be acknowledged fully because to do so might empower the laboring classes and, more critically, might undercut the claim to the providential basis of that social order. As Caygill concludes, "The equivocation of the idea and sense in the realm of circulation masks a violence at the level of production which cannot be known" (61). The embarrassing problem posed by the fact that Providence must be supplement by, in effect, the wisdom of the wealthiest property owners in society, therefore, can only be expressed as the inseparability of pleasure and violence (witness the rhetoric surrounding the "trickle-down" economics of the 1980s). In the mirror realms of political economy and aesthetic theory, this inseparability is signified by the "invisible hand" and, on the other hand, by the *je ne sais quoi*. In Kant's third *Critique*, the name given to this equivocation of pleasure and violence, sense and idea, is "play." In mid-nineteenth-century British discourses, the name more often given for that same aesthetic operation is, tellingly enough, "work," art-as-work, which in effect is work *as* play. In one sense, then, Victorian play is the labor of production that "cannot be known" if private interest and public good are to be reconciled through means less violent than state intervention.

Kantian Play

It is this feeling of freedom in the play of our cognitive powers, a play that yet must also be purposive, which underlies that pleasure which alone is universally communicable although not based on concepts.
Immanuel Kant, *Critique of Judgment*

The German constructs art as he constructs the camel out of the depths of his moral consciousness.
E. S. Dallas, *The Gay Science* (1866)

Aesthetic theory was born as the German alternative to Britain's moral theory of taste, "aesthetics" having been coined in 1735 by Immanuel Kant's predecessor, Alexander Baumgarten. Kant's *Critique of Judgment* was a response to the British tradition of theory represented by the works of Shaftesbury, Kames, Burke, Hume, and Smith, among others. While Kant borrowed from and cited these works, he felt they lacked philosophical rigor, a situation that he set out to correct. This cycle was continued by early to mid-Victorian British theorists of art, who in turn generally strove to refute German idealism.[6] In a certain sense, there was no aesthetic theory in England until the Aestheticism of late century. The antipathy of such thinkers as John Ruskin to idealist aesthetics can be understood as a reaction against what was thought to be Kantian play. The necessary first step here is to delineate how play is figured in Kant's third *Critique*.

At the risk of treating Kant reductively (which, given the scope of his work, is perhaps unavoidable), one can summarize the central assumption underlying the third *Critique* as follows: Aesthetic judgments of the beautiful must have an a priori, disinterested, and universal foundation, because otherwise humans would have no alternative but to conceive of Nature as an array of random particulars with no governing universal order, and that simply is inconceivable. In his introduction, Kant defines judgment as "the ability to think the particular as contained under the universal" (18.iv),[7] continuing as follows: "Hence judgment must assume, as an a priori principle for its own use, that what to human insight is contingent in the particular (empirical) natural laws does nevertheless contain a law-governed unity. . . . [W]e present this unity as a purposiveness of objects. . . . This is also why we rejoice (actually we are relieved of a need) when, just *as if it were a lucky chance favoring our aim*, we do find such systematic unity among merely empirical laws, even though we necessarily had to assume that there is such unity even though we have no insight into this unity and cannot prove it" (23–24.v) (emphasis added). By "purposiveness of objects" Kant means "the object's being commensurate with the cognitive powers that are . . . brought into play when we judge reflectively, and hence [expresses] merely a subjective formal purposiveness of the object" (30.vii). It is purposiveness in this sense that is "lucky." Yet to express it as such is to reveal the precariousness of the concept, since chance, as opposed to necessity, is precisely what Kant is concerned with limiting. (Similarly revealing is Kant's subsequent statement that if we found "our understanding could not unify nature's particular laws under universal empirical laws," "we would certainly dislike it" [27–28.vi].)

Thus the terms of Kant's aesthetics point simultaneously in two directions that might seem to be opposed: toward freedom and toward law, toward human subjectivity and toward "the supersensible." The third *Critique* handles the former of these with greater sureness than it does the latter. Kant does not shy away from positing the centrality of a universalized subjectivity as the (tautological) proof of his entire system:

But there is one fact that virtually proves the principle that the purposiveness in the beautiful in nature is *ideal*, that we ourselves lay this principle at the basis of all our aesthetic judgments . . . namely, the fact that whenever we judge any beauty at all we seek the standard for it a priori in ourselves. . . . This could not be so if we adopted a realistic interpretation of the purposiveness of nature, because then we would have to learn from nature what to consider beautiful, and a judgment of taste would be subject to empirical principles. In fact, however, what counts in judging beauty is not what nature is, nor even what purpose it [has] for us, but how we receive it. If nature had created its forms for our liking, such a purposiveness of nature would always be objective; it would not be a subjective purposiveness, based on the play of the imagination in its freedom, where it is we who receive nature with favor, not nature that favors us. (225.58)

"Subjective purposiveness" — the "lucky" matching of forms in nature to intersubjective forms — is *of* nature *for* human conceptual understanding, which never has access to "the thing in itself," only to conceptual forms. This constitutes a radical freedom for the subject, one that verges on an ability (perhaps a responsibility) for creating the universe, though it is the Romantic thinkers following Kant who first entertain that possibility.

At the same time, however, the third *Critique* is underpinned by the law of a moral theology, though Kant takes pains to de-emphasize this. One glimpses it throughout the text as the largely unexplained figure of the supersensible (for example, the "supersensible vocation" by which humanity finds a "moral foundation" in its response to the category of the sublime [158.39]). In the final sections of the *Critique*, Kant turns to the topic that he has attempted to keep from undermining the rigor of his philosophy, "teleological judgments." While he qualifies such judgments as reflective, not determinative, and disclaims any debt to the "argument from design," he turns at last to the explanatory necessity of "final causes," to which he gives the traditional name, if parenthetically: "The purposiveness that we must presuppose even for cognizing the inner possibility of many natural things is quite unthinkable to us and is beyond our grasp unless we think of it, and of the world as such, as a product of an intelligent cause (a God)."[8] Without an underwriting by the "intelligent cause," the Kantian system could not stand, at least not as Kant, as opposed to some twentieth-century Kantians, conceived of it. The supersensible therefore marks the margins of the third *Critique*, what Jacques Derrida's *Truth in Painting* terms the "parerga." I point to the margin of the text not to attempt to undermine it but to locate an aporia that lies at the center of the framing. Perhaps contrary to Derrida, I would argue that the third *Critique* consciously works with its framing and with this aporia, or does so as much as does Derrida in reading it.[9] The figure in the third *Critique* for this aporia is the figure of play. Kant uses play, on the one hand, to demonstrate the autonomy of the subject and, on the other hand, to demonstrate the lawfulness of the moral order. The text hinges entirely on the auto-deconstruction enacted by the figure of play.

Recall that aesthetic judgment is introduced by Kant in the third *Critique* as that which dialectically completes the system of philosophy developed in the first and second *Critiques*. It is the synthesis, the mediating term between "pure reason" and "practical reason." The following table from the third *Critique* provides a useful summary overview (the middle row representing the concerns of the third *Critique*):

All the Mental Powers	Cognitive Powers	A Priori Principles	Application to
cognitive power	understanding	lawfulness	nature [form]
feeling of pleasure and displeasure	judgment	purposiveness	art
power of desire [will]	reason	final purpose	freedom
			(38.ix)

The centrality of play to this system becomes obvious when one recognizes that the mediating oscillation between understanding and reason, necessity and freedom, is characterized throughout the third *Critique* as nothing other than play. In an exemplary passage, Kant writes: "The spontaneity in the play of the cognitive powers, whose harmony with each other contains the basis of this pleasure [in judging the beautiful], makes that concept of purposiveness suitable for mediating the connection of the domain of the concept of nature with that of the concept of freedom" (39–38.ix). The *Critique* proceeds to argue the disinterestedness and universality of aesthetic judgments on the basis of subjective purposiveness, which is epitomized by the spontaneous play between the mental powers: "When this [aesthetic pleasure] happens, the cognitive powers brought into play by this presentation [*darstellen*, the 'representation' or 'picturing' in the mind that constitutes the beautiful object] are in free play, because no determinate concept restricts them to a particular rule of cognition" (62.9).[10] Kant then develops this understanding of play in relationship to terms that will become more central to Romanticism than they are in Kant, specifically "feeling" and "imagination," continuing as follows: "This state of *free play* of the cognitive powers, accompanying a presentation by which an object is given, must be universally communicable; for cognition, the determination of the object with which given presentations are to harmonize (in any subject whatever) is the only way of presenting that holds for everyone." Phrases such as "free play of imagination" and "harmony of cognitive powers" mark the threading of the figure of play throughout the remainder of the third *Critique*.

Critically, play is not synonymous with pleasure in the third *Critique*;

play takes place in the act of judgment as the spontaneous play among mental powers. Pleasure results from the activation, recognition, and sustaining of a mental process (or the repetition of it — enter Sigmund Freud). Thus, while there may be implications of an impulse to liberate play as a sign of ecstatic merging between subject and object (and this is one way that subsequent British thinkers misread Kant), the third *Critique* in fact works to purify play. This is necessitated by the fact that play constantly threatens to become "merely subjective" pleasure: "Cognitions and judgments . . . must be universally communicable. For otherwise we could not attribute to them a harmony with the object, but they would one and all be a merely subjective play of the presentational powers, just as skepticism would have it" (87–88.21). In order to remain free from individual interest and sensuous pleasure, the play of subjective purposiveness must be preserved at the loftiest of heights as the famous *Zweck ohne Zweckmassigkeit*, the "purposiveness without purpose" in the apperception of the beautiful.[11] But it is precisely here that the abyss of play yawns. At the very point where the universality and disinterestedness of play are being defended through an appeal to its "uselessness," its freedom from any moral prejudice, play threatens to exchange universality for absolute relativism, undercutting all moral foundation. In reading the third *Critique*, I picture Kant continually circling and recircling the crumbling edge of this abyss. To the Zweck ohne Zweckmassigkeit he throws another oxymoron: the "*free lawfulness* of the imagination" (91.22). He sees a swinging footbridge disappear into the sublimely immense distance above the abyss. That bridge is play.

How does Kant use play to recuperate moral order out of freedom? From two directions: as part of the beautiful and as part of the sublime. The spontaneous subjective purposiveness of aesthetic judgment of the beautiful finds a surprising analog in the moral law, just as the beautiful is claimed to be "the symbol of the morally good" (228.59). Thus the "harmony" among the mental powers that is produced as the play of aesthetic judgment "also promotes the mind's receptivity to moral feeling" (38–39.ix). Judgment "is not based on any interest, *yet it gives rise to one*," which again is "moral feeling" (167.42). The rationale for these claims rests on a reversion to originary definitions: moral law is formal in the same way that aesthetic judgment is. Humankind's "moral vocation" must issue from the same subjective and spontaneous purposiveness without a purpose, which is nothing other than play (168.42). Aesthetic play is "free" to obey or disobey moral law, but since it originates from the same source, it always freely chooses to correspond with moral law.[12]

As in the beautiful, an analogy operates in the discourse of the sublime such that the experience of it parallels the form of the ultimate sublimity, God (123.28). The sublime speaks of moral foundations in part because it points to that which supersedes nature, as represented by nothing so much as the human power to conceptualize nature even in its most terrifying magnitude. Thus the sublime is defined as "an object (of nature) the presentation of which determines the mind to think of nature's inability to attain to an exhibition of ideas" (127.29). Nature's (material or real) supremacy over humans reminds them of their (conceptual or ideal) supremacy over nature. Though Kant has no intention of making man into God — quite the contrary — this implication, which exists in his work, was not overlooked by some who followed (Friedrich Nietzsche, for instance). In effect, if one could play as one plays in judging the beautiful but in response to the natural sublime, thereby entirely transcending the fear of mortality, then one would *be* God. The sublime thus conceived is unbounded, absolute play. However, such play for humans becomes a form of self violence (116.27). The sublime is a "negative pleasure," "a pleasure that is possible only by means of a displeasure" (98.23; 117.27).[13] Therefore, play must be rationalized further in the sublime than it is in the beautiful, as Kant writes: "It is in fact difficult to think of a feeling for the sublime in nature without connecting with it a mental attunement similar to that for moral feeling. It is true that the pleasure we take directly in the beautiful in nature also presupposes, as well as cultivates, a certain *liberality* in our way of thinking, i.e., an independence of the liking from mere enjoyment of sense; but here the freedom is still presented more as in *play* than as subject to a law-governed *task*. But the latter is what genuinely characterizes man's morality, where reason must exert its dominance over sensibility" (128.29). The sublime threatens to tie humankind too strongly to the materiality of the body, to "mere enjoyment of sense," albeit as the negative pleasure of fear. At the very same instant, the level of play that the sublime would require in order to produce ideal pleasure (pleasure without enjoyment, pleasure without the body) threatens to dissolve entirely the human particular into the universal.[14] This, then, is the aporia of play. Kant, unlike Nietzsche or Nietzsche's postmodern disciples, is not quite able to cross this abyss, even with the bridge of play, though that abyss and that bridge are outlined clearly in the third *Critique*. In the sublime, play finally must be subsumed under "a law-governed task," must become, at last, work.

The Romantic Replacement of Play

Friedrich von Schiller is the first heir to Kantian aesthetics, and his *Aesthetic Education of Man* (1795) is one of the most important vehicles after Kant for transmitting the figure of play into British Romantic and subsequent British discourses. Given my purposes, I provide only the briefest consideration of his work here.[15] In short, Schiller simplifies the architecture of Kantian aesthetics and, in the process, unabashedly centers play as the defining activity of the liberal-intellectual, humanist man of whom he writes, as in this most-quoted passage: "Man shall *only play* with Beauty, and he shall play *only with Beauty*. . . . For, to declare it once and for all, Man plays only when he is in the full sense of the word a man, and *he is only wholly a Man when he is playing*" (80).

Following the structure but not the content of the Kantian dialectic, Schiller theorizes a "formal impulse," a "sensuous impulse," and — replacing aesthetic judgment as the mediating term — the "play impulse" (64–75). Unlike Kant, Schiller directly posits the possibility of a complete reconciliation between nature and culture, necessity and freedom. Play is endowed with the power to effect what amounts to a merging of object and subject. The play impulse will "be directed towards annulling time *within time*, reconciling becoming with absolute being and change with identity," thereby bringing "form into the material and reality into the form" (74, 75). At the same time, Schiller undercuts Kantian subjectivism and disinterestedness, linking play in one direction to the sensuous body and in the other direction to the social collective (or, more accurately, to an emerging form of culture that he helps to theorize).[16] He is not troubled in making the link that is implicit in Kant between aesthetic play and social order explicit: "If we are to solve the political problem [meaning the specter of class revolt] in practice, follow the path of aesthetics, since it is through Beauty that we arrive at Freedom" (27). Similarly, he sees no conflict between a claim for the universality of play and an attribution of moral utility (and thus "interestedness") to play: "So the play impulse, in which both [of the other two impulses] combine to function, will compel the mind at once morally and physically; it will therefore, since it annuls all mere chance, annul all compulsion also, and set man free both physically and morally" (75).

Thus one can see that Schiller moves the figure of play in two potentially contradictory directions. On the one hand, the ideality of play is heightened, or at least play becomes less theorized and more mystified as that which magically heals difference and so erases the violence required to reconcile diversity and unity. On the other hand (and as part of his intention to ameliorate empiricist and idealist theories of beauty), Schiller also grants value to the sensuous particular, if only to dissolve the universal into it. The combined result is to anchor universal social harmony to a particular intersubjective state through a process that cannot bear rigorous investigation. Thereafter, "[a]ll improvement in the political sphere is to proceed from the ennobling of the character" (50). It is as if one can witness in Schiller the transition as it is taking place from juridical forms of power to the internalized form of the bourgeois subject. His theory marks a point halfway between the German aesthetics of the centralized state and the British theory of taste within civil society (using Howard Caygill's distinctions). Perhaps for this reason, his "revisionary version of Kantian aesthetics and play" was more readily adopted by British and American thinkers than was Kant's, becoming "the 'true Kant' not only for the Romantics but also for . . . many present-day Anglo-American and Continental scholars" (Spariosu, *Dionysus* 65). Schiller marks a critical, transitional position in the history of play concepts, signaling the forms that the figure of play takes in Romantic and Victorian discourses.

Though it may not have been evident to contemporary readers of Samuel Taylor Coleridge, he was the original siphon of Kantian idealism into British culture. Rosemary Ashton's book *The German Idea: Four English Writers and the Reception of German Thought, 1800–1860*, is not the only study to conclude that "[t]here is no doubt, however, that he [Coleridge] was the first and most important interpreter of Kant [in England], and the first theorist of literature to respond to the new aesthetic movement in Germany which followed Kant's philosophy" (66).[17] Indeed, Coleridge was one of the few English thinkers of his time to read Kant at all, which meant reading in German, much less to take his theories seriously. Coleridge told a friend in 1812 that he had "learnt more from Kant than from any other philosopher" (qtd. in Ashton, *German Idea* 36). In the ninth book of the *Biographia Literaria*, Coleridge proclaims that "the writings of the illustrious sage of Konigsberg, the founder of Critical Philosophy, more than any other work, at once invigorated and disciplined my understanding" (256). Despite this evidence, however, one would be hard pressed to find recognizably Kantian terminology in any of Coleridge's works, or citation of Kant sufficient to the degree of his influence on Coleridge. One might explain this in terms of the way that Coleridge sampled German idealism in fabricating British Romanticism, one result of which was the effective replacement of play or aesthetic judgment (in the Kantian senses) by "the imagination." I would argue that the relative absence of overt reference to Kant, coupled with the extensive intellectual debt to his work, represents not simply an oversight or plagiarism but an active repression.[18] Further, the figure of play was to some extent the specific target of that repression. This claim receives support when one considers the fate of the figure of play following Coleridge. Coleridge was the gatekeeper for Victorian access to Kantian/Schillerian play. After Coleridge closed that gate (though obviously not for this reason alone), play as such remained a submerged element in British theory for half a century.

Nancy Webb Kelly pursues these issues in her essay "Homo Aestheticus: Coleridge, Kant, and Play," where she writes: "In effect, the very absence of 'free play' in Coleridge's borrowings from German Romanticism becomes the ground of its presence: from that critical juncture we can trace the rhetorical usage of 'play' as a denigrated category in human experience generally, and in cultural or aesthetic experience more specifically" (201). Kelly goes on to offer an explanation for Coleridge's omission of play in terms of the economic needs of a newly emerging profession to which he was, by dint of economic necessity, an extremely interested party.[19] That profession, the profession of producing culture, roughly lumped together the self-supporting (rather than patronage-supported) artist, the professional critic in the media, and the salaried intellectual in academia. The figure of play was, on the surface, less compatible with middle-class industriousness and the desire to control the working class, while the figure of imagination designated a special province to which the artist and the art critic could lay claim as the inner spring of a unique vocation. Coleridge's arguments in favor of the "work" of the artist-critic and of the professionalization of what he dubbed "the clerisy" can be understood as part of the nineteenth-century trends that privileged work and propagated professionalization. As Raymond Williams notes, the making of art "was coming to be regarded as one of a number of specialized kinds of production, subject to much the same conditions as general production" (*Culture and Society* 32). In the same moment — and with the appropriateness of paradox — "a theory of the 'superior reality' of art, as the seat of imaginative truth," and "the idea of the independent creative writer, the autonomous genius," were coming into wide circulation. Williams summarizes the conflicting pressures of the period using terms of particular relevance to this study: "In practice there were deep insights, and great works of art [from the Romantics]; but in the continuous pressure of living, the free play of genius found it increasingly difficult to consort with the free play of the market, and the difficulty was not solved, but cushioned, by an idealization. The last pages of Shelley's *Defence of Poetry* are painful to read. The bearers of a high imaginative skill become suddenly the 'legislators,' at the very moment when they were being forced into practical exile; their description as 'unacknowledged,' which, on the theory, ought only to be a fact to be accepted, carries with it also the felt helplessness of a generation" (47). Resolving the relationship between the "free play of genius" and the "free play of the market" was an even more conflicted issue for the Victorians than for the Romantics. Thus this issue appears as a compelling concern in the aesthetic and social theories of Ruskin, the theory of culture developed by Arnold, and the struggles to re-define the artist in Thackeray's *Pendennis* and Kingsley's *Alton Locke*. These Victorians denounced, hungered for, and transformed the cushioning ideal-ization signified by the figure of play.

Before moving to analysis of Victorian aesthetic play, I want to outline three points for further development. First, to summarize, aesthetic theory and political economy came of age in conjunction with one another in the eighteenth century as discrete domains of discourse that we now call philos-ophy and economics. These disciplines produced during the eighteenth century their own cultural forms (as I define that concept in chapter one), which served as specialized and, increasingly, professionally regulated vehi-cles for their respective discourses. The cultural form for aesthetic theory was the theoretical treatise or philosophy book on subjects like taste, the beautiful, and judgment, for instance, which the eighteenth century cer-tainly did not invent but did produce in unprecedented numbers. British political economy and the "science" of economics in general was given its own discrete cultural form roughly in the decades between Adam Smith's *Enquiry into the Nature and Causes of the Wealth of Nations* (1776) and John Stuart Mill's *Principles of Political Economy* (1848). But there was a third cultural form that also developed alongside the theoretical treatise and the economic manuscript and that shaped and was shaped by the other two cultural forms. I mean, of course, the novel, which during the same period transmuted through epistolary, Gothic, and historical forms, among oth-ers, eventually claiming the epithet of "realism" in the nineteenth century. As Eagleton observes, "If one wished to name the most important cultural instrument of this hegemony [of bourgeois civil society] in the nineteenth

century, one which never ceases to grasp universal reason in concretely
particular style, uniting within itself an economy of abstract form with the
effect of lived experience, one might do worse than name the realist novel"
(*IA* 43–44). I do name that form and more specifically analyze the mechanism by which it participated in the aestheticization of the social, but also
the socialization of the aesthetic. That mechanism was the figure play, and
through it nineteenth-century realist novelists and their texts exercised a
prerogative *not* to restrict themselves from the domains colonized by political economy and aesthetic theory.

Second, I note that play appears to disappear from British discourses
about art in the first half of the nineteenth century. Between Coleridge's
replacement of "play" with "imagination" and the revival in the 1880s of an
overtly play-based aesthetics by the Decadents, play became a more pressurized and sublimated figure.[20] To make this claim is not to subscribe to a
reductionistic "repressive hypothesis," according to which the Victorians
were simply repressive of play. Rather, it is in the first place to view the
permutations of the figure of play during the early- to mid-Victorian decades as specific to a more "rational" stage in the long cyclical history of play
concepts, in contrast to the more "prerational" play of the Romantics and
then the Decadents (using the categories developed by Mihai Spariosu). It
is in the second place to acknowledge that play took on discursive roles and
performed ideological functions that were specific to this historical period,
functions that were only more socially significant for being more intensely
regulated. That regulation took a variety of forms, including the anti-
aesthetic and frequently masculinist Utilitarianism of early Victorian culture, the anti-idealism of prominent Victorian art critics such as Ruskin,
and the reading middle class's preference for practical "art criticism" over
what was perceived as the more patrician form of "philosophical criticism"
(traditional aesthetic theory). Andrew Hemingway argues that in early-
nineteenth-century Britain art criticism ("occasional writings on art in the
newspaper and periodical press") became the vehicle for the middle-class
preference for a naturalistic as opposed to a picturesque aesthetic, gaining
in popularity over two other forms of writing about art, aesthetic philosophy and academic theory (which theorized the techniques and effects of
specific works of art) (10). The cultural form of art criticism — short, non-
theoretical pieces in the accessible and inexpensive medium of the periodical — came to dominate other forms of discourse about art, especially those
most closely associated with "theory." If play disappeared — or appeared to
disappear — from discourse about art, it was in part because the cultural

form that had been the guardian of play as an aesthetic concept since Plato, and especially since Kant's revival of it, had for the moment lost cultural market share.

Third, aesthetic play did not disappear; it was expressed through a different cultural form. In the first half of the nineteenth century, realist novels were engaged in establishing the dominance of their cultural form, which historically meant competing with and if possible displacing previously more dominant forms, which in material terms meant gaining market share through the sale of the various media in which novels were printed and read. During this period the realist novel did in part displace the Romantic lyric, for instance, and the aesthetics associated with it by many Victorians. The novels read in this study thematically represent the historical competitions between cultural forms in which they were engaged, depicting discursive contests between figures that represent idealist and Romantic aesthetics and other figures that stand for the aesthetics of novelistic realism. Novels became the primary vehicle for and expression of the cultural work of play at a time when neither Romantic poetry nor aesthetic theory served that function. Play did not disappear from discourses about art; rather, a new cultural form assumed the authority to speak not only for "literature" but for "art" in general and, what is more, incorporated play as the basis for its form.

The Labor of Art / The Art of Labor

> The imagination, when at play, is curiously like bad children, and likes to play with fire.
>> John Ruskin, *Modern Painters* (MPIII 131)

John Ruskin never read Kant.[21] Indeed, Ruskin's "theocentric" aesthetics combines the two extremes that Kantian aesthetics strives to avoid: an empirical privileging of the sensuous particular and a transcendental vision overtly wedded to a didactic mission.[22] The merging of subject and object implied by Kant's "subjective purposiveness" is precisely the sort of thinking that Ruskin wishes to correct with his theory of the "pathetic fallacy." Further, a reading of *Modern Painters* (1843–60) and *The Stones of Venice* (1851–53) finds no uses of the figure of play in the sense developed in Kant's third *Critique* or Schiller's *Aesthetic Education*. The consideration here of Ruskin, then, is justified not by any obvious relevance but, con-

versely, by the apparent lack of relevance coupled with the widely recognized importance and representativeness of Ruskin's thought to mid-
Victorian aesthetics.

To the extent that the figure of play is discernible in Ruskin's aesthetic
writings, it is expressed in relation to the grotesque. Ruskin initially associated the grotesque with the Gothic, the style for which he became such a
widely read champion that he can be said to have generated more new
Gothic buildings in Victorian England than the number of Venetian ones
about which he wrote.[23] In the second volume of *The Stones of Venice*, in the
chapter titled "The Nature of the Gothic," Ruskin develops the dichotomies
that reappear throughout his writings: north/south, English/Italian, Middle Ages/Renaissance, Christian/pagan, originality/imitation, truth/effect, noble/ignoble. His privileging of the first of each of these pairs of
terms and his use of them to characterize the Gothic served more than
aesthetic interests, or precisely the type of interests that the aesthetic always
unavoidably serves. As John D. Rosenberg notes, the mid-Victorian Gothic
revival was both "an escape from the tensions and ugliness of industrial
civilization" and "an attempt, however fated to failure, to revolutionize that
civilization" (52). For Ruskin as for contemporaries like A. W. Pugin, "The
medieval town is a kind of Heavenly City, ideally beautiful, humane, and
at peace; the modern town is an inferno filled with sulphurous smoke and
the restlessness of unsatisfied needs." Within this context Ruskin set about
defending the Gothic through the definition of six "moral elements of
Gothic": Savageness, Changefulness (or variety), Naturalism, Grotesqueness, Rigidity, and Redundance (*SV* II 184). His treatment of two of these
elements — Naturalism and Grotesqueness — is of immediate relevance.

Ruskin defines the naturalism of the Gothic as "the love of natural
objects for their own sake, and the effort to represent them frankly, unconstrained by artistical laws" (*SV* II 215). Naturalism is the term that Ruskin
opposes to idealism, and it is one platform for his defense of what he saw as
the irreducible factuality of material objects and the objective basis for
judgments of beauty.[24] His defense of Gothic Naturalism therefore is of a
piece with what may be his central tenet: seek through art the truth above
all else, or "be true to Nature." Ruskin admits, however, that Gothic Naturalism requires defense, naturalism and the Gothic having acquired connotations of rudeness, vulgarity, and attention to unseemly subjects. He
therefore must distinguish Naturalism, on the one hand, from an idealized
aesthetic that is too removed from nature and humanity and, on the other
hand, from an aesthetic that can house the potentially vulgar aspects from

which the Gothic must be distanced. The former, idealist position he associates with the Purist, while the latter, vulgar one is labeled as Sensualist (*SV*II 224). Ruskin then characterizes the difference between the Purist, the Naturalist, and the Sensualist using a textbook description of the natural sublime as it had been handed down from eighteenth-century aestheticians, though he avoids using the term sublime.[25] In short, the Purist withdraws from the terrifying in nature, rendering himself less sensible to its grandeur and beauty. In characterizing the Naturalist he writes, "That man is greater, however, who contemplates with an equal mind the alternations of terror and of beauty" (*SV*II 225). And here is the Sensualist: "But separate from both by an immeasurable distance would be the man who delighted in convulsion and disease for their own sake; who found his daily food in the disorder of nature mingled with the suffering of humanity; and watched joyfully . . . while the corners of the house of feasting were struck by the wind from the wilderness" (*SV*II 225–26). The Sensualist takes unmediated pleasure in the natural sublime *for its own sake*, and therefore fails to regard the human consequences.

Perhaps because the sublime, in its evocation of visceral emotions such as terror, awe, and fear for mortality, is more directly tied to the human body than is the beautiful, Ruskin further distinguishes the three aesthetics in terms of their representations of the body. While the Purist's artistic portrayal of the body "effaces from the countenance the traces of all transitory passion," and the Naturalist "takes the human being in its wholeness, in its mortal as well as its spiritual strength," the Sensualist revels in the body, its passions and functions, as a means of self-titillation (*SV*II 226). The Sensualist artist therefore focuses on "poverty or decrepitude, fury or sensuality," choosing as subject matter "drunken revels and brawls among peasants, gambling or fighting scenes among soldiers, amours and intrigues among every class, brutal battle pieces" (*SV*II 227). The class basis of Ruskin's distinctions is evident here. Worst of all, however, the Sensualist does this "for the sake merely of the excitement, —that quickening and suppling of the dull spirit that cannot be gained for it but by bathing it in blood, afterward to wither back into stained and stiffened apathy" (*SV*II 227). The Sensualist masturbates with Beauty or, rather, violates the virgin body of Art, only to fall back unsated. This is the most evil form of play for Ruskin, though it is not until later that he will make the connection of Sensualism to play explicit.

Ruskin's treatment of Gothic Grotesqueness (following on his portrayal of the Sensualist) is truncated surprisingly to a single short paragraph, the main function of which is to direct the reader to a subsequent volume on the Renaissance (*SV*II 239). In other words, while Ruskin admits a popular association of grotesqueness with the Gothic, he wishes to displace it from its primary association onto the Renaissance. In the third volume of *The Stones of Venice*, in a chapter titled "Grotesque Renaissance," one finds Ruskin at pains to distinguish the Gothic grotesque from the grotesque that arose during the supposed fall or decline of Venice into the Renaissance. The first result of that decline was the "unscrupulous *pursuit of pleasure*," and this, it seems, produced the Grotesque Renaissance style (*SV*III 135). Ruskin's strategy here is to distinguish between two categories of the grotesque, the "terrible grotesque" and the "sportive grotesque." The first of these he associates with the sublime; he characterizes the second in terms of "playfulness" (*SV*III 151). In this way Ruskin arrives at the following question: "What are the conditions of playfulness which we may fitly express in noble art, . . . what is the proper function of play?"

But Ruskin's answer is not theoretical; in a characteristic, historicizing move, he analyzes play as recreation, defining four types of play, which then are tied to historical stages of artistic output, each having a moral valence. The four types are wise play, necessary play, inordinate play, and lack of play (*SV*III 152). In short, wise play, which makes "its lightest words reverent, its idlest fancies profitable, and its keenest satire indulgent," and necessary play, which is the rustic sportiveness of the working classes that makes daily toil bearable, both are seen to contribute to the *noble* grotesque of the Gothic. The source for the Gothic Renaissance, on the other hand, is inordinate play (*SV*III 153). The inordinate player is described as an aristocratic idler in terms similar to those used previously to describe the Sensualist (and used elsewhere to describe the aristocratic gambler, as discussed in chapter two). Inordinate players injure society not only by "leav[ing] the work undone" but by squandering their talents on pleasure seeking (*SV*III 154). Their "want of reverence" results in grotesque satire and parody of power and the powerful, which does "infinite mischief by exposing weakness to eyes which cannot comprehend greatness" (*SV*III 155). In other words, inordinate play poses a direct threat to social order. Further, inordinate play "will not be so hearty, so simple, or so joyful," becoming in the end, like the masturbatory excess of the Sensualist, "a restless and dissatisfied indulgence in excitement, or a painful delving after exhausted springs of pleasure" (*SV*III 161). Thus, the art of inordinate players, though evil, is not potent, more "an elaborate and luscious form of nonsense," depicting "nymphs, cupids, and satyrs, with shreddings of heads and paws of meek wild beasts, and nondescript vegetables" (*SV*III 162).

But there is much more at stake for Ruskin in the grotesque than the dismissive passages about the inordinate player might suggest. For Ruskin, the grotesque is no less than the human response to the sublime, which is the figure for the highest moral imperatives exercised on humanity by God's emissaries, Death and Sin (*SV*III 165). The issue of the sincerity and nobleness of grotesque art is therefore of paramount importance, as Ruskin writes: "I believe that there is no test of greatness in periods, nations, or men, more sure than the development, among them or in them, of a noble grotesque" (*SV*III 187). In line with this greatness, the category of the "terrible grotesque" is at once a registering and a necessary turning away from the awful, a sincere mixture of denial, fear, surrender, and reverence. It is in fact only a mediated reflection of the sublime itself (*SV*III 178). In certain works of art, such as the grotesque etchings of Albrecht Dürer, "every now and then, the playfulness and apathy of the painter passes into perfect sublime" (*SV*III 171). But the "sportive grotesque," with which the figure of play is associated, is more troublesome. Here is the dilemma: "For observe, the difficulty which, as I above stated, exists in distinguishing the playful from the terrible grotesque arises out of this cause: that the mind, under certain phases of excitement, *plays* with *terror*, and summons images which, if it were in another temper, would be awful, but of which, either in weariness or in irony, it refrains for the time to acknowledge the true terribleness. And the mode in which this refusal takes places distinguishes the noble from the ignoble grotesque" (*SV*III 166). The refusal, then, is a natural response to overwhelming fear.

What matters to Ruskin is, in the first place, the *seriousness*, and therefore consciousness of vulnerability, with which one fronts the sublime: "The true grotesque being the expression of the *repose* or play of a *serious* mind, there is a false grotesque opposed to it, which is the result of the *full exertion* of a *frivolous* one" (*SV*III 170). What matters in the second place is the *sincerity* through which one translates the unavoidable turning away, the refusal or "apathy," into "true," as opposed to "false," art. It is a matter, finally, of feelings: "In the true grotesque, a man of naturally strong feelings is accidentally or resolutely apathetic; in the false grotesque, a man naturally apathetic is forcing himself into temporary excitement" (*SV*III 168). The distinction seems to be whether one has strong feelings before responding to the sublime and whether they are genuine or artificially generated. The falsely grotesque artist is somehow already apathetic, jaded, decadent. In the true grotesque the response to the sublime is "true, and of true things, however fantastic its expression may be";, in the false grotesque, the terribleness is "manufactured," mechanically reproduced (*SV*III 168).

The true or noble, which appears to be synonymous with the category of the terrible grotesque, is an unavoidably feeble but at least serious and sincere response to the sublime. The false or ignoble, which characterizes the sportive grotesque, is a perverted response to the sublime, a carnivalization of that which is most powerful; thus Ruskin characterizes the sportive grotesque in terms of the dangers of satire and parody.[26] The "wild and wonderful images" of Gothic gargoyles and monsters, which have their origin in "the dusty and dreadful whiteness of the charnel-house," always border on making light of Death (*SV*III 186). The satyrs and nymphs cannot but point the way to the sins of the flesh. Any sign of levity in church — not to mention outright sniggering — threatens to become a mockery of God. The caricature of the king holds the seeds of armed revolt. For Ruskin, the grotesque is the site for the appropriate or inappropriate response to power, emblematized by the ultimate power of the sublime.

But the real danger that troubles Ruskin's analysis of the grotesque is less the parodic nature of the sportive grotesque than the precariousness of this distinction between the terrible grotesque and the sportive grotesque. Play is that which both separates *and* connects the terrible from the sportive grotesque. The play that Ruskin recognizes as good and healthy, the "play of a serious mind," might at any moment slip into sportiveness. The grotesque always threatens to become parodic, playful in the bad sense. Play therefore requires vigilant supervision. What emerges as the central issue in Ruskin's analysis of the grotesque is the dire importance of *governing play*. This amounts to policing an invisible boundary, for instance, between the Gothic and the Renaissance. This boundary becomes doubly invisible when it is given an intersubjective locus. Ruskin does just that in turning, as did his Romantic predecessors, to feeling and imagination. Ruskin's expression of the problem of governing play is as the problem of the "ungovernableness of the imagination." The imagination as manifested in dreams, he writes, is "entirely deprived of all aid from reason, and incapable of self-government." The problem becomes one of regulating the human unconscious (though, of course, this term was not yet available). It is made infinitely more difficult by the recognition that "the noblest forms of imaginative power are also in some sort ungovernable" (*SV*III 178). This is the problem then: how to discern between products of the imagination, between the internal states of artists, determining which are serious and governed and which are frivolous and ungoverned. The problem is compounded when those internal states must be read, in effect, blindly from the features of external objects, the works of art. The task that Ruskin sets himself as society's moral interpreter of art is to be a reader of the minds of objects.

When in the third volume of *Modern Painters* (1856) Ruskin returns to the grotesque in a chapter titled "Of the True Ideal: — Thirdly, Grotesque," he acknowledges the good form of play as the "healthful but irrational play of the imagination in times of rest" (*MP* III 131). In order to demonstrate the ability to read the difference between healthful and unhealthful play, serious and frivolous play, he finds it necessary to provide a concrete example: a comparative reading of two carved bas-relief griffins (or of drawings of them). One is a Lombard-Gothic griffin, the other of classical Roman origin. His argument in favor of the former ultimately comes to rest on the claim that the Lombard artisan "simply saw the beast; saw it as plainly as you see the writing on this page" (*MP* III 143). This statement is problematic for a number of reasons. In the first place, since griffins are mythical beasts, none ever has been "seen." Ruskin places himself in a position of having to argue for the "true nature" of the griffin, making claims such as this: "We may be very certain that a real griffin is, on the whole, fond of eating, and that his throat will look as if he occasionally took rather large pieces" (*MP* III 144). If one did not know how serious Ruskin was in all this, one might think his hyperbolic readings of the smallest details of the two artifacts to be, in his own terms, frivolous. For example, he argues that the classical griffin's cocked ears would produce "a continual humming of the wind on each side of his head, and he would have an infallible ear-ache when he got home" (*MP* III 144). Further, the smallest aspects of the artifacts take on profound semiotic functions, signifying abstract qualities such as "power" and "indolence." In his pursuit of the "true" and the "natural," Ruskin pushes objectivity until it disappears. It is as if, in an attempt to locate the invisible in the visible, he cranks his microscope closer and closer, until tiny details are blown-up into allegories of giant emotions. Clearly, then, the writing on Ruskin's page is far from plainly written or unequivocally read. Further, when Ruskin writes that the Lombard workman "did really see a griffin in his imagination, and carved it from life," he conflates the imagination with nature and life with the imaginary (*MP* III 141). He claims to be able to read from an object the inner state of a human, unavoidably reading his own projections, which are based on an idealized definition of "griffinness." In other words, Ruskin commits the "error" that he spends his entire writing life criticizing, the error that he condemns in a chapter that soon follows the one just discussed with the epithet "pathetic fallacy." In this Ruskin is far from alone, since his notion of the pathetic fallacy is in a sense definitive of aesthetic judgment, the exercise of which frequently is accompanied by an explicit or implicit denial that one's own subjective, cultural, historical, and political hallucinatory projections of beauty are just that.

In "Of the Pathetic Fallacy," Ruskin constructs a triad of positions in relation to the subject-object split that once again reproduces the Purist-Naturalist-Sensualist triad. There is "the man who perceives rightly, because he does not feel" and, at the other extreme, "the man who perceives wrongly, because he feels, and to whom the primrose is anything else than a primrose: a star, or a sun, or a fairy's shield, or a forsaken maiden" (*MP* III 209). The privileged middle position is occupied by "the man who perceives rightly in spite of his feelings, and to whom the primrose is for ever nothing else than itself." Indeed, only if the feeling is strong *and* it is under command is the artist great: "the greatness of a poet depends upon the two faculties, acuteness of feeling, and command of it" (*MP* III 215). (This, of course, could be taken from Wordsworth's preface to *Lyrical Ballads*.) Once again, the emphasis is on strong feeling coupled with strict governance of the imagination. It is as if one should have strong feelings *so that they can be governed*. The subject and the object must approach merging, demonstrate an ability to do so, but resist doing so. One must cultivate an ability to play in order to exercise control over it repeatedly. Play is the essential catalyst that must become the waste product of the reaction in order for the product to remain pure (as in Robert Browning's *The Ring and the Book*). One might hypothesize at this point about the pleasures of the exercising of control, as well as about the social functions that an internally directed repetition of this pleasure might serve.

Second, "Of the Pathetic Fallacy" is as close as Ruskin comes to a direct response to what he calls in a footnote "our German friends" (*MP* III 203). In short, for Ruskin the "pathetic fallacy" is symptomatic of the selfish subjectivism he takes to be characteristic of German idealism, to which he refers in this statement: "From which position, with a hearty desire for mystification, and much egotism, selfishness, shallowness, and impertinence, a philosopher may easily go so far as to believe, and say, that everything in the world depends upon his seeing or thinking of it, and that nothing, therefore, exists, but what he sees or thinks of" (*MP* III 202).[27] It is clear, finally, that for Ruskin the ultimately bad form of play is idealist aesthetics itself, to which he assiduously opposes the "Theoretic Faculty" and its concern with "the moral perception and appreciation of ideas of beauty": "And the error respecting it is the considering and calling it Aesthetic, degrading it to a mere cooperation of sense, or perhaps worse, of custom; so that the arts which appeal to it sink into a mere amusement, ministers to morbid sensibilities, ticklers and fanners of the soul's sleep" (*MP* II 35–36). "Ticklers and fanners" is once again an allusion to the masturbatory Sensualist, and this association completes the chain of associations expressed in the following equation: Sensualism = the sublime, when approached frivolously = the body = pleasure for pleasure's sake = inordinate play = lack of inner vision (on the part of the artist) = the pathetic fallacy = idealist aesthetics. This, then, is the connective thread that traces the figure of play through the works of Ruskin considered here.

In his characterization of the evils of idealism, Ruskin appears to confuse sensualism with idealism. This is representative of a wider Victorian confusion about German idealism. It may be that he sees the two extremes of the autonomous sensuous particular and the universalized ideal as coterminous. Indeed, even though he had read none of the major works of German aesthetics, he understood well enough that the autonomy of the aesthetic object and the "purposelessness" of aesthetic pleasure threaten to free art from any moral utility. This he could not allow. On the other hand, in his discussions of the grotesque he admits play as a potentially productive and beneficial activity, at least as tied to healthy recreation and the noble imagination. His primary concern still remains the governing of play, which never in his writings about it loses its possibility for violence. Like Schiller, he focuses on the disciplining of the individual imagination, from which noble art and social order then are presumed to follow. Unlike Schiller, for whom the "play drive" is the mediating term and itself the means to achieve personal and social harmony, Ruskin sees play as that which must be controlled by reason, objectivity, selflessness, and seriousness. At the same time, and similarly to the British Romantics whom he follows, Ruskin privileges the imagination in ways that parallel the privileging of play by Kant and Schiller. But as has been shown, it is here that he is unable to escape the violence of the subject-object dialectic. In discussing the Lombard griffin, for example, Ruskin effectively gives the imagination the power to determine the real, claiming that "the imagination is *always* right" (*MP* III 145). Yet here, without knowing it, he has made what amounts to a Kantian claim: that the real is contingent on an internal faculty or, expressed less categorically, that an internal faculty and an external object can be in such perfect correspondence that they must be taken as indistinguishably co-determining. This contradicts Ruskin's empiricist foundation. Finally, it is telling that the figure of play becomes an issue for Ruskin in relation to the grotesque, thereby becoming an exponent of the sublime. His writings appear to deny and reverse the primary meaning given to the figure of play by Kant, where it is more in relationship to the beautiful than to the sublime. Therefore, Ruskin subscribes to play only to the extent that it can be conceived as the most mortally dire form of labor.

One of the reasons that the grotesque is the troubled focal point for Ruskin's aesthetics is because his treatment of it, and of the Gothic in general, always verges on the issue that will become the center post for his social theory. That issue is labor, which for Victorians was inseparable from the issue of play. For example, it is through discussion of the "Savageness" of the Gothic that Ruskin arrives at his thesis about the correlation between the conditions of artistic production and the aesthetic qualities of the artifact. This is a logical result of his central premise that through the features of an art object one can read, in an allegorical fashion, the moral qualities of the age, country, and people that produced that object.[28] Thus, for Ruskin, subjected labor is mechanical and repetitive, a form of slavery that produces artificially "perfect" objects, while the expression and invention allowed in free labor produce original and therefore "imperfect" artifacts, such as those found in Gothic, as opposed to Renaissance, ornamentation. It is with statements such as the following that Ruskin was to become a hero within the Working Men's College Movement and a mentor figure for William Morris: "And observe, you are put to stern choice in this matter. You must either make a tool of the creature, or a man of him. You cannot make both. Men were not intended to work with the accuracy of tools, to be precise and perfect in all their actions. If you will have that precision out of them . . . you must unhumanize them. . . . On the other hand, if you will make a man of the working creature, you cannot make a tool. Let him but begin to imagine, to think, to try to do anything worth doing; and the engine-turned precision is lost at once" (*SV* II 192).[29] An aesthetics of the Gothic becomes the basis, on the one hand, for an indictment against the mechanization of an age and, on the other hand, for a theory of artisanal workmanship that shares similarities both with the Kantian notion of "free art" as opposed to "mercenary art" and, in the other direction, with the Marxist critique of alienated labor.[30]

While Ruskin starts his career concerned with the labor of the artist, he ends it concerned with the art of labor, remaining throughout a disciple of Thomas Carlyle's "gospel of work." His early writings reflect an interest in defining artistic creation as a form of labor that is serious, disciplined, and productive, as when he writes: "Art, properly so called, is no recreation; it cannot be learned at spare moments" (*MP* II 26). In this he both follows the Romantics (for instance, Shelley's *Defense of Poetry*) *and* distances his portrayal of the artist from the Romantic stereotype. The legitimizing of art as work—not play—can be understood as part of a trend toward professionalizing the artist and, in turn, professionalizing the art critic. After 1860, following his famous loss of faith, Ruskin turns more directly to social issues, and work emerges as that which he offers as a solution to the troubles of Victorian society: "Since Ruskin no longer believes that man's purpose is to glorify God and thus gain a heavenly reward, he has to discover—or invent—a purpose. And this purpose is work" (Landow 311).[31] What I would emphasize, however, is that Ruskin's aesthetic and social writings are of a piece and that his mission to redeem the artist through work translates naturally into his mission to transform the worker into an artist. The artist into whom he would fashion the English laborer is the Gothic artist, just as he would refashion the slag heaps of Manchester into the wholesome, agrarian dung heaps of the medieval village. While it is important not to underestimate the value of the critique Ruskin launched against modern industrial society in such works as *Unto This Last* (1862), one also must recognize the utopian, sentimental, and recuperative nature of his vision. For instance, he ends his 1865 lecture "Work," delivered to the Working Men's Institute, with the instruction to work "cheerfully," to be as "modest" and "faithful" in work as a child, "[t]aking no thought for the morrow; taking thought only for the duty of the day; trusting somebody else to take care of tomorrow . . . and always ready for play—beautiful play" (*CWO* 430).[32] While Ruskin uses work—moral arduousness as well as labor—to save the artist from the dangers of play, he then turns around and offers "beautiful play" as compensation to workers, hoping to save society from the dangers he perceived in artistic and nonartistic laborers alike.

The Victorian Revival of Kant as Culture

Matthew Arnold is the Victorian champion of play, or so one might think if certain key passages from *Culture and Anarchy* (1869) are taken at face value.[33] Indeed, play—the "free play of the best thoughts upon . . . stock notions" or the "disinterested play of consciousness"—is the defining activity of the Hellenism that Arnold called on to balance what he saw as the excessive Hebraism of his day (*CA* 5,140). While the "governing idea of Hellenism is *spontaneity of consciousness*; that of Hebraism is, *strictness of conscience"* (*CA* 88). Spontaneous play of this sort opens the way to "sweetness and light" or "perfection" in thought and so in social relations, and this was the antidote that Arnold prescribed for the "anarchy" he attributed to "middle-class liberalism," religious dissent, and the threat of lower-class revolt (*CA* 42–43). The name that Arnold gave to this process — the generating of social harmony through play — was "culture." Play produces culture. Perhaps particularly in late-twentieth-century western society, when cultural issues have come to the fore as focal points of social debate, Arnold's notion of culture needs to be recognized as both context-specific and far from self-evident.[34] To understand that notion, it is necessary to ask: What is the play of which Arnold was a champion?

Arnoldian play shares characteristics with Kantian play, and for good reason. Arnold, unlike Ruskin, had read and studied Kant. Despite Arnold's professed refusal of idealism, it can be argued, as Hilary Fraser has, that the "implications of Kantian metaphysics invade [his] intellectual interest in every sphere" (138). Arnold characterizes play in particular and culture in general with the recognizably Kantian terms disinterestedness and spontaneity. While for Arnold play is an "inward working" (and so is another model for the internalized subjectivity of the bourgeois subject), it is not the means of aesthetic judgment (*CA* 26). Even so, culture clearly is an aesthetic and aestheticizing concept; recognizing this, Arnold felt compelled to defend it against charges of effeminacy, idealistic speculation, and playfulness in the wrong sense. He defends it in the opposite direction from equation with scientific rationalism, which might link it to Comtean positivism, utilitarianism, skepticism, or moral relativism. Thus he writes: "Culture is then properly described not as having its origin in curiosity, but as having its origin in the love of perfection; it is *a study of perfection*. It moves by the force, not primarily of the scientific passion for pure knowledge, but also of the moral and social passion for doing good" (*CA* 31). Culture and play in particular function as mediating operators between rationality and morality. This is precisely the structural position of play in Kantian theory: play, as the key of aesthetic judgment, mediates between "pure reason" and "practical reason," understanding and reason, necessity and freedom. In one sense, Arnold's play concept is an undertheorized translation of Kantian play from the conceptual stratosphere of German aesthetics to the practical and smoggy atmosphere of nineteenth-century London. In the process of translation, the moral and political subtext of Kant's writing becomes explicit in Arnold's writing.

A primary reason that Arnoldian play must differ from Kantian play is the difference in historical contexts. For Kant, writing in the late eighteenth century, play is posited as that which undoubtedly *will* mediate between culture and nature, subject and object. Failure of that mediation is unthinkable or is presented as such. Play is the sign of an unshaken faith in participation between God and human and, in turn, between human and the material world. In contrast, for Arnold, whose "Dover Beach" is paradigmatic of the ennui of the postindustrial, middle-class, intellectual male, the figure of play is instead the sign of a lack. It is the site where certainty once was supposed to reside. As Fraser suggests, Arnold's midcareer shift from poetry to prose (similar to Ruskin's from art criticism to social criticism) and from his near aestheticism in the 1840s to a moral poetics in the 1850s indicates "a loss of faith in his own power as a poet to realise the union of imagination and reason which he was formulating in his criticism" (148, 150). I would suggest that Arnold's criticism, far from offering a haven from this anxiety over loss of faith, is founded upon it. Play, and culture in general, is necessitated as an internalized, order-providing mechanism precisely because, as Arnold quietly notes, "in the world outside us we find a disquieting absence of sure authority" (*CA* 108). Neither can the blindered faith of Hebraism provide a solution, because its adherent lacks the perspective of "a larger conception of human nature, showing him the number of other points at which his nature must come to its best." "There is no *unum necessarium*, or one thing needful, which can free human nature from the obligation of trying to come to its best at all these points" (*CA* 100). In the absence of any "one thing needful," the world takes on a pervasive indeterminacy that Kant could not or would not have theorized. Arnold worked to attribute to his play concept a flexibility and openness that was commensurate with the indeterminacy that he encountered, while at the same time striving mightily to limit or ameliorate that indeterminacy. He was unable to provide, as Kant had, an ideally stable play concept, though he tried to do so; the other option—to celebrate indeterminacy—was not yet (or again) available.

In contrast to Kant and to the Romantics, Arnold represents what Lawrence Starzyk describes as a "crisis in participation" (1986: 219). If one finds in Coleridge's *Biographia Literaria* (1817) a belief in "the essential 'coincidence,' 'coalescence,' or 'reconciliation' of object and subject, thought with thing, image with reality," what one finds in Arnold's later writings is a loss of this "participatory faith" (1990: 29). Though this formulation appeals to a traditional definition of Romanticism that has come under critical question, it still provides a useful description of Arnold's struggle to realize a natural "coincidence" between artist and artifact, citizen and society. His ultimate failure to do so is expressed as a traumatic severing of subject and object, which is recognizable as the symptom of what might be called the modern crisis of representation. Initiated by Cartesian metaphysics, this is the crisis that Kantian idealism claimed to heal and that a series of philosophers starting with Nietzsche claimed to obviate. Between Kant and Nietzsche, Arnold represents himself and Victorian society as caught in an epistemological crack. Unable to heal this fissure either by idealist or empiricist means, Arnold struggles to reunite two halves of an imaginary whole, the "harmonious perfection," "totality," or "whole man" toward which his writing of *Culture and Anarchy* is aimed (*CA* 8, 9, 103).

The dilemma as Arnold seemed to have understood it was that neither dissevered, epistemological half — neither the autonomous subject nor the autonomous object — was sufficient to provide the basis for a whole society composed of whole yet mutually responsible subjects. The threat of the autonomous subject appears in *Culture and Anarchy* as the "ordinary self" (as opposed to the "best self") "doing as [it] likes" (*CA* 48). Doing as one likes is that "central idea of English life and politics" that Arnold opposes: "the assertion of personal liberty" over the claims of collective well-being or social good (*CA* 50). The equal but opposite threat posed by the autonomous object appears as the ever-present backdrop in Arnold's criticism of "the world," a particular post-Darwinian world of pitiless necessity, random justice, or, worse, active hostility toward civilization (or at least toward cherished middle-class propriety and property). This threat appears specifically in the figure of "machinery" or the "mechanical" (*CA* 105). Combining this Carlylean concern with a Malthusian preoccupation, Arnold associates the mechanical with the body and with "animality," which manifest organically on a collective scale as "the great sexual insurrection," the specter of a mechanical "multiplying of population" with which the last pages of *Culture and Anarchy* are fearfully concerned (*CA* 121, 127).[35] A separate but related type of social machinery results from the "concern for making money, and the concern for saving our souls," which Arnold argues are linked in the blindly applied practices of the Philistines (*CA* 105). He implicates in particular the doctrine of free trade, using a term that Karl Marx (*Capital*, 1867) was using in a similar way at the same time: "We have already seen how these things, — trade, business, and population, — are mechanically pursued by us as ends precious in themselves, and are worshipped as what we call fetishes" (*CA* 123). For Arnold — as for Ruskin before him and William Morris after him, though in their different ways —

the mechanical pursuit of "fetishes" was the antithesis of cultural play, the evil for which the play of culture was to be the antidote.

Finally, then, while the autonomous subject promises freedom, it threatens, as Terry Eagleton puts it, "an object drained of intrinsic value with a subject now forced to generate all value from itself" or, in terms perhaps closer to those of *Culture and Anarchy*, a social collective drained of collective authority and citizens eager to generate value free of social responsibility (66). On the other hand, while the autonomous object promises the empirical stability of "reality," it threatens to drain the subject of any intrinsic value apart from the material and to invest the object with the authority to generate all value, thereby subjecting the rights of subject and society to the rights of "machinery" and things. What Arnold feared was the combination of (the illusion of) infinite, individually consumed liberty with a moral order founded on the mechanisms of commodity exchange, which indeed was becoming the dual, contradictory basis of society.

Where, then, does Arnold turn for the new source of authority that he felt was needed? The short answer is the state, though not the state as an overarching legal entity that imposes order from above (as in Howard Caygill's analysis of the German police state, for instance). Rather, the state must be produced by each citizen appealing to her/his "best self" and continuously cultivating "perfection," as opposed to succumbing to the animal desires and "taste for the bathos" of the "ordinary self" (*CA* 64). Here is a familiar combination of the Victorian fable of growth or improvement and the directive to look not to social conditions but into one's own soul.[36] A second, related mandate is to "see things as they really are," which is where Arnold most directly calls for the free play of consciousness upon social issues. This is familiar rhetoric after reading Ruskin, though it might appear that "things as they really are" are different things for Ruskin than for Arnold. For the early Ruskin, access to things as they really are — to truth — is through Medieval Gothic Christianity, which is in effect Hebraism, while for Arnold such access is through Hellenism, the Enlightenment tradition of the Renaissance that Ruskin opposes. Yet Arnold's "reality" essentially is the same as Ruskin's to the extent that it too is an idealized category masquerading as an empirical fact. In his argument against lower-class organization and protest, for instance, Arnold criticizes "class-instinct" for limiting its concerns to "ordinary self"-interest and the material conditions of labor and remuneration; he argues that it is "wholly occupied, according to Plato's subtle expression, with the things of itself and not its real self, with the things of the State and not the real State" (*CA* 70–71). The real self, in other words, is the ideal self; the real State is the image of the state that the citizen carries inside him-/herself. Thus seeing things as they really are is "to see them in their beauty." For the Hellenistic thinker, "Difficulties are kept out of view, and the beauty and rationalness of the ideal have all our thoughts" (*CA* 90). This is necessary because "things cannot really appear intelligible, unless they are also beautiful . . . ; behaviour is not intelligible, does not account for itself to the mind and show the reason for its existing, unless it is beautiful" (*CA* 103). The process for creating social harmony is an aesthetic one; the ideal citizen is the *aesthetic citizen*.

As may be apparent, the bent of Hellenism is the same as that of Schiller's play drive. Culture is Arnold's word for Schiller's aesthetic education (regardless of whether Arnold consciously was responding to Schiller). As Schiller's *On the Aesthetic Education of Man* was written on the heels of the French Revolution, so Arnold's *Culture and Anarchy* was written in part as a prescription against the violence of the Hyde Park riots and the general unrest surrounding the passage of the second Reform Act. Schiller wrote, "It is therefore one of the most important tasks of culture to subject Man to form even in his purely physical life, and to make him aesthetic as far as ever the realm of Beauty can extend, since the moral condition can be developed only from the aesthetic, not from the physical condition" (*AE* 110). The parallel between Arnold and Schiller is blatant when one compares this passage by Arnold: "But culture indefatigably tries, not to make what each raw person may like, the rule by which he fashions himself; but to draw ever nearer to a sense of what is indeed beautiful, graceful, and becoming, and to get the raw person to like that" (*CA* 34–35). The "get the raw person to like that" makes the disciplinary objective overt. What aesthetic education means, for Arnold as for Schiller, is the aestheticization of the social. This is to be effected through the dissemination of an internally borne image of the beautiful wholeness of society by which social difference — indeed, the plane of social materiality and action in its entirety — is erased into a transcendentally shared sense of unity. Culture, if one is willing to trust in its educational process, will take care of the unruly passions rooted in animality and, in particular, the bodily excesses of the Barbarians; will take care of the mammonistic machinery of the Philistines and their penchant for "doing as one likes"; will take care of the dangerously volatile Populace by shining "light" into their darkness; will, in short, remove any basis for difference by dissolving social particularity into cultural wholeness. Culture will be satisfied only when all its aesthetic citizens have joined what Arnold refers to as "the main stream of human life": "It is not satisfied until we *all* come to a perfect man" (*CA* 21, 47). The "perfect man" is to be modeled on the "aliens" within each class, those who are led "not by their class spirit, but by a general *humane* spirit, by the love of human perfection," those, as it turns out, like Arnold himself (*CA* 73). Social order will issue from a universal aesthetic or, rather, from the aesthetic that springs spontaneously and disinterestedly from the Hellenist, the ideal model for which happens to be a quite specific nineteenth-century British middle-class intellectual male.

Arnold is the paradigm of what Daniel Cottom analyzes as the "liberal intellectual," a figure that arose in the mid-nineteenth century as in effect a specialized subcategory of the bourgeois subject. Arnold, like George Eliot, George Henry Lewes, and other liberal intellectuals, represents the fruition of Coleridge's dream of a clerisy, an institutionalized, professionally recognized intellectual/artist. The function of the liberal intellectual is to produce, disseminate, and guard liberal intellectual discourse, which is synonymous with Arnoldian culture. The modus operandi of the liberal intellectual is to propagate an image of society as culture, to replace the social with liberal intellectual discourse. That discourse defines itself as that which is "disinterested," untouched by class, politics, or history. One component of it is the fable that, as Cottom puts it, "power governs society only when that society is tyrannical," or, as Arnold puts it, "we are only safe from one another's tyranny when no one has any power" (*SF* 16; *CA* 64). Liberal intellectual culture exercises power through the illusion that no power is being exercised; its technique of power is "the dissimulation of prescriptive legislation as descriptive analysis, whether this be exercised through the work of science or through the values of the culture promoted by a novelist like Eliot" (*SF* 25). While naturalization of ideology might be a part of any dominant order, it is the distinguishing characteristic of nineteenth-century liberal-intellectual order, which "made this appeal to universality a sophisticated program of analysis that was continually able to reconfirm the identities of intellectuals, of the middle classes, and of middle-class truths" (*CA* 25–26). Universal harmony can be achieved, the story goes, if we all become liberal intellectuals, which is to say aesthetic citizens. What the subject of culture must do in order to bring this about is to *do less* and know more, to pursue internal "perfection," in the Arnoldian sense, by reading, observing, reflecting, and, in sum, cultivating inaction. What culture offers is the *process* of acquiring culture. Taking part in liberal intellectual discourse replicates liberal intellectualism; it is performative, constituting what it claims to report from reality. The primary technique that Arnold forwards for practicing and replicating culture is play.

Play takes on a practical function in *Culture and Anarchy*. It supplies a procedure for issue resolution or adjudication between competing points of view. It is not, however, a decision-rule, because the point is to defer any decision. The point is to concentrate on and perpetuate the process. Play is that process of allowing one's mind to flow freely around a recalcitrant issue in order to "float" and "soften" the prejudices and set notions that prevent seeing "things as they really are" (through what sounds like a laxative process) (*CA* 132). The assumption is that the answer or solution that pops spontaneously into the mind of the liberal intellectual thus engaged will represent "right reason" and will serve all levels of society with objectivity. Play, therefore, is a form of rationality; Arnoldian play is "rational play" in the sense developed by Mihai Spariosu.

In order to demonstrate the credibility of the procedure he recommends, Arnold applies it to four case examples: the disestablishment of the Anglican Church in Ireland, the Real Estate Intestacy Bill, the bill to enable a man to marry his dead wife's sister, and free-trade policy. Striving for open-mindedness, Arnold admits, for example, that the monopoly on church property exercised by the Anglican Church in Ireland is unfair and unreasonable, in spite of his own strong allegiance to the Anglican Church. His argument, however, is that the dissenting Irish Catholics, in insisting violently on their rights (presumably out of a prejudice against the Anglican Church), use the wrong means and so do not deserve their ends. He writes that "it is more important to make our [their] consciousness play freely round the stock notion or habit on which their operation relies for aid, than to lend a hand to it straight away" (*CA* 112). What Arnold demands, then, is that everyone involved in a social dispute become a practicing liberal intellectual *before* considering any resolution to the social problem. This indeed would obviate most social differences by erasing them.

My point is not that Arnold is uniquely misguided or biased, nor that while attempting to demonstrate the objectivity of the play method he instead demonstrates its subjectivity, though these claims may be true. For example, one suspects in his treatment of the four issues, particularly the issue of marriage to a dead wife's sister, that the solutions produced by the play method tend to uphold the conservative Anglican party line of which Arnold was a proponent.[37] Gerald Graff may be correct in claiming that "Arnold is committed to the Hellenic free play of reason only as long as its dictates coincide with those of unreflective custom, tradition, and consensus" (188). In a sense, however, Arnold's specific biases are irrelevant, as is the issue of whether his solutions to the four case issues really are reached "objectively." To ask the question in this way is to endorse Arnold's definitions from the onset — to speak as a liberal intellectual (which in the culture of which I am a part may be unavoidable to some extent). The real point is that regardless of whether play works as a form of rationality or not, "rationality" cannot but be defined in an interested and context-specific way. Arnold's rational play cannot but reproduce the liberal intellectual ideology by which he defines its rationalness; to be rational is to be a liberal intellectual.

A distinguishing characteristic of Arnoldian play is the presumption of what might be called a democracy of thought. The premise is that if ideas are allowed to circulate freely and to compete openly, then the best idea (like the "best self") naturally will rise to the top and be recognized by all. Play takes the form of a radically egalitarian democracy or, rather, of the perfect competition posited by laissez-faire political economy, according to which unfettered exchange always produces the most equitable outcome. This market model is consistent with Arnold's objective to disseminate culture through the perpetuation of play, which means extending this circulation and competition of ideas into an indefinite future. In Arnold's words, "our main business at the present moment is not so much to work away at certain crude reforms of which we have already the scheme in our own mind, as to create, through the help of that culture. . . a frame of mind out of which really fruitful reforms may with time grow" (*CA* 133).

Uncharacteristically for a Victorian (or for the stereotype of a Victorian), Arnold privileges play even above work in order to advocate aesthetic citizenry. It is, of course, true that if everyone concentrates on the process, then there can be no violent conflict over outcome, assuming that the process is liberal-intellectual play. But two crucial problems undercut this market model of play. In the first place, it replicates the ideology that it claims to circumvent. There is a consistent if paradoxical logic in the fact that Arnold mounts a cogent humanistic attack on dogmatic individualism and laissez-faire economics by forwarding a technique of play that he defines in terms of unfettered competition. The principle that is unacceptable objectively is recommended subjectively, and thus it is ratified ideologically: "free trade" must be internalized. The overt ideology serves as the vehicle for an opposite, covert ideology. In the second place, and predictably enough given the first contradiction, within this logic competition becomes perpetual deferral of resolution. As Cottom analyzes it, "Argument is always deferred to time or to the illimitable correction of other viewpoints, while the assumption is concurrently made, through the reverent characterization of this deferral as a mystery, that there is an agreement or common identity implicit in the field" (*SF* 30). He concludes, "This is precisely the

theory of competition in liberal economics and politics and ideas: that
blatant conflict should be regarded as mysterious consensus, the diversity of
individuals as the common abstraction of society, and diverse societies as
one humanity." What Arnoldian disinterestedness becomes in its supposed
consideration of all sides is a jury that is out, permanently. Equality of treatment becomes in effect endless equivocation, which unavoidably serves the
existing social order. In the same way, the "perfection" that is the ultimate
aim of Arnold's project must be deferred by its very definition to an ideal
future, the unreachable horizon of liberal-intellectual nirvana toward which
only the practice of culture can guide society.

Arnold poses a genuine dilemma for the heirs of liberal intellectualism,
which by definition includes everyone who has been socialized by and en-
culturated into the institution of academia. Arnold is an important source
of twentieth-century critical practice. This is neither a hagiographic statement or a history-of-ideas-type generalization; Arnold contributed in identifiable ways to the historical process through which a primary method
underlying contemporary criticism or theory within "arts and sciences" or
the "humanities" was constructed. Arnold's definition of Hellenism rests on
the intention, however realized or unrealized, "to try the very ground on
which we appear to stand" (*CA* 100). This could be the motto of late-
twentieth-century criticism. We who criticize Arnold may differ from him
only in degree, not kind, and may rely on the tools that he helped to
formulate. As Terry Eagleton observes in a more general vein, "If we can
and must be severe critics of Enlightenment, it is Enlightenment which has
empowered us to be so" (*IA* 8). Indeed, the dangers of replicating Arnold's
blindnesses are strongest for those whose criticism of him rests on a claim to
greater reflexivity or for those, in the opposite direction, whose theories
imply for themselves a status above or outside social particularity and an
immunity to ideology. Both claims are inherently Arnoldian.

These difficulties make it doubly challenging to separate the necessary
criticism of Arnold's liberal-intellectual, bourgeios humanism from a sympathy with his social critique. Arnold was a keen-sighted critic of his society.
He and other liberal intellectuals, in particular George Eliot, mounted a
cogent attack on middle-class self-righteousness and against the greed and
exploitation that were a part of the booming capitalism of their—and
our—day. It also is not difficult to be sympathetic toward a policy that
places thinking and talking before acting (or shooting) and that stresses
educational training for thinking and talking. Similarly, it seems advisable
to favor a policy of having the means justify the end, as opposed to the end

justifying the means, if one is interested in producing a peaceful and equitable society. In short, rational play as a process of resolving disagreement through a democracy of ideas has its appeal. That appeal is realized by those of us who generally practice humanist tenets in day-to-day life, even while fiercely critiquing them. The resulting problem is a familiar one: the difficulties of critiquing social practices and cultural forms of which one is a part or in which one unavoidably takes part. These difficulties do not prevent me from seeing that Arnold's formulas leave all of the most important issues unanswered: *whose* definition of education, *whose* mode of thinking, *whose* style of talking, *whose* means, equitable *for whom*? Arnold never asked, never considered the necessity of asking, who defines the ground rules for the process of play and who participates in it. He failed to recognize the essential distinction between *the perpetuation of a discourse* that contains the image of equality or the image of democracy and, on the other hand, *the social practice* of equality or democracy.

Learning to Play by the Rules in *Pendennis*

> When you want to make money by Pegasus (as he must, perhaps, who has no other saleable property), farewell poetry and aerial flights; Pegasus only arises now like Mr. Green's balloon, at periods advertised beforehand, and when the spectators' money has been paid.
> W. M. Thackeray, *Pendennis*

William Makepeace Thackeray's *Pendennis* and Charles Kingsley's *Alton Locke*, both published in 1850, are particularly appropriate in a consideration of mid-Victorian aesthetics and in relation to one another. They are among the clearest examples of the nineteenth-century *Kunstlerroman*.[38] Each charts the artistic maturation of a protagonist bearing widely recognized similarities to his author; *Pendennis* was admitted to be autobiographical. Each is set in the socially volatile 1830s or 1840s, and *Alton Locke* focuses on the Chartist movement. Most significantly, both texts explicitly confront the role of art and of the artist in society, and they each do so through the figure of play.

There is nothing subtle in Thackeray's naming of his protagonist in *Pendennis*: Arthur Pendennis, Art Pen for short. The early trials through which the young Pen must pass in order to reach artistic maturity result from what I will call the *problem of excess*. This problem is expressed as an excess of aesthetic play. Pen, like Alton (and like Aurora Leigh in Browning's verse novel), wishes to assume the high Romantic mantle of the Poet. For Pen this means staying up all night in the bath to write melodramatic epics with titles like "Seneca, or the Fatal Bath," then saddling up at dawn and galloping across the downs "spouting his own poems, and filled with quite a Byronic afflatus as he thought" (*P* 60). There is no shortage of Thackerian irony in the coloring of Pen's artistic ambitions, though this irony may take on poignancy when considered in relation to Thackeray's own troubled artistic ambitions.[39] *Pendennis* accuses its protagonist in the way that Aurora Leigh is accused, and later accuses herself, of "play[ing] at art, as children play at swords, / To show a pretty spirit, chiefly admired / Because true action is impossible" (Browning 2.229).[40]

In the self-conscious discourse within *Pendennis* about the art of writing, the falseness or artificiality of poetry is opposed to the "true action" of prose. While for Thackeray, as for many other Victorians (John Ruskin in particular), it is acceptable to "fail in art," to fail at truth is grievous, because "[i]f there is not that, there is nothing" (*P* 33). Indeed, failure in artifice may be taken as the proof of genuineness. As a result of indulgence in the excesses of aesthetic play, Pen fails at truth. The sign of this failure is his confusion of artifice and essentiality. Thus in his infatuation with the actress Emily Costigan, Pen commits the sin of confounding surface, and therefore false, beauty with inner, and therefore true, goodness. The text points to this most egregious of misjudgments in Victorian fiction when Pen claims to his mother that Emily "is good as she is beautiful" (*P* 99). Pen compounds this error by then making a fetish of the beautiful, compromising his ability to discern between image or mimesis and the real or original. The narrator comments: "But what did our Pen care? He saw a pair of eyes, and he believed in them — a beautiful image, and he fell down and worshipped it" (*P* 88). Only later in the story, when he at last is working, not playing, at art, does Pen come to the lessons that the text intends about truth in art and about the merits of nonexcessive "fair play." The converted Pen will exorcise his former errors by writing the novel within the novel, *Walter Loraine*, in which Walter decries his theatrical counterpart, Leonora, as "False as thou art beautiful!" (*P* 433).

One problem that ensues from aesthetic excess is that it leads to other forms of excess. In both *Pendennis* and *Alton Locke*, Romantic aestheticism breeds romance, love of the wrong sort. As in many other Victorian novels, romance here involves the figure of the theatrical woman, the female character who is shown to perform her self duplicitously and who generally must be foiled in the end by the nontheatrical (sincere, genuine, selfless, domestic) female character. Thus, while Pen works his way through Emily Costigan, Blanche Amory, and Fanny Bolton, all of whom are thoroughly theatricalized, Laura Bell waits like the "angel in the house" for Pen to stop playing around and come home to Fairoaks. Pen's attachment to Emily "the Fotheringay," like his subsequent one to Blanche "the Sylphide," only spurs him to a higher pitch of poeticizing, as here for example: "He was biting a pencil and thinking of rhymes and all sorts of follies and passions. He was Hamlet jumping into Ophelia's grave: he was the Stranger taking Mrs. Haller to his arms. . . . [A]ll the love-songs he had ever read, were working and seething in this young gentleman's mind, and he was at the very height and paroxysm of the imaginative phrensy, when his mother found him" (*P* 104). Concerning the object of Pen's affections, the narrator makes no secret of his prejudices when he comments that "her profession was sufficient to characterise *her*" (*P* 150). The text shows Emily mechanically reproducing the exact same performance of "the lady" onstage each night, then stepping offstage to eat, drink, and sleep with the delicacy of a sailor. Issues such as "manners" and "proper language" are used by the text to stigmatize her character, explicitly tying class to a gendered aesthetics. Emily provides an alternative perspective to Pen's on the beautiful when, in discussing her feelings for him, she says: "He's a most worthy young man, I'm sure. I'll thank ye hand me the salt. Them filberts is beautiful" (*P* 147).

The linkage between aesthetic play, romantic excess, and theatricality is even more explicit in the character of Blanche, who may come under greater censure from the text for *not* being a professional actress. The portrayal of her as the parodically saccharine and lachrymose high priestess of the Muse would make Elizabeth Barrett Browning shake her head. Laughter appears to be the response that Thackeray had in mind in writing passages such as the following, which describes Blanche's collection of poetry: "A faded rose inspired her with such grief that you would have thought she must die in pain of it. . . . What a talent she must have had for weeping to be able to pour out so many of 'Mes Larmes'!" (*P* 250). Meanwhile, Blanche is as dry-eyed as a banker about the business of romance and marriage. Perhaps paradoxically, being businesslike about love is proved by the text to be the most reprehensible form of play, an improper mixing of business with pleasure, perhaps because to make the connection explicit is to reveal the social mechanisms behind the mystifications surrounding love, art, and culture alike. The sin for which Blanche's character ultimately is condemned by the text (if with a bit of grudging admiration for her style and hubris) is that of playing at love. Readers are made aware of this early on by a condescending if not misogynistic narrator: "The impetuous little lady played at love with these imaginary worthies, as a little while before she had played at maternity with her doll. Pretty little poetical spirits! it is curious to watch them with those playthings" (*P* 253). Not until hundreds of pages later, when he too has become a player at love, does it begin to dawn on Pen that "the worldly little flirt . . . had been playing at love for the last dozen years of her life" (*P* 679). The narrative's final judgment is unequivocal: "For this young lady was not able to carry out any emotion to the full; but had a sham enthusiasm, a sham hatred, a sham love, a sham taste, a sham grief, each of which flared and shone very vehemently for an instant, but subsided and gave place to the next sham emotion" (*P* 757). Thus a central Victorian contradiction becomes clear: the excesses of Romanticism, which are expressed as aesthetic play and as the playing at love that is associated with it, are condemned. In the same instant, the cure given for these excesses is a deep genuineness of feeling, an inner spring of truth, which originates in part from the same Romantic tradition.

Pen's contact with aesthetic, romantic, and theatrical play appears to culminate in a generalized infection of excess. Away at the University of Oxbridge, Pen is characterized as having an "appetite for pleasure" that is "insatiable" (*P* 213). He becomes "one of the men of fashion," fashion being a theatricalized term; he dallies with gambling, that other tabooed form of play; he begins to spend like a lord, buying cases of fine wine and art works for his wall, which he pays for by passing his signature on "stamped paper" (much as Fred Vincy "post-obited" in *Middlemarch*); and he generally indulges what are described as "a universality of taste" (*P* 204, 205, 210, 216). This is aristocratic excess, which *Pendennis* seems even more bent on exorcising than the lower-class excesses of which Emily Costigan and her father, Captain Costigan, are figures. Because of his inexhaustible and too liberal taste, as well as his want of "a little regularity and constancy of occupation," Pen is "plucked" at Oxbridge and must retreat in disgrace (*P* 218). The message is clear: excess must be curbed, or given its proper outlet; play must be disciplined. The rehabilitation to which Pen's character then is subjected is represented through two discourses: taste and work.

Poems and filberts taken together point to what might be called the *problem of taste*. In short, taste hopes to be disinterested and universal but always threatens to become a relative matter of individual pleasure. As the writings of theorists as far apart as Kant and Ruskin both attest, if taste is not tied finally to a universal standard, then aesthetic judgments can no longer be attributed a moral foundation, and as a result, the unity and harmony that culture promises to a society are dissolved.[41] Thackeray, unlike Kant and perhaps even Ruskin, has no qualms initially about debunking any notion that smacks of idealism or Romanticism. In *Pendennis*, he pointedly reserves the title of "the artist" for one character alone, the Claverings' chef, Alcide Mirobolant. It was not unusual for chefs, particularly French ones, to be referred to as "artists." My point is that Thackeray, in a novel that concerns the role of the artist, plays on this designation with a vengeance. Mirobolant regularly expounds on "the poesy of [his] art" and is described by the narrator in terms such as these: "It is a grand sight to behold him in his dressing gown composing a *menu*. He always sate down and played the piano for some time before. If interrupted, he remonstrated pathetically. Every great artist, he said, had need of solitude to perfectionate his works" (*P* 244–45, 259). The distinction between the connoisseur of fine art and the gourmand thus is deflated. Thackeray seems intent on collapsing the former into the latter, though not without complications (and he eventually becomes squeamish about jettisoning all aesthetic standards).

For Pen's uncle and worldly adviser Major Pendennis, distinctions remain to be drawn not between art critics and restaurant critics but among gourmands. The Major's maxim of life, which he repeats on multiple occasions to Pen, is as follows: "I've told you before it is as easy to get a rich wife as a poor one; and a doosed deal more comfortable to sit down to a well-cooked dinner, with your little *entrées* nicely served, than to have nothing but a damned cold leg of mutton between you and your wife" (*P* 402). The novel will demonstrate that while the Major disapproves of playful excess, he does so neither for the right reasons nor thoroughly enough. His reasons are instrumental: he wants Pen to marry upward. While he is glad to foil Emily's attempt to do this in trying to marry Pen, he prompts Pen to play at love for the same mercenary reasons, even after he knows that foul play is afoot in relation to the intended match with Blanche. For the Major, it is not how you play the game but whether you win or lose. The text thus requires that Pen "mature" beyond his uncle's influence. Major Pendennis's participation in the discourse of taste is to reduce taste in art and taste in women to a taste for French cuisine. This places him in a category with Mirobolant in a contradictory but also appropriate way, given that aesthetic play (Blanche, Mirobolant) and romantic play (Blanche, the Major) each are to be proved misguided. The course of the novel steers Pen away from a taste for French cuisine—its associations of playful excess—toward the more wholesome fare described in the following statement by Pen's new mentor at Lamb Court, Mr. Warrington: "Well, you may get bread and

cheese, Pen: and I own it tastes well, the bread which you earn yourself"
(*P* 345).

Pen's rehabilitation also is to be effected through that familiar Victorian prescription, namely, work. Because *Pendennis* is a *Kunstlerroman*,
the work in question is the work of the artist, and the discourse of work in
the novel therefore cannot help but foreground the author's own art, which
is the novel's apparatus. Thus, it is precariously that the character of Warrington becomes a mouthpiece for the doctrine of art-as-work. The center
of the novel is dominated by lengthy dialogues between Pen and Warrington in which the latter convincingly defends the integrity of the "prose
labourer" against the fancies and posturings of such poets as Blanche Ar-
mory, Percy [Bysshe Shelley] Popjoy, and Pen himself, whose early poetry
he characterizes as "miserable weak rubbish" (*P* 340, 355). When Pen defends the necessary "eccentricities of genius," Warrington sets about debunking the Romantic figure of the genius, arguing in effect that genius is a
much rarer commodity than the average poet would like to think and that
even genius is a commodity. He concludes, "Rags [as in "the starving
artist"] are not a proof of genius; whereas capital is absolute, as times go,
and is perforce the bargain-master. It has a right to deal with the literary
inventor as with any other. . . . I may have my own ideas of the value of my
Pegasus, and think him the most wonderful of animals; but the dealer has a
right to his opinion too, and may want a lady's horse, or a cob for a heavy
timid rider, or a sound hack for the road, and my beast won't suit him"
(*P* 355).

As much if not more than any nineteenth-century text, *Pendennis* re-
cords anxieties about the ongoing historical transition from the patronage
system of artistic support to the market system and the resulting commercialization of art and professionalization of the artist. The text does this in
the first place by offering a character who, like his author, is forced by
necessity to make his living through his art. In the second place, the commercialization of art and the ensuing debate about its benefits to and compromising of "artistic integrity" emerge as the central and deeply troubling
issues of the novel. Thackeray himself was troubled by these issues. As a
result of reactions to the serial publication of the first sections of *Pendennis*,
Thackeray became embroiled in what is known as the "dignity of literature"
debate. He may have written certain later sections of the novel in part as a
rebuttal to critics of his early portrayals of the writer, sections in which Pen
now defends artistic sensibility (along with the legitimacy of marketing
it).[42] Thus, while *Pendennis* ultimately disciplines play, affirming work over

play, necessity over freedom, it does so at the risk of revealing a loss of faith on the part of the novelist in his art. What results is the figure of *the anxiety of the artist*, and it appears in the text where the discourse of work intersects the discourse of taste.

Early in *Pendennis*, the narrator, in one of his characteristically skeptical asides, comments, "Ah, sir [the implied reader] — a distinct universe walks about under your hat and under mine — all things in nature are different to each — the woman we look at has not the same features, the dish we eat from has not the same taste to the one and the other — you and I are but a pair of infinite isolates, with some fellow-islands a little more or less near to us" (*P* 177–78). This is recognizable as a variety of the ennui of the Arnoldian modern man. What is interesting, however, is that the source of the ennui is taken to be the relativity of taste. The same issue surfaces again in a somewhat different guise during one of Pen and Warrington's dialogues about the commercialization of art. Pen already has conceded that the Public is the "great landlord" of Genius, but he still protests the artist's subjection to market mechanisms. Warrington responds: "What is it you want? Do you want a body of capitalists that shall be forced to purchase the works of all authors who may present themselves manuscript in hand? Everybody who writes his epic, every driveller who can or can't spell, and produces his novel or his tragedy — are they all to come and find a bag of sovereigns in exchange for their worthless reams of paper? Who is to settle what is good or bad, saleable or otherwise?" (*P* 355). Precisely. "Who is to settle what is good or bad?" may be the central question motivating the course of eighteenth- and nineteenth-century aesthetic theory from Lord Shaftesbury through Immanuel Kant to Matthew Arnold. But that question became especially pointed for the proliferating number of nonaristocratic, professional artists who in the nineteenth century looked not toward patronage but toward the market for support. Having surrendered idealist forms and Romantic genius, Thackeray has left himself and his characters with nothing but taste, the moment-to-moment desires of self-satisfying individuals, which the text portrays as a disintegrating condition. The anxiety of the artist is produced, according to *Pendennis*, by the recognition of public taste as the arbiter of artistic merit.

The aftermath of such a recognition is represented most graphically by the character of Mr. Bows, Emily Costigan's devoted instructor in the performing arts, who says to Pen: "You go to dine with great people. Who ever gives a crust to old Bows? And yet I might have been as good a man as the best of you. I might have been a man of genius, if I had had the chance;

ay, and have lived with the master-spirits of the land. But everything has failed with me. I'd ambition once, and wrote plays, poems, music — nobody would give me a hearing" (*P* 519). The point is not that Bows is a pathetic failure but rather that even talented artists may fail (and so not get to taste the fruits — or French *entrées* — of their labors). Later, in conversation with Bows for the last time, Pen says, "I have known so many brave and good men fail, and so many quacks and impostors succeed, that you mistake me if you think I am puffed up by my own personal good luck, old friend. . . . Do *you* think the prizes of life are carried by the most deserving? and set up that mean test of prosperity for merit?. . . . It is you that are peevish against the freaks of fortune, and grudge the good luck that befalls others" (*P* 748).[43] This, then, is the most troubling aspect of the problem of taste for the characters of *Pendennis* (and, it seems, for Thackeray): public taste is fickle and unpredictable. It is a matter of probability, little more than a gamble.

To summarize, in the course of *Pendennis* Pen's character is made to give up one sort of play, the play of aesthetic excess, for work. Art-as-play must become art-as-work. However, a contradiction becomes apparent through the problem of taste: one sort of play is to be replaced by another sort of play. The artist now is to be made subject to the play of the market, which is the play of public taste, which, finally, is shown to be no more than the "freak of fortune" that may win one "the prize in the lottery," as Bows says (*P* 748). The tragedy of this for Bows (from the middle-class perspective that Thackeray represented) is that not even hard work as an artist can guarantee success. Having relinquished the freedom of play — which had been the artist's measure of reward — and taken on the necessity of disciplining art, the middle-class, liberal-intellectual Victorian artist then finds that work also cannot deliver what was promised in its name: a standard of merit. If neither genius nor diligence ("seriousness" is Ruskin's word) pays off, then what is left to the artist? What *Pendennis* leaves is the diffused anxiety of "infinite isolates" and — to replace what is presented as the dangerous old play — a new form of play that is precariously similar to gambling.

It is no wonder then that Pen's conversion to the gospel of work does not solve all of his problems. Pen's "lucky" success with the publication of *Walter Lorraine*, rather than relieving the anxiety of the artist with freshened optimism, produces instead an unhealthy skepticism. This newfound "worldliness" becomes apparent in conversations with Warrington about courtship and about Warrington's as yet unexplained reluctance to participate in the "game" of love, which Pen describes as a boat race: "You see a man sink in the race, and say good-bye to him — look, he has only dived under the other fellow's legs, and comes up shaking his poll, and striking out ever so far ahead. . . . It's good sport, Warrington — not winning merely, but playing" (*P* 473). Here is a new, more virile (indeed, bluntly phallic and "ho(m)mo-sexual") form of play.[44] This play is analogous to a doctrine of *l'art pour l'art* in that it represents a doctrine of *le jeu pour le jeu*. It is unlike aesthetic play and like a sport in that it is explicitly agonistic. It also is like gambling, and the novel frequently describes it in the language of gambling, as here Pen draws out the parallel between winning a suitably provisioned wife and placing a bet: "You must have a certain stake to begin with, before you can go in and play the great game" (*P* 482). Thus, ultimately, it appears as a more masculinized version of the romantic play that the first half of the novel condemns. Pen becomes a player at love, and the first result is his unfortunate entanglement with a woman of a lower class, Fanny Bolton, in which each is nearly "ruined" by the other (though Pen's greater power in the situation makes him much more culpable). The second result is Pen's belated, half-hearted, and "convenient" engagement to Blanche Amory, about which Warrington ruefully comments, "You're going to sell yourself" (*P* 650).

It would appear that Pen's character takes the lessons administered through the problem of taste and the anxiety of the artist too much to heart and so begins to play the market, as it were, with a vengeance. Warrington expresses his criticism of Pen's *blasé* attitude toward things of moral import through the discourse of taste: "What a monstrous Cynicism it is, which you and the rest of you men of the world admit. I'd rather live upon raw turnips and sleep in a hollow tree . . . than degrade myself to this civilisation, and own that a French cook was the thing in life best worth living for" (*P* 643). The narrator's comment is that Pen has gone "fatally astray, whilst the natural truth and love which should illumine him grow[s] dim in the poisoned air," the poisoned air of love that is not "true" because it is played (*P* 486).

Further analysis of this most recent permutation of play finds it to be intertwined in the text with a series of comments about "the struggle of life," which also happens to be expressed in terms of play. Immediately following Pen's first exhortation to Warrington to join the play of love, the narrator asks, "Was Pendennis becoming worldly, or only seeing the world, or both? and is a man very wrong for being after all only a man? Which is the most reasonable, and does his duty best: he who stands aloof from the struggle of life, calmly contemplating it, or he who descends to the ground, and takes his part in the contest?" (*P* 474). This obviously is a highly gendered, agonistic form of play. What is not so obvious is how the text will square what becomes a recommendation to engage in one sort of manly play—the struggle of the world—while prohibiting another sort of manly play—virile love-play—which may in fact only be a variation of the former. It is not surprising that the text should confuse itself on this issue, as it does. Is the Pen who takes part in cynical love-play taking part in "the struggle of life" by playing the world's game by the world's rules? Or is the Pen who cynically accepts the world's hypocrisy and corruption and thus refuses to take part in the idealistic "fight for truth" (as the narrator approvingly calls it) avoiding the struggle of life, as Pen has accused Warrington of doing (*P* 649)?

"Both and neither" seems to be the answer. In Pen and Warrington's longest debate on this issue, for example, Pen aligns himself with the figure of the jaded politician who once in office forfeits his youthful ideals for political expediency, "march[ing] as the world marches towards reform, but at the world's pace (and the movements of the vast body of mankind must needs be slow)" (*P* 644). Pen's reasons for taking this position again point to the anxiety of the artist: after all, one can do nothing about the "lucky speculation[s]" that bring one person to power while another is left oppressed, so why not just accept the dominant social order (*P* 645)? The anxiety of the artist here becomes synonymous with the anxiety of the citizen (given the perspective of a bourgeois, liberal-intellectual who was embroiled in a cultural discourse through which that transformation was enacted). Pen fatalistically responds, "Who are we to measure the chances and opportunities?" (*P* 647). However, as already noted, the radical equality of the hand of fortune—according to which anyone may win the lottery—is little comfort to Pen and even less to Warrington. Now it is Warrington's turn to argue in favor of taking part in "the struggle." His character makes the parallel between political action and artistic judgment explicit when he finally charges Pen with dissolving the basis for discerning between "the hymn of a saint, or the ode of a poet, or the chant of a Newgate thief" (*P* 646, 647). By the time this dialogue is finished, social justice, artistic integrity, and moral judgment have been mixed together in a rough fashion that bares but does not address the foundational linkages between them.

Within five pages of *Pendennis*, Thackeray pours out a heterogeneous range of Victorian discourses in a form little less condensed than dream material. What is perhaps most jarring is that Warrington and the narrator, who speaks out in favor of Warrington's side, are situated in opposition to Pen and therefore in the uncomfortable rhetorical position of supporting two views that the dominant discourses of the text oppose: active political reform and idealist aesthetics (or at least an aesthetics that subscribes to an abstract standard of merit). The tension thus produced in the text has the effect of flushing the narrator and perhaps the author out of hiding. Pen is given such a convincing voice in favor of laissez-faire politics, moral relativism, and utilitarian self-satisfying that Warrington appears to be left speechless. At this emergency, the narrator peremptorily steps in and delivers a rebuttal to Pen's position, arguing that "[i]t leads a man to a shameful loneliness and selfishness," and so on (*P* 649). Then, without skipping a beat, and thus as if in direct reply to the narrator, not Warrington, Pen recommences his side of the dialogue. Most tellingly, Pen restarts the discussion not from the point at which he had left off with Warrington but from the topic that the narrator just has left. The artifice of the realist text appears to be crumbling under the tension it has produced.

The scene just described can be understood as the point of crisis in this text, the point at which it no longer can bear — or no longer submerges — the burden of its contradictions. One reasonably might suspect that these contradictions were quite pressing for Thackeray in his own life as a working artist. The anxiety of the artist that Pen suffers erupts through the surface of the text at this point as the author's anxiety. Thus the author/narrator interrupts his character only to disclaim responsibility for him: "We [the royal author] are not pledging ourselves for the correctness of his opinions . . . the writer being no more answerable for them than for the sentiments uttered by any other character of the story" (*P* 648). Even by Thackeray's standards, this is a flagrant challenge to the reader's credulity and thus to the artifice of the realist novel. The anxiety expressed in this rupturing of the text is symptomatic of the tensions produced by the overlapping and contradictory ideological currents of Thackeray's time. In five pages in *Pendennis*, one clearly can read the outlines of Wordsworth and Ruskin, Paine and Disraeli. By what mechanism, then, short of continuous rupturing of the mimetic surface, is *Pendennis* going to resolve the dilemma created by placing the protagonist between two contradictory but affiliated sorts of manly play? How is Pen's character going to be gotten from a loveless engagement to Blanche Amory, an ill-gotten seat in Parliament, and an attitude of jaded acquiescence to a marriage with Laura Bell, a life of rural wholesomeness in his mother's house, and an active participation in the struggle for truth? In short, this is brought about through yet another permutation of play, the figure of *fair play*.

Although he comes to the brink of selling his integrity, Pen is shown from the first to be a character with character in the most Victorian sense.[45] This is made explicit in a scene in which Pen is exhorted by fellow journalist Captain Shandon to attack in print the books published by a rival regardless of their true quality. Shandon says, "My good young friend, for what do you suppose a benevolent publisher undertakes a critical journal, — to benefit his rival?" Pen replies, "To benefit himself certainly, but to tell the truth too" (*P* 378). Thus Pen's character comes to embody his author's belief in truth as expressed in the preface to *Pendennis*. However, it does so at the cost of posing a potential contradiction to the prevalent discourse of taste, according to which there is no truth to be had, or at least no justice in whose work is picked and whose is panned. This contradiction, which proves to consist of an unquestioning belief in fair play, is what will save Pen's character from skepticism. After Pen refuses to sully truth at the "loss of character or remorse of conscience," Shandon (who can no longer financially afford a conscience) replies, "Well, I am glad that your conscience gave you leave to play for us." Pen responds: "Yes, but . . . we are all party men in England, and I will stick to my party like a Briton. I will be as good-natured as you like to our own side . . .; and I will hit the enemy as hard as you like — but with fair play, Captain, if you please. One can't tell all the truth, I suppose; but one can tell nothing but the truth: and I would rather starve, by Jove, and never earn another penny by my pen . . . than strike an opponent an unfair blow" (*P* 378). Here — in a familiar confluence of patriotism, masculinity, war, and honor — Pen names the form of play that the text ultimately offers as the palliative for the more dangerous forms of play.

It is this sense of fair play that prompts Pen to refuse the Clavering seat in Parliament and all the income and prestige that would come with it after he knows that his uncle, the Major, procured it by blackmailing Francis Clavering. Pen's character thus is brought to the unavoidable crisis of facing down his father-figure in order to become "a man." As Pen marches with resolve toward the Major's private chamber, the enigmatic narrator comments, "It is strange to take one's place and part in the midst of the smoke and din [of the war of becoming a man], and think every man here has his secret *ego* most likely, which is sitting lonely and apart, away in the private chamber, from the loud game in which the rest of us is joining!" (*P* 729). In the impassioned exchange that follows, Pen proves Warrington right by admitting that to marry Blanche for money and prestige would be "prostituting [his] honour" (*P* 732). He denounces the Major's philosophy of skepticism in the following terms: "Don't you see that we have been playing a guilty game?"[46] Major Pendennis goes down on his knees and pleads with Pen not to "fling this chance away," this winning ticket in the family lineage lottery that would ensure a proper place for the name of Pendennis. But Pen is determined not to rely on chance but rather to embrace necessity with a stiff upper lip.

According to a paradoxical logic, this submission to necessity thus is made to appear as the exercise of will. Not only is Pen set on winning fairly, he also determines to lose with honor: he honors his engagement to Blanche even knowing that now they would not be able to afford a French chef. Within the logic of Victorian realist novels, this is the only way that he can be released from that obligation in such a way that he thereby will *earn* the love and respect that he is to receive in full and for the rest of his fictional life from Laura Bell. This is the only way that the text can speak the moral that it places in the mouth of an unsuspecting Mr. Huxter (who is sold on the idea of his son's downward marriage to Fanny Bolton by Pen and Laura) when he says, "And love is better than money, isn't it?" (*P* 764). This, finally, is the way that the text is able to recuperate dangerous play: by refashioning it into another form of play, one that is productive of proper British manliness, conscience without consciousness, activity without activism, sport without sportiveness. Fair play is the earning of honor. As such, it is a type of work, work that offers the ideological advantages of never being finished and of producing no tangible output other than proper forms of behavior. These forms of behavior, though aristocratic and idealist in origin, relied on a new intensity of internalization while at the same time serving the very practical and material interests of domesticity, productivity, and patriotism.

An analysis of the figure of play in *Pendennis* reveals not one figure of play but five moments in the transformation of the figure of play. Initially, play appears as aesthetic excess, which is consistent with Victorian responses to Romantic and idealist theories of art and self. This sort of play is shown in the second moment to lead to the playing of love and to the theatricalization of authenticity, both of which are gendered feminine. These forms of play are corrected in the third moment by the transformation of art-as-play into art-as-work, a form of unplay. It then briefly appears that the gospel of work will solve the problems of play. However, the demystification of idealism that accompanies this process also produces an undesirable level of anxiety about the figure of the artist and a skepticism that undermines the moral foundation of judgments of merit or value. This proves particularly dangerous to discourses of social harmony when the dominant ideologies connected with utilitarianism, Protestant individualism, and laissez-faire capitalism begin to appear as nothing more than rationalizations for isolation, avidity, unchecked competition, and lack of compassion. The negative analogue to the doctrine of equality surfaces as the gambler's creed of universally even odds (though, as the character of Bows demonstrates, not everyone starts with the same chances). One result is the spawning in the fourth moment of a more virile and virulent form of love-play that threatens to reduce love — that unimpeachable source of value in Victorian fiction — to a combination of mercenary convenience and individual sensual pleasure. This cannot be permitted. Thus the figure of fair play emerges in the fifth moment as that which ameliorates or avoids the problems found with the previous permutations of play, as well as serving certain identifiable interests. Excess is moderated by exposing the idealized self to the practical necessities of accepting one's circumstances with a stiff upper lip. Theatricality is regulated by the demand for authenticity. Artistic anxiety is palliated by the partial reinternalization of the standard of merit. Work is elevated above socially contentious questions such as "for whom?" and "for what?" through an aestheticized doctrine of *le travail pour le travail*. Market forces, otherwise considered unpredictable and uncontrollable, are regulated supposedly by a mechanism that is internal to the subject, or to the collective subject under the name of "the market." The institutions of love and marriage are policed by the same code, which says that both romance without love and marriage without love are dishonorable, though for different reasons. Further, as a masculinized figure, fair play is represented as overcoming the stigma of feminization that accompanies most other forms of play in the Victorian context. While considered an appropriately manly activity, fair play nevertheless directly serves the purposes of domestication by channeling play energies that might disrupt domestic politics — personal and national — toward the more "healthy" outlets of organized athletics, chivalrous competition for a lady, gentlemanly business transactions, and war. Thus, while "feminine" play is masculinized, "masculine" play serves to domesticate the Victorian male. Finally, the preceding analysis suggests that inscribed within *Pendennis* in the form of the five moments just outlined is a genealogy of the figure of play as it was refashioned from eighteenth-century aristocratic ideologies and idealist aesthetics to meet the needs of nineteenth-century bourgeois ideology and taste.

Alton Locke's Colonization of Play

> The example of *Kim* reminds us of the fact that the function which an author attributes to play commits him necessarily to a political position in the nineteenth century, and, indeed, in our own.
>   Daniel Bivona, *Desire and Contradiction*

As a novel within the Victorian Condition-of-England tradition, the "auto-biography" *Alton Locke* varies significantly from *Pendennis* in that it is written from the point of view of a working-class protagonist. Like *Pendennis*, and like the majority of Condition-of-England novels, which also purport to be from a lower-class perspective, *Alton Locke* is dominated by the middle-class morality of its author. While one must not underestimate the value of *Alton Locke*'s graphic portrayal of sweatshop labor exploitation or of its direct critique of "buy-cheap-and-sell-dear commercialism," one also must recognize the interests served by the text's predominant message (*AL* 372). That message is that it is selfish and socially irresponsible to become engaged in political activism; that one should accept existing social conditions as part of the Divine order; that "there is no real rank, no real power, but worth; and worth consists not in property, but in the grace of God"; and that the working classes should strive not for social equality but for "spiritual liberty," "endeavouring to make, them[selves], not electors merely, but fit to be electors" (*AL* 364, 377, 383). This summary, though potentially reductive, provides the background against which the figurations of play in *Alton Locke* must be read.

One important difference between *Alton Locke* and *Pendennis* is that in the former the issues of artistic merit and of the artist's role in society are tied more explicitly to questions about the political functions and responsibilities of art. Should art and politics mix (as if this could be prevented)? Should Alton's character write heartfelt, and therefore "true," protest poetry, or should he compromise the feelings of his verse in order to produce a perhaps more socially responsible—meaning balanced toward the middle—poetry? While such questions as these are diffused throughout *Pendennis*, they are central to *Alton Locke*.

In a number of other ways, however, the figure of play operates in *Alton Locke* similarly to its operation in *Pendennis*. For example, like Pen, Alton indulges in the play of aesthetic excess. Alton's characteristic flights of fancy are described in terms that draw a parallel with Pen: "Now I was the corsair in the pride of freedom on the dark blue sea. . . . Now I was a hunter in tropic forests—I heard the parrots scream and saw the humming-birds flit on from gorgeous flower to flower. Gradually I took a voluntary pleasure in calling up these images. . . . And as the self-indulgent habit grew on me, I began to live two lives—one mechanical and outward, one inward and imaginative" (*AL* 80). The text justifies this opposition of fanciful play to work by the severity of the sweatshop working conditions for the tailors in Smith's garret. It initially sanctions imaginative escape as necessary in the face of the "ugliness" of the London slums, which Alton presents as a form of aesthetic oppression more onerous than bodily hunger and sickness (though one suspects that subsistence-level tailors might have been more concerned with the latter than with the former) (*AL* 6). Here also are two issues that will recur throughout *Alton Locke*: the issue of the Other as exotic, "tropical," or "southern," and the issue of the free labor of the artisan versus the mechanical production of alienated labor.

Another similarity to *Pendennis* is that Alton's aesthetic excess also is linked to romantic excess, which again leads to the idolization of beauty. In his momentous first visit to an art gallery, Alton's initial fixation on Guido Reni's portrait of St. Sebastian pierced with arrows is translated — as if by the fairy potion of an aesthetic Robin Goodfellow — into a fixation on Lillian Winnstay, the daughter of Alton's future benefactor, Dean Winnstay, whom Alton meets in the gallery.[47] Lillian is the typical, idealized female icon of beauty; for Alton she is "beautiful, beautiful, beautiful, beyond all statue, picture, or poet's dream," a "newfound Venus Victrix" to whom he whispers "the extravagances of [his] idolatry" (*AL* 71, 73, 77). Later in the story, when Alton has been invited to stay at the Winnstay's country house (for the purpose of giving the Dean an opportunity to assess Alton's worthiness for patronage), the conversation turns directly to the issue of beauty. The specific question concerns the difference between the superficial beauty of dress and the "real beauty of persons as well as the higher beauty of mind" (*AL* 177). In what reads like a summary of *Sartor Resartus, sans* irony, Alton defends the beauty of external appearances (and, coincidentally, his trade), with significant glances toward Lillian, in the following terms: "How many lovely and loveable faces there are, for instance, among the working classes, which, if they had but the advantages which ladies possess, might create delight, respect, chivalrous worship, in the beholder — but are now never appreciated, because they have not the same fair means of displaying themselves which even the savage girl of the South Sea Islands possesses!" (*AL* 177). Alton's ambition to be a Henry Higgins to the working class thus is revealed, as is the more latent desire to be alone with Lillian on a tropical island (with Lillian fashioned in a grass skirt, one suspects). More to the point, Alton's ambition is to be the Pygmalion to his false idol of Aphrodite, which as it turns out is both Lillian *and* the British working class.

The novel links Alton's worship of superficial beauty with his belief in "circumstance" and his resulting commitment to Chartism. "Circumstance" here signifies material social conditions in a sense similar, though not identical, to its use in George Eliot's determinism (as analyzed in chapter two). The text shows belief in circumstance and in Chartism to be misguided, and for similar reasons: each mistakes the (false) outer for the (true) inner. External beauty is to true inner beauty as circumstance is to the "spiritual body" of the nation, which is equivalent to Arnoldian "culture" (*AL* 364). In each pair, one is to deny the importance of the former and to concentrate on the latter. One should "try no more to meet Mammon with his own weapons" (*AL* 365). This is the message delivered at the end of the novel to Alton's character by the redeeming female figure of Eleanor Staunton. In the closing confessional dialogues between Alton and Eleanor, even Eleanor, the paragon of the text, confesses that in her youth she too worshiped aesthetic pleasure and made an "idol-temple of self" (*AL* 373,374). She admits that "the beautiful was [her] God," prior to her conversion to Christian charity. She then uses the same terms to characterize Alton's commitment to Chartism: "You regarded the Charter as an absolute end," she says. "You made a selfish and a self-willed idol of it" (*AL* 378).

Thus aesthetic excess leads in *Alton Locke* to a more dangerous form of excess: political activism. The novel represents participation in social reform as a misconception about the basis for aesthetic judgment, revealing the Victorian translation of politics into aesthetics. Alton's error, the error of anyone who attempts to change social circumstances through material action, is an aesthetic confusion about the proper relationship between the subject-citizen and the object-society. The subject must neither confuse its true self with the object, which is Alton's error in viewing social change as personally vital, nor grant the object complete autonomy from the self (the collective, universal self), which would admit the empirical skepticism underlying market capitalism. What *Alton Locke*, like other texts of the period, recommends is to create an ideal sphere in which the subject (individual) and the object (society) correspond to one another without material contact. Social conditions are to be changed only by the citizen looking inward and changing itself, which assumes an original autonomy of the subject from social conditions. It is perhaps surprising, given mid-Victorian antipathy to idealist aesthetics, to find here a subscription to those very aesthetics. This is merely the unavoidable outcome, however, of making politics into aesthetics. Once the social is aestheticized, then by definition the material already has been idealized. Thus, while idealist aesthetics are taboo, idealist politics are recommended. Politics has been made the domain for aesthetic theory.

This transformation cannot be achieved, however, without challenging the text's ability to rationalize it without contradiction. The difficulties that the text sets for itself are intimated by Alton's character as narrator in the third paragraph of the novel: "I used once, when I worshipped circumstance, to fancy it my curse, Fate's injustice to me, which kept me from developing my genius, and asserting my rank among poets. I longed to escape to glorious Italy, or some other southern climate, where natural beauty would have become the very element which I breathed; and yet what would have come of that? Should I not, as nobler spirits than I have done, have idled away my life in Elysian dreams, singing out like a bird into the air, inarticulate, purposeless, for mere joy and fullness of heart; and taking no share in the terrible questionings, the terrible strugglings of this great awful blessed time—feeling no more the pulse of the great heart of England stirring me?" (*AL* 6). How is Alton's character going to assert his "rank among poets" *without* resorting to the excessive aesthetic play of art that is "purposeless" (a term that harkens back to Kant's *Zweck ohne Zweckmassigkeit*, purposiveness without purpose)? How is Alton going to take part in the "terrible strugglings," which in *Pendennis* are called the "struggle of life," *without* crediting the importance of "circumstance" or becoming actively involved in social reform? How is art to be useful without being dangerous? How, finally, is the convergence of the exotic "southern climate" with the "great heart of England" to be effected?

In the first place, the young Alton's aesthetic excess must be corrected. The initial correction comes not through the character of Eleanor Staunton but through the radical Scottish bookshop owner, Sandy Mackaye, Alton's father-substitute. Inspired by his encounter with Lillian in the Dulwich gallery, Alton undertakes his first poem. The topic he chooses is the voyage of "a pious sea-rover" who, Alton comments, "set forth under the red-cross flag to colonise and convert one of my old paradises, a South Sea Island" (*AL* 84, 85). Unexpectedly, but also as one might expect, the ship enters a lagoon in which "a troop of naked island beauties" happens to be swimming; at this point, Alton finds it difficult to continue writing and decides to show the verses to Mackaye. Mackaye proceeds to give Alton a sound lesson in the frivolousness of "wasting God's gifts on your ain lusts and pleasures" (which recalls Ruskin's critique of the Sensualist) and concludes by saying, "True poetry, like true charity, my laddie, begins at hame" (*AL* 87, 88). The artistic subject that Mackaye commends is the exploitation and degradation of the lower classes, the "tragedy" of "man conquered by circumstances" (*AL* 89). The young Alton follows Mackaye's advice, thereby finding his vocation as the "People's Poet" and beginning on the road of "the struggle of life" that will lead him to violent revolt, prison, near suicide, and final repentance at the knee of Eleanor Staunton (*AL* 94). In this way, the text places Alton's character between two undesirable forms of excess: the Romantic excess of the selfish, purposeless imagination and, at the opposite extreme, the excess by which art becomes too "useful," too close to the struggle of politics.

The second stage in the correction of Alton's character comes during Alton's stay at Dean Winnstay's. The Dean has sent a sheaf of Alton's poems to a publisher who has offered to publish them "if certain passages of a strong political tendency [are] omitted" (*AL* 179). The Dean and Alton engage in a debate over artistic integrity versus artistic success (publication), though the Dean's approach is to raise a question about the appropriate subject for poetry. He argues, "The poet, like the clergyman and the philosopher, has nothing to do with politics" (*AL* 180). His concluding advice is as follows: "Or, if you must be a poet [as opposed to a natural scientist, which is what the Dean wants Alton to become], why not sing of Nature, and leave those to sing political squabbles, who have no eye for the beauty of her repose?" (*AL* 181). The situation is very complex for Alton's character, since publication not only means recognition, which he craves, and financial reward, which he sorely needs, but the continued good favor of the Dean, which guarantees continued access to Lillian. The aggrieved Alton comments: "If I had acted on the first impulse, I should have refused, and been safe. These passages [the ones to be expunged] were the very pith and marrow of the poems. They were the very words which I had felt it my duty, my glory, to utter. . . . Could I not, just once in a way, serve God and Mammon at once? — or rather, not Mammon, but Venus. . . . In short, between 'perhapses' and 'mights,' I fell — a very deep, real, damnable fall; and consented to emasculate my poems, and become a flunkey and a dastard" (*AL* 182–83).

Here is the crisis in this text. The speaker is Alton as narrator — the older, wiser man looking back in retrospect — and so the views here demand to be taken as those of the text. However, they appear to contradict the dominant message of the end of the novel, which effectively supports the views of the Dean over those of Mackaye (which is surprising also in that the latter character is treated much more sympathetically than the former). Further, in the above passage, God is aligned on the side of maintaining artistic integrity *and* an actively political function for art. This again appears to contradict the intention of the end of the novel. This tension results in, and perhaps results from, a certain productive schizophrenia within the narration, which might be labeled Alton-the-(Ch)artist. This can be read at one level as a confusion on the part of Charles Kingsley about the two potentially contradictory and equally heartfelt messages of the novel: (1) the suffering of the lower classes, which is symptomatic of capitalist greed and exploitation, is real and must be alleviated; and (2) any such alleviation must not take upon itself the revision of the social order and, at all costs, must avoid class conflict. It can be read at another level in the uncertainty of the narrative voice, which wobbles between the points-of-view of the future narrator and the past character. On the other hand, this ambivalence is represented overtly in the struggle enacted in the story over Alton's allegiance. As Mackaye says to Alton, "Can you deny that you've been off and on lately between flunkeydom and The Cause, like a donkey between two bottles of hay?" (*AL* 249). Should Alton's character be true to Lillian and artistic success or to Chartism and artistic integrity? Answering this catch-22 question proves more than Alton or the text can bear with ease. As a result, the text falls back on what amounts to a deus ex machina: Alton's character falls deliriously ill and dreams a series of visionary scenarios through which he and the text are led to a much needed salvation from undecidability.

The unique stream-of-consciousness dream sequence in *Alton Locke* — perhaps the most widely noted aspect of the novel, in part because of its "use of pre-Darwinian evolutionary ideas"—traces the evolution of the human species, with each stage of development represented in a separate dream (Cripps xviii). This chapter raises many interesting questions, particularly concerning Alton's masculinist response to the anxiety of the artist, but I will overlook most of these to move to the primary issue. In the last stages of evolution, in a series of events that closely parallels the Exodus, the human tribe has been directed to march "westward ever," claiming the land in the name of the "All-Father."[48] They come to a mountain and are compelled by faithfulness to "His" decree to bore a hole through it in order to continue expansion. This proves difficult, enthusiasm flags, and squabbling over land, belongings, and power breaks out among the brethren. The figure of Alton in Alton's dream becomes, in effect, the new Messiah who preaches as follows: "Oh ye hypocrites! have ye not forgotten the old traditions, that each man should have his equal share of ground, and that we should go on working at the mountain, for the sake of the weak and the children, the fatherless and the widow?" The Sadducees, figuratively speaking, of the tribe attempt to bribe the Alton figure from continuing to stir up discontent by offering him a beautiful young woman, whom the dreaming Alton recognizes as Lillian. She beseeches in these terms: "Come! I will be your bride, and you shall be rich and powerful; and all men shall speak well of you, and you shall write songs, and we will sing them together, and feast and play from dawn to dawn." As one might expect, the Alton figure's response to this offer of play is work: "Wife and child, song and wealth, are pleasant; but blessed is the work which the All-Father has given the people to do." Alton becomes the disciple of work who uses his art, his poetry, to rouse the industriousness of the people to "pierce the mountain" and, having done so, to behold the promised land. The promised land is described in terms that suggest — at least to this twentieth-century reader — the prospect of conquerable indigenous peoples and infinitely renewable resources. Here, as clearly as anywhere in Victorian literature, is the dream of endless colonization, draped in the sanctimonious garb of spiritual redemption. The novel offers the dream of empire as the solution to domestic strife, as well as to what is clearly a masculine sexual anxiety. With it is coupled a gospel of self-sacrifice, work, and what accurately might be called communism: "Work for all, and all employ— / Share with all, and all Enjoy." As the sequence closes, a female figure tells the Alton figure that his "penance is accomplished" and that he has "learned to be a man," which recalls Pen's learning to be a man through fair play. The voice commands him, with the authority of a hypnotist, to awake, and Alton opens his eyes to behold Eleanor Staunton (now Lady Ellerton), his personal savior.

In light of this reading, the ending of *Alton Locke* is perhaps less unexpected and "weak" than many readers have found it to be, and perhaps it is *more* contradictory. With the aid of Eleanor, Alton comes to the realization that the only "perfect Artist, the Fountain of all Genius," is God, and that, in effect, it is blasphemy for the human to attempt that greatness. Even Jesus, according to Eleanor, "was tempted, like every genius, to use His creative powers for selfish ends — to yield to the lust of display and singularity" (*AL* 356). Alton must seek neither the Romantic illusion of genius, which is the source of the claim to artistic integrity, nor the Mammon of artistic success and notoriety, nor, certainly, the folly of attempting to change social conditions with art. Yet he still is to become, or be made into, "the poet of the people," now conceived very differently from Sandy Mackaye's idea (*AL* 384). How? By the combination of two factors. First, Alton must be sent "westward ever" to the southern colonies. It is from this remove, apparently, that he best can serve the British worker. At last he is to become the "Tropic poet," as Eleanor calls it, that he longed in youth to be (*AL* 384). What the opening of the novel portrays as Romantic excess the end of the novel portrays as the appropriate vocation of the poet. What was taboo when indulged in imaginatively is recommended when undertaken in actuality. In the course of the novel, the following formula emerges: *the Imagination → "nature" ← the social*. The true poet is to indulge in neither the excesses of the Romantic imagination nor the excesses of social activism, but is to concentrate on "nature." This is what the Dean had recommended to Alton: the poet is to become the scientist, distanced, objective, realistic. This is what Eleanor recommends at the end: "I do not send you to look for society, but for nature" (*AL* 385). The poet should be a Romantic, but without Romanticism. All play is to be reserved for God, the "perfect Artist," and to be found only in the natural world, "in which the God-given life . . . can have its free and normal play" (*AL* 371). Poetry is not play; it is work, and Alton's new work as the people's poet is described to him by Eleanor as follows: "See if you cannot help to infuse some new blood into the aged veins of English literature; see if you cannot, by observing man in his mere simple and primeval state, bring home fresh conceptions of beauty, fresh spiritual laws of his existence, that you may realise them here at home — (how, I see as yet but dimly; but He who teaches the facts will surely teach their application) — in the cottages, in the play-grounds, the reading-rooms, the churches of working men" (*AL* 384). Alton is to bring back exotic "new blood" and "facts" to reinvigorate England through "applications" that are as yet only dimly realized, at least by Eleanor's character. However, history provides a perspective on what the applications were to be. The "natural" topic for the poet in *Alton Locke* is in fact the object of imperial conquest.

This becomes even more apparent when one reads the final poem written by Alton (and published later in verse collections by Charles Kingsley) before his death onboard the ship bound for the Americas. The first stanza laments the plight of "pauper, dolt, and slave," recommending "Work! or the grave!" (*AL* 389). The second stanza concludes: "He that will not live by toil / Has no right on English soil." And here is the final stanza:

> Up, up, up, and up,
> Face your game, and play it!
> The night is past — behold the sun! —
> The cup is full, the web is spun,
> The Judge is set, the doom begun;
> Who shall stay it! (*AL* 390)

These closing lines of the novel appear purposely enigmatic. One might wonder what game and what play *Alton Locke* finally recommends. Comparison with a well-known stanza from the poem of another Victorian poet, Sir Henry Newbolt, points to an answer.

> The sand of the desert is sodden red —
> Red with the wreck of a square that broke;
> The Gatling's jammed and the Colonel dead,
> And the Regiment blind with dust and smoke.
> The river of death has brimmed his banks,
> And England's far and Honour a name,
> But the voice of a schoolboy rallies the ranks:
> "Play up! play up! and play the game!"

The question of Kingsley's possible influence on Newbolt is irrelevant; rather, the strong parallel between the two poems bespeaks a mutual participation in a shared cultural discourse, which also is evidenced by the fact that generations of public school boys were required to memorize Newbolt's poem. Finally, then, the form of play to which *Alton Locke* subscribes, to which it would mold all other dangerous forms of play, is the same as that recommended by *Pendennis*: public school fair play. Alton grudgingly admires this aristocratic form of play once early in the novel when he witnesses the boat races at Oxbridge, commenting: "The true English stuff came out there . . . the stuff which has held Gibraltar and conquered at Waterloo — which has created a Birmingham and a Manchester, and colonised every quarter of the globe — that grim, earnest, stubborn energy, which . . . the English possess alone of all the nations of the earth" (*AL* 132). Though the theme of colonization generally is not explicit in *Alton Locke*, it clearly is represented in the handling of the figure of play and in the use of the tropical Other to signify the "natural" aesthetic object that the fair play of British imperialism intends to create.[49]

The second factor that is to confirm Alton as "the poet of the people" is his return to what appears to be an archaic, aristocratic system of patronage. In accepting Eleanor's patronage (and that of other subscribers rallied by her), Alton's character surrenders the autonomy of the artist, thereby also escaping the competition of the market and the anxiety of the artist, which proved so troubling in *Pendennis*. Eleanor's character clearly understands this when she says, "You are my servant now, by the laws of chivalry, and you must fulfill my quest," the conquest of "the paradisaic beauty and simplicity of Tropic humanity" (*AL* 384). Eleanor has the same sort of solution in mind for the general problem of the condition of the working poor. While Alton is safely packed off to the New World, Eleanor, like Dorothea

Brooke in *Middlemarch*, will undertake an "experiment of associate labour" dedicated to training participating workers to "devote themselves, body and soul, to the great end of enabling the artisan to govern himself; to produce in the capacity of a free man, and not of a slave; to eat the food he earns, and wear the clothes he makes" (*AL* 380–81). The workers will need to consent to instruction by "a clergyman or two among them," and will be allowed to govern themselves as long as they leave overall government to the institution of patronage, which demands loyalty and obedience in exchange for support. Part of this system is the translation of the laborer into "the artisan," just as Alton is translated from the dangerous kind of artist to the prescribed kind of artist.

Throughout the novel the following formula emerges: *artist* → *"the artisan"* ← *worker*.[50] The artist is to become a worker, while labor is to become an art. This is parallel to John Ruskin's appeal to the image of the medieval artisan happily carrying out his work without a thought of protest beneath the benevolent eye of the overseeing landlord. *Alton Locke* embraces this image, a very fancifully playful image within the context of nineteenth-century British society, as the solution to unemployment, dissension among workers, and social revolt. In the process, the text very neatly makes the solution to the problem of alienated labor, and the attendant excesses of social activism, coterminous with the solution to the problem of aesthetic play. Alton can become the "poet of the people" because "the people" are to become appropriate subjects. The system of patronage to which Alton submits, while appearing to meet the needs of the lower classes by employing the surplus and assuaging the guilt of the upper classes, ultimately serves the interests of the industrial and commercial middle classes by removing them from consideration of an endemic problem (in a way that appears to herald George Bush's "thousand points of light" initiative in the 1980s). While Eleanor Staunton's intentions toward Alton and toward the working class are represented as and should be read as sincerely humanitarian, they serve the ultimate goal of providing the rationale for denying societal responsibility for structural inequalities.

The Novelization of the Aesthetic

In *Alton Locke*, as in *Pendennis*, the central plot concerns the training of the protagonist to put his "Pegasus into Harness," as one of Kingsley's chapters is titled. *Pendennis* uses the figure of Pegasus first in Warrington's lectures to

Pen and then, as if to affirm Warrington's view, through the narrator. The narrator observes, "Often Pegasus does his work with panting sides and trembling knees, and not seldom gets a cut of the whip from his driver. Do not let us, however, be too prodigal of our pity upon Pegasus. There is no reason why this animal should be exempt from labour. . . . If he gets the whip, Pegasus very often deserves it, and I for one am quite ready to protest . . . against the doctrine which some poetical sympathisers are inclined to put forward, viz., that men of letters, and what is called genius, are to be exempt from the prose duties of his daily, bread-wanting, tax-paying life, and are not to be made to work and pay like their neighbors" (*P* 380). Pegasus, the winged charger of the Muses that caused the Hippocrene fountain of poetic inspiration to spring from Mount Helicon, must become a dray horse. Poetry must be converted from play to work, or be replaced by a form of play more appropriate to that work. The form recommended as the necessary replacement for poetry is none other than novelistic realism. The discourse about poetry in these novels displaces it as the "queen of the arts" by aligning the figure of the poet with a type of play that is demonized. By contrast, the work of realist novels is founded on another variety of play, the mimetic play that defines their form. What the discourse of poetry-versus-novel in the novel hopes to demonstrate is that Romantic poetry, and the idealist aesthetics for which it serves as a metonym, no longer are able in the Victorian age to heal the rift between beauty and truth, subject and object, diversity and unity. A new art form, a new aesthetics, and a new form of play are required for this purpose or to announce the social conditions in which such a healing no longer is possible by any means.

At the thematic level, *Pendennis* and *Alton Locke* chart the maturation of their protagonists away from poetry toward prose. *Alton Locke* itself is the tangible fruit of that process, the autobiographical masterwork of a protagonist whose claim to the vocation of poet is supported only by a few pieces of weak verse quoted in the novel that is the vehicle for them. In *Pendennis*, the novelization of the poet is less immediately realized. Pen's character must pass in a three-stage process from being a poet through the filter of being a professional literary critic and only then on to being a novelist. In the middle stage, Pen is to be a practitioner of practical "art criticism" rather than "academic theory" or "philosophical criticism," using Andrew Hemingway's terms. This stage is required in order for Pen to learn discipline, market sense, and the allegiance to truth required of the Thackerian novelist. In the process of translating Pen's character along the chain of poet-critic-novelist, the distinctions between these categories are blurred in significant ways.

For example, the lengthy debate between Pen and Warrington about poetic genius is centered not on the figure of the poet but on Captain Shandon, a professional critic whom Pen nevertheless describes as a genius. In a chapter entitled "Contains a Novel Incident," Pen's character presents the novel's first convincing argument in favor of the poet's claim to a heightened "sensibility"; he does so, however, in reference not to poetry but to his novel *Walter Lorraine* (*P* 434). The point is not that these categories should be kept separate — that poets also do not write novels, for instance — but that *Pendennis* appears to blur the distinctions upon which it elsewhere relies when doing so favorably replaces the figure of the poet with the figure of the novelist. Two other points are clear in the novel's treatment of Pen's writing of *Walter Lorraine*. First, while the romantic excesses of the young poet have been shown to be inappropriate for the poet, the text presents them as quite appropriate — in fact, recommended — as material for the novelist. After all, the most obvious modus operandi of many Victorian novels is to expose and then correct such excesses of play as gambling, theatricality, and aestheticism. Second, while *Walter Lorraine* functions as the figure of the novel, the novel itself is implicated in the characterization of *Walter Lorraine* as merely a "fashionable novel" (*P* 435). *Pendennis* not only is above and beyond Romantic poetry, the reader is to understand, but is above and beyond other types of prose as well, since it, unlike *Walter Lorraine*, is a *realist* novel.

The portrayal in midcentury realist novels of discursive contests between figures representing novelistic realism and figures representing other cultural forms — in this case the Romantic poem and the romance novel — was a response to and a construction of historical contests between cultural forms in which the realist novel was engaged especially in the first half of the nineteenth century. *Alton Locke* and *Pendennis* worked to effect by fiat the victory of their own "prose duties" over poetic play at the very time when the novel in fact was supplanting the Romantic lyric as the more dominant vehicle for cultural material within British society (dominant in terms of greater market share, wider distribution, more readers, and therefore greater contribution to the construction of the subject in society). In representing this competition, novels enact the transformation of aesthetic play in the figure of the poet into the work of truth in the figure of the novelist. The realist novel performatively embodies the replacement of a predecessor genre by its own genre, by itself in the act of performing that replacement. Realist novels convert play into truth, the truth that they constitute; however, this truth is in turn itself based on a form of play.

But Romantic poetry, as represented in novels like *Pendennis* and *Alton Locke*, functions as a synecdochic sign of the broader category of idealist aesthetics. The broader historical contest in which realist novels were engaged in the first half of the nineteenth century was with the theorization of art and its cultural form, the philosophical treatise on aesthetics. This contest is of course more than familiar; it is a foundational agon within western metaphysics that reaches back to its origins in the Platonic distinction between philosophy and poetry and, at the same time, forward to postmodern debates within academia about what ought to be the relationship between "theory" and "literature." Literature and aesthetic theory enter the nineteenth century engaged in a discursive contest, a version of the Platonic contest, over which type of knowledge, definition of reality, and genre of writing will have truth-telling authority and, what is more, which will be the representative for the play of signification itself.

The novels analyzed here not only convey these discourses but embody and act out this contest at the level of their form. This is unavoidable given the fact that the primary formal characteristic of the realist novel is the very form of play — mimetic play — against which Plato mounted, in the name of philosophy, his critique, which in turn is the German cousin to the form of play that Kant reactivated in attempting to explain how aesthetic experience works. In between Plato and Derrida, Kant and Nietzsche, realist novels staked out a defense of their own form, which is to say a defense of a specific type of mimetic play. This was by extension a defense of the prerogative of art, as opposed to philosophy, to maintain custodianship of the play concept in the form of play-as-art. By making "Realism!" the rallying cry behind which realist novels would strive to retrieve moral truth-telling authority, Victorian novelists and critics reclaimed from philosophy control of the figure of play in the name of Literature and of Art.

Realist novels therefore took as one of their antagonists the immediately preceding discourse of play-as-theory and the cultural form that had been the vehicle for that discourse and a defining intellectual form of the preceding cultural period. But where the eighteenth-century treatise on aesthetic philosophy had spoken largely to and for the very small, elite culture of the educated upper classes, the realist novel spoke for and to a much broader constituency. Realist novels not only claimed to speak for the broadening middle but, by midcentury, in fact *did* speak to a correspond-ingly broad middle sector of society. By the 1840s, the realist novel became a dominant cultural form by dint of the economics of the distribution and consumption of novels and the resulting dissemination of a subject position for which realist novels were the model. In these quite material ways, then, novels became during that period the primary vehicles for and expressions of the cultural work of the figure of play. Nineteenth-century realist novels perform their claim to victory as a cultural form in a historical contest, or, expressed from the opposite but complementary perspective, they dem-onstrate the way in which discourse produces social and material conse-quences. Where as the eighteenth century had aesthetic theory, the nine-teenth century had the realist novel. The realist novel *is* the aesthetic theory of the mid-Victorian period.

This claim is recognizably parallel to the claim in chapter two that the realist novel strove to be the political economy of its time and to the claim in chapter three that it worked not only to replace melodrama with realism, performance with reading, but also to be the cultural form that controlled the definition of the theatrical. Throughout this book I have analyzed suc-cessively the nineteenth-century realist novel's historical competitions with and resulting discursive representations of political economy, melodramatic theater, and aesthetic theory. These four cultural forms were in competition each with the others in the first half of the nineteenth century as in no prior or subsequent period in British history. This claim, though perhaps sensa-tionally phrased, is really only to say that cultural forms are historically specific, that the realist novel became a dominant cultural form in Britain at a certain time, and that a particular configuration of competing forms was specific to that time and place. These statements, and the findings that support them, are consistent with the understanding of the concept "cul-tural form" that this book has attempted to demonstrate since the provi-sional definition in chapter one. I have told the tale from the perspective of the novel, and so whatever counterrepresentations may appear in the other three cultural forms have been excluded from consideration by necessity. However, there is a critical difference in this regard between the realist novel and the other cultural forms in relationship to which it worked out its form. A defining characteristic of the nineteenth-century realist novel is the extent to which it incorporates other domains of discourse, omnivorously cannibalizes competing cultural forms, and re-presents that material in and as its own form.

The Recuperation of Aesthetics and the Art of Subversion

> The criticism, from the vantage point of play, of depth and seriousness and the whole domain of inwardness is, however, as ideological as inwardness itself, since it justifies mindless participation or rote activity for its own sake.
>
> T. W. Adorno, Aesthetic Theory

If the realist novel was the aesthetic theory of the nineteenth century, there remain several potentially contradictory ways of interpreting that claim. One way is to note that the realist novel is in a sense the realization of Friedrich von Schiller's dream of "aesthetic education." Thematically, through such figures as sympathy, for instance, these novels instruct readers in a doctrine of self-reflexiveness, refinement of sensibilities, connectedness to others in society, acceptance of responsibility for one's actions, and resolution of differences through a civil sharing of ideas among individuals (rather than social activism or physical violence). Not only do many realist novels convey this doctrine, but they effect it directly by training subjects in and through the practice of reading. As a regularly exercised discipline and source of pleasure, reading is particularly suitable training for producing subjects that are isolated, inwardly directed, socially deactivated, and positioned for passive consumption of cultural material. In one sense this may be especially true of the reading of novels (not to mention the succeeding cultural forms of television, cinema, and video), since sustained narrative that focuses on the inner workings of sympathetic characters additionally trains readers in identification with others. Stated conversely, the *subject effect* of realist novels occurs when the play between reading subject and text generates a position for the subject through the pleasure that the subject derives from the sustained impression that the text is a reflection of the self.[51] The subject thereby recognizes himself as the artifact to be created precisely through the ongoing iterative process of dialogue between self and other that is the process of reading a novel. In other words, the novel, as a widely consumed cultural form, becomes a machine for producing *the aesthetic subject*. Mimetic play is the technology of that machine; novels engage people in the cultivation of play. Contrary to the cliché, Victorian novels do not repress play; rather, they strive to promulgate their own play as the potentially infinite process of generating meaning and identity. Understood in these terms, the Victorian novel indeed is Schiller's dream of aesthetic education come true.

Another interpretation, which carries the previous one to its logical end, is that the idealist definition of the object of aesthetics is enacted in and as the form of the realist novel. From this perspective, nineteenth-century realism *performs* eighteenth-century aesthetic theory. What better actualization is there of the merging of the aesthetic subject and object than the moment when an engaged reader "loses" herself — and therefore simultaneously finds herself — in a "good book"? In Kant's terms, this is the "subjective purposiveness" through which a beautiful object spontaneously corresponds to intersubjective forms. In more practical terms, this is the experience of surrendering one's disbelief to a narrative while simultaneously engaging one's imagination in the creation of that narrative — namely, the pleasure of reading a story. But to summarize the experience in this way risks trivializing an incredibly complex interaction and, more important at the moment, obscures the extent to which the nineteenth-century realist novel is unique as a cultural form. No other cultural form so intensely engages readers for such extended periods of time in oscillating back and forth between an object that so complexly refracts social reality and a subject that is split between self and other with such disturbing potential. The nineteenth-century realist novel, more than any other cultural form, takes mimetic play seriously.

To say that the novel enacts the aesthetic is to say what is perhaps obvious but not simple, which is that a novel *is* art. This in turn relies on a sometimes disputed distinction between aesthetic experience and the theorization of aesthetic experience, between art and other areas of knowledge, especially aesthetic theory. This distinction became significant in a newly intensified way after the aesthetic revolution of the eighteenth century and its contribution to rising bourgeois civil society of an ideology that aestheticized social difference. After analyzing this aestheticization of the social throughout *The Ideology of the Aesthetic*, Terry Eagleton arrives at the ominous conclusion that "aesthetics is born at the moment of art's effective demise as a political force, flourishes on the corpse of its social relevance" (368). While Eagleton apologizes for the "exaggerated" nature of this claim, I contend that early Victorian realist novelists, situated as they were in the wake of the advent of civil society, perceived just this sort of threat from the rationalization represented by art theory to their art's social relevance. Their texts, among other things, defend the concrete, local, and particular meaning of art and the moral utility of art against being usurped by the abstract universality and moral disinterestedness of aesthetic philosophy and, equally, of that aesthetic abstraction called "the market." The discursive contest that I have identified between the figure of aesthetic theory and the figure of the novel depicts and enacts the novel's *resistance in the name of art to the turning of art into discourse in the name of philosophy*, whether aesthetic or economic. Early to mid-Victorian novels resisted what they perceived as "aesthetic alienation," "art's alienation from truth which is caused by art's *becoming* aesthetical," as J. M. Bernstein puts it in *The Fate of Art: Aesthetic Alienation from Kant to Derrida and Adorno* (4).[52] While unavoidably reproducing dominant discourses, nineteenth-century realist novels also resisted the aestheticization of the social that was part of the ideological infrastructure of the ascendant social order of civil society and its laissez-faire political economy. In making these claims, I am opening a reading of realist novels as resistant to certain aspects of dominant bourgeois ideology.

This is not to deny, however, that in presenting itself as Art the realist novel unavoidably participates in, while protesting, the rationalization of art in bourgeois society. This apparent contradiction is the basis for a double bind that may be insurmountable, in part because it is a version of the old argument between empiricism and idealism, which finally is unresolvable. The double bind for the realist novel is the claim to an aesthetic foundation for truth while proving such a foundation to be unsupportable. Realist novels simultaneously defend the truth-telling authority of the aesthetic *and* work to offset the explanatory power of any universalized truth that neglects the sensuously particular and socially contingent nature of truth. In defending (itself as) art as a social space in which the linkage between beauty and truth — the aesthetic and the ethical — still is possible, realist novels resist a theorization of play, which, according to the discourse of those novels, places that figure at the service of recuperative rationalization. A paradox arises, however, in that to the extent that the novelistic text consciously and directly engages in the defense of play against such rationalization, it *becomes* aesthetic theory. By their own definitions, novels then lend themselves to the recuperation of the subversive potential of art — art-as-play — that they set out to prevent.

This is most evident when novels become what Mikhail Bakhtin describes as "monological," either in making the novel a platform for a diegetic address by the narrator/author or allowing character voices to be dominated by the authorial voice.[53] One of the best-known examples of the former is chapter seventeen of *Adam Bede*, in which Eliot's narrator indeed lectures the implied reader on the very topic of art's responsibility to truth (although that truth proves to be anything but unequivocal, as I have shown in relation to some of Eliot's other novels). One example of the latter is the dream sequence that occurs toward the end of *Alton Locke*. That scene, fascinating as it is, marks the point in this novel where its own "heteroglossia" becomes so threatening to central moral tenets of the day that "authoritative discourse" steps in and demands "unconditional allegiance," "permit[ing] no play with the context framing it, no play with its borders, no gradual and flexible transitions, no spontaneously creative stylizing variants on it" (Bakhtin, *Dialogic* 343). Thus in the dream sequence Alton's character is ventriloquized by a voice that speaks in the diction and tone of the Old Testament, the ultimate patriarchal voice as invoked by Charles Kingsley, the middle-class Anglican minister. The effect is to silence the other "images of languages" that the text up to that point had allowed to spark off of one another, such as the voices of Alton-the-Chartist or Sandy Mackaye or Alton's cousin, George.[54] In Bakhtinian terms, *Alton Locke* stops being a dialogical novel. In the terms of this chapter, *Alton Locke* becomes aestheticized.[55]

On the other hand, even a novel like *Alton Locke* also makes a space for othered voices; the fact that they are recuperated in the end does not erase their presence from the text. This certainly is not to claim that all realist novels or any specific realist novel includes all possible voices, because no text of any type does; nor is it to deny that any given novel excludes specific voices, because all novels unavoidably do. Rather, it is to claim more generally that at the moment nineteenth-century realist novels reproduce dominant discourses they also open up a play space within the text and within the reading subject in which the voice of the Other might be heard.[56] Thus Charlotte Brontë's *Shirley* keeps readers on the edges of their seats with the conflicts generated by a configuration of characters with incommensurable gender roles and class codes, the result of which is to foreground some of the potentially tragic contradictions in society's expectations about women and men. Even *Alton Locke*, with its lapses into monological discourse, brilliantly places its working-class protagonist in an unresolvable double bind between, on the one hand, love plus artistic success and, on the other hand, political activism plus artistic integrity. The resulting struggle by the text to generate the desired combination — love plus artistic integrity — also highlights not only the shortcomings of each of these but also the possible advantages of artistic success (commodification of labor, in this case) and political activism (resistance to commodification of labor). In novels like *Villette, Pendennis,* or *Daniel Deronda*, tensions produced by the dialogue between contradictory ideological imperatives foreground the text's own

formal apparatus, and dilemmas of representation erupt on the textual surface. Some realist texts sustain an almost continuous dialogue between the
thematic and formal levels about the relationships between the two, which
is a dialogue about the novel's own mimetic play. This sort of dialogue
between heterogeneous interests, voices, and contexts of meaning within
society is definitive of even the so-called bourgeois realist novel.

It is this understanding of the novel that Bakhtin indicates when he
writes in this well-know passage that the "prose art presumes a deliberate
feeling for the historical and social concreteness of living discourse, as well
as its relativity, a feeling for its participation in historical becoming and in
social struggle; it deals with discourse that is still warm from the struggle
and hostility, as yet unresolved and still fraught with hostile intentions and
accents" (*Dialogic* 331). Thus the dialogue between voices and histories
within the dialogical word is the play of the *social word*, or, as Julia Kristeva
expresses it, the "ambivalence" of the "historical word," which provides a
space where multiple contexts of meaning and potentially conflicting ideologies can converge intertextually (*Desire* 66). This play is of a piece with
the play that readers experience between the image of society in the text and
their image of their own society, between the "inside" and the "outside" of
the text. Readers experience play at that level as an oscillation between the
imaginary and the real, the fictional world and the social world. One effect
is to destabilize the reality of reality, to open up the reader's conception
of social reality to revision, which is the means by which works of literature
contribute to the constitution of social reality through the "ideological
becoming of a human being" and the "historical becoming of language"
(*Dialogic* 330, 341). At the same time, however, that the realist novel provides a space for play at multiple levels—the word, the image of society,
the reader—it also subjects these processes to "the dynamic unity of its
own style" (*Dialogic* 331). The dialogical text allows for play among different images of languages but *within* the form-giving structure of the
novel. Thus "novels are never in danger of becoming a mere aimless verbal
play," "purely formalistic playing about with words" (*Dialogic* 357). The
mimetic play of realist novels operates in a range between "no play" and
"all play."[57]

Realist form makes of itself a space within which readers can engage in
the very sorts of debates that I have been raising about the novel's status as
art, its dialogue between formal and thematic levels, or its oscillation between the real and the imaginary. These debates can take place in critical
texts like this one in part because realist novels made them part of their form

in the first place. Realist novels are not naïve about the issues of representation that they raise. Rather, as Sandy Petrey puts it, "the dilemmas of representation, far from being realism's blind spot, figure among its major narrative strategies" (*Realism* 1). Realist novels theorize their own process in the process of creating it and in the process of the participation by readers in that creation. This in part is what Bakhtin describes as the novel's "*auto-criticism of discourse*," which he argues is "one of the primary distinguishing features of the novel as a genre" (*Dialogic* 412). As he describes it, "Discourse is criticized in its relationship to reality: its attempt to faithfully reflect reality, to manage reality and to transpose it (the utopian pretenses of discourse), even to replace reality as a surrogate for it (the dream and the fantasy that replace life)." Realist novels do not adhere to any strict delineation between the imaginary and the real, between art and theory (while, of course, they milk those distinctions for all they are worth). Even if the way in which I have framed the historical competition between literature and philosophy risks reifying traditional definitions of art and theory, nineteenth-century realist novels work to deconstruct those definitions. The realist novel's theorization of the social signified as its own form reflects an understanding "that language is at one and the same time independent of objective reality and inextricable from social reality" (Petrey, *Realism* 49). Novels theorize meaning production as social negotiation, as what words *do* between people, and according to Petrey, "When we *do* things with words, the referent is neither captured nor alienated; it's produced through a process that contradicts both the historical assumption that written description is perfect and the deconstructionist conviction that writing is supra-historical" (*Speech Acts* 120). In many ways it is the theory of meaning production that nineteenth-century realist novels themselves theorized-while-enacting that is still the center of debates about representation.

The possibilities of participating in the making of language, the making of society, and the making of one's self constitute the primary pleasures that readers derive from reading novels. Wolfgang Iser articulates this point in *The Fictive and the Imaginary*: "Human beings, as the unfolding of themselves, can never be fully present to themselves, because at any one stage they possess themselves only in the possibility realized, and that is what they are not: one limited possibility of themselves. Therefore continual self-unfolding has to be sustained by playing out the plenum of possibilities through a constant alternation of composing and decomposing fabricated worlds" (236). He goes on to argue, "Such an enactment [in and as the reading process] can only be played; its inception is the boundary-crossing of fictionalizing, which allows referential realities as well as other writings to recur in the text; these, even if they appear to be mere reproductions, always recur with a difference, giving rise to a back-and-forth movement between what is in the text and the reality that is being referred to." The categories of "the fictive" and "the imaginary" are not merely abstractions, despite Iser's tendency in that direction; they are an attempt to describe the way that specific texts interact with specific readers to produce social meanings within history. Texts remain "open to the imprint of history," because the oscillating "doubling" between contexts of meaning that takes place in the act of reading "manifests itself as a play space in which all the different discourses come together to form the matrix that enables the text to end up with a potentially infinite variety of relations to its surroundings" (xii, 228).

In my revised, more historically committed interpretation of Iser's model, "the fictive" can be understood as an oscillating transaction of meaning production that takes place between a text and the historically specific social context from which it was written. That context is preserved in the text as interpreted, condensed, and coded languages and representations of discourses, and each reading (intentionally as well as unintentionally) accesses and reactivates these. Thus a similarly modified definition of "the imaginary" emerges as an oscillating transaction of meaning production that takes place in the act of reading between that text and a reader, who unavoidably reads from within his or her specific historical moment, whether that be the same year and country in which the novel was written or five hundred years afterward in a very different language and society. Understood in this way, reading is an incredibly complex, continuous series of iterative and comparative reality checks between the *context of inception* and the *context of reception* of the work of literature. The fact that literary works continue to have powerful impact upon generation after generation of readers need not be explained by resort to abstractions such as "greatness" or "genius" but rather by analysis of the specific ways in which the formal and the ideological participate alike in a historical process of social meaning production.

Realism, at the most general level, is the process of reading the Other in the same and the same in the Other. That descriptor might apply to any cultural form that engages readers in a continuous oscillation between contexts of meaning to which the readers themselves actively contribute. In this view, one might describe any long printed narrative that uses, revises, and reflects upon mimetic strategies as a realist novel, although I would not want to lose sight of the historical and geographical specificity of cultural forms, especially the nineteenth-century British realist novel. Even so, perhaps it is time to expand and redefine the concept of realism to encompass not only Charles Dickens's *Our Mutual Friend* and Victor Hugo's *The Hunchback of Notre Dame*, for example, but also James Joyce's *Ulysses* and Toni Morrison's *Beloved*. The broadened definition that I am hypothesizing would include modernist and postmodern fictional works that make the play along the boundaries of textuality part of their subject matter. In a certain sense that I have tried to raise to the level of perceptibility, nineteenth-century realist novels only do this in a way that is more continuous, subtle, and intensified and therefore perhaps has even more potential for disrupting the boundaries of identity and social meaning.

What realist texts do they do through no single narrative style or strategy, as often is implied and often pejoratively with the phrase "bourgeois realism." Rather, what we call realism is a bundle of shifting, historically specific, and potentially contradictory textual strategies operating simultaneously at multiple levels ranging from the word to the cultural form.[58] To recognize this is to eschew the pitfalls of critical condescension by giving realist texts credit for using all of their strategies and levels: those that add to the illusions of verisimilitude and those that disrupt it, those that disguise the narrative apparatus and those that call attention to the dilemmas of mimesis, those that enlist readers in the dominant ideologies of the time and those that provide us with the opportunity to congratulate ourselves for seeing through those same ideologies. What realist texts do is perform play in and as a series of interrelated gaps — the gap within the word between different "images of languages," the gap between the reader's image of her self and other images of selfhood initiated by the text, the gap between the context of inception and the context of reception, the gap between when a reader starts reading and when he realizes that two hours have passed unnoticed. This is the space of play.

Notes

*Chapter 1. Nineteenth-Century Discourses of Play and the
Novel as a Cultural Form*

1. No doubt like many of my readers, I too am suspicious of studies that make general claims about "the novel." Many types of novels were written in the eighteenth and nineteenth centuries, including gothic, romance, history, and sensation novels, not to mention fictionalized diaries, working-class narratives, and verse novels. All of these used mimetic techniques in varying degrees. Yet one sub-genre of novel came in the 1840s and 1850s in England to claim for itself a special cultural significance on the basis of its greater realism, particularly in the writings of middle-class liberal intellectuals like William Makepeace Thackeray, George Eliot, George Henry Lewes, Edward Bulwer-Lytton, Elizabeth Gaskell, and Anthony Trollope, for example. It is this form of novel that I mean in this study when I write "the realist novel" or "the Victorian novel." Even in saying this, I recognize that this category is heterogeneous and that its boundaries are porous. Eliot's realism is not Trollope's; early Eliot is not late Eliot. One might legitimately question whether Charlotte Brontë's *Villette* is primarily a realist novel; certainly it is a boundary-marking text in this regard. The same can be said about Charles Dickens's novels, which were seen by contemporary critics as too melodramatic and caricatured to be considered realistic. (See chapter three, note three, for an explanation of my decision not to include works by Dickens in this study.) Recognizing these caveats, this book is among other things a defense of the validity of writing about the nineteenth-century realist novel as a generic category.

2. My claims concerning the novel's form and play should be distinguished from another category of claims about the gamelike structure of plots or character relations or the games that authors may play with readers by applying various narrative techniques. See, for example, Peter Hutchinson's *Games Authors Play*, Nancy Morrow's *Dreadful Games*, and R. Rawdon Wilson's *In Palamedes' Shadow*. Another category of studies concerns probability or game theory as it appears in or applies to literary works. See, for example, Robert Newsom, *A Likely Story: Probability and Play in Fiction* and Thomas M. Kavanagh, *Enlightenment and the Shadows of Chance*.

3. This agonistic model and macroeconomic terminology may reproduce part of the capitalist ideology of the culture that I am studying, not to mention twentieth-century American culture; this seems to me unavoidable, and I work to remain reflexive about it.

4. Joseph Allen Boone's *Tradition Counter Tradition: Love and the Form of Fiction* provides an articulate summary of what has become a standard ideological

critique of the nineteenth-century realist novel: "For the classic mode of realist narrative is also a system of representation, working to naturalize, or recuperate, the image of 'reality' that it creates in the form of a coherent, intelligible world. Presenting the reader with fictions that appear 'real,' but whose 'realism' is predicated on a series of narrative manipulations working to present that reality as stable, ordered, and trustworthy, novelistic structures therefore undertake a mission analogous to that of society's dominant ideological structures" (8). I agree at a broad level with much of what Boone writes. At the same time, I work to substantiate an alternate and equally valid reading, one that recognizes, for instance, that the worlds portrayed in Victorian novels are in significant ways not "coherent" and that the realities they construct are often far from "stable, ordered, and trustworthy."

5. Stephen Marcus, *The Other Victorians: A Study of Sexuality and Pornography in Mid-Nineteenth-Century England*, 283, uses "negative analogue" in this sense, which I find generally useful throughout this study.

6. See Barthes's *Pleasure of the Text*, esp. 27 and 37.

7. Heraclitus, *Presocratic Philosophers*, Fragment 52. Here are two other translations: "The course of the world is a playing child moving figures on a boardthe child as absolute ruler of the universe" (Fragment 52, qtd. in Fink, "Oasis" 29). "Lifetime is a child playing, moving in a backgammon (?) game; kingly power (or: the kingdom) is in the hands of a child" (Heraclitus, *Fragments*, Fragment 52).

8. For commentary on the role of the play concept in Nietzsche's philosophy, see the works by Lawrence M. Hinman, Richard Detsch, Peter Heller (esp. 321–36), and Rose Pfeffer (esp. 201–7). For some of the specific references to play in Nietzsche, see *The Birth of Tragedy*, 183–84; *Daybreak*, 81; *The Gay Science*, 302–3; *Human All Too Human*, 385–86; *Philosophy in the Age of the Greeks*, 108, 114, 156, 160; and *Will To Power*, 163, 419, 432.

9. Kant, *Critique of Judgment*, 62.9 and 173–74.45. Also see 38.ix and 225.58. Citations to this work are made parenthetically throughout in the following format: the page number is listed first and is separated by a period from the section number.

10. Kant discusses *Zweck ohne Zweckmassigkeit* on 73.15, 84.17, and 92.22, for example.

11. Play is recognized as a pivotal concept in Heidegger's philosophy, especially *Der Satz vom Grund*, as it is in a different way in Gadamer's *Truth and Method*, esp. 105–20. Fink is representative of a more recent generation of ontologists of play, as here: "But the perplexing world-formula, according to which Being in its totality functions like play, may perhaps make us aware of the fact that play is no harmless, peripheral or even 'childish' thing — that precisely in the power and glory of our magical creativity we mortal men are 'at stake' in an inscrutably threatening way" ("Oasis" 29). Hans's *Play of the World* is a post-Lacanian, post-Derridian theorization of play as the basis for an ecological ethics that relies on a "productive" model of desire (as opposed to a consumptive model of desire conceived as "lack") and a "free play" among socially contingent fields of meaning and action, "not in Derrida's sense, but in the sense that they [the fields] are always open to the new productions which change the field and make it more adequate to its everchanging context" (Hans 155). In a related way, Susan Stewart's *Nonsense: Aspects of Intertextuality in Folklore and Literature* conceives of play as an adaptive activity through

which social meanings become negotiable; play occurs in and as the gap of indeterminacy between a society's conceptions of nonsense and common sense.

12. I refer to *Critique of Judgment,* 236.61, 261–64.68, 270.72, and esp. 282.75. On the eighteenth-century concept of the *je ne sais quoi*, see Howard Caygill's *Art of Judgement,* 39, 61, 86.

13. I agree with the double-edged argument in Christopher Norris's *Derrida*, which takes to task both those who criticize Derrida's philosophy under the false assumption that it can be reduced to "the rhetoric of 'freeplay'" as well as those who celebrate Derrida's work under the same false assumption (20). Thus, while it may appear in places that I lump Derrida into a group with postmodern theorists such as Gilles Deleuze or Jean Baudrillard, I agree with Norris that there is an important distinction to be made between Derrida and "the adepts of post-structuralist apocalyptic discourse" (225).

14. One can trace Derrida's consistent use of play in defining his key terms through these texts: *Speech and Phenomena*, "Difference," 129–60, esp. 130, 135, 140–41, 146, 154, 159; *Writing and Difference*, "Structure, Sign and Play," 278–93, esp. 279–80, 289–92; *Dissemination*, "Play: From the Pharmakon to the Letter and from Blindness to the Supplement," 156–72, and "The Double Session," 173–286; and "Economimesis," 4–6. The most balanced readings of Derrida's use of play are to be found in Jonathan Loesberg's *Aestheticism and Deconstruction: Pater, Derrida, and De Man*, esp. 84–91, and in Mihai Spariosu's *Dionysus Reborn: Play and the Aesthetic Dimension in Modern Philosophical and Scientific Discourse*, 153–64.

15. Or, as Derrida puts it in *Writing and Difference*: "The absence of the transcendental signified extends the domain of the play of signification infinitely" (280).

16. *Sophist,* 977. Also see 976, 983.

17. This observation, which I admit is precariously general, nevertheless has become so commonplace that it appears in *The Encyclopedia of Contemporary Literary Theory*: "In the late 18th century, literature acquires its most familiar modern sense as an aggregate term for imaginative writings" (582). Some may argue that this should make it all the more suspect.

18. I am aware that not everyone subscribes to Foucault's story about literature, and I too retain critical distance from it. See for example Adrian Marino, *The Biography of "The Idea of Literature" from Antiquity to the Baroque*. On the other hand, a diversity of scholars ranging from Roland Barthes in *Writing Degree Zero* to Raymond Williams in *Culture and Society* to J. G. A. Pocock in *Virtue, Commerce, and History* to Michael McKeon in *The Origins of the English Novel* support and convincingly apply arguments that a major cultural paradigm shift occurred at the end of the eighteenth century that is marked in part by new conceptualizations of literature, criticism, and culture itself.

19. Among Oscar Wilde's many well known statements on related topics are these: "As a method Realism is a complete failure, and the two things that every artist should avoid are modernity of form and modernity of subject matter"; "Life goes faster than Realism, but Romanticism is always in front of life" (319).

20. Along similar lines, Bruce Haley's *The Healthy Body and Victorian Culture* argues that "in their sports, however, Victorians turned play into work, investing it

with just those higher meanings Ruskin claimed it lacked . . . reconciling the plea-sure of bodily self-awareness with the duty of moral self-improvement" (258).

21. Huizinga summarizes his definition of play as follows: "Play is a voluntary activity or occupation executed within certain fixed limits of time and place accord-ing to rules freely accepted but absolutely binding, having its aim in itself and accompanied by a feeling of tension, joy and the consciousness that it is 'different' from 'ordinary life'" (28). The other most frequently cited general study of play is Roger Caillois's *Man, Play and Games*, which delineates four major types of play: agon (interpreted as conflict *and* merit), alea (chance, as in gambling), mimicry, and ilinx (vertigo, as in spinning games and drunkenness). For a general, com-parative critique of Huizinga and Caillois, see Jacques Ehrmann's "Homo Ludens Revisited."

22. Ronald Bogue argues a similar point in his introduction to *Mimesis in Contemporary Theory*, 4. Perhaps the most famous (or infamous) remark concerning the importance of realism was made by Bertolt Brecht in "Against Georg Lukàcs": "Realism is an issue not only for literature: it is a major political, philosophical and practical issue and must be handled and explained as such — as a matter of general human interest" (45).

23. In this regard, Christopher Prendergast notes in *The Order of Mimesis* that one of the casualties of what he describes as the "war" between postmodern critical schools has been "the notion of mimesis" (1). In *Realism and Revolution*, Sandy Petrey takes a similar stand: "My point of departure is the recent critical assault on representational categories long identified with the achievements of realist prose; I argue that the dilemmas of representation, far from being realism's blind spot, figure among its major narrative strategies" (1). I agree with Petrey. I also agree with Linda Hutcheon's observation in *A Poetics of Postmodernism* that "[t]he link between realism and the ideology of liberal humanism is a historically validatable one . . . but the postmodern contesting of both is just as ideologically inspired, and considerably more ambivalent" (180).

24. Bulwer-Lytton quoted in Richard Stang, *The Theory of the Novel in England 1850–1870*, 175. Lewes defines realism in opposition not to idealism, but to "falsism" ("Realism" 87). Thackeray opens *Pendennis* with the promise to deliver writing that "strives to tell the truth," for he writes, "If there is not that, there is nothing" (33).

25. David Lodge clarifies the Classical mimesis/diegesis distinction in *After Bakhtin*, 25–44.

26. With some similarity to Barthes, Hayden White's *The Content of the Form* analyzes the nineteenth-century disciplinization of history in relation to realist fic-tion as an attempt to "discipline history from fiction" while simultaneously effecting the "domestication of history" (65, 75).

27. Some theorists would argue that this same logic applies equally to a barom-eter in a scientific report, while I would argue for a distinction between "barometer" that is understood to have a concrete referent and "barometer" that is understood not to have a concrete referent. For one "barometer," people will carry their um-brellas, perhaps risking a naïve understanding of the nature of signification in order to stay dry. Of course, it is possible to understand signification *and* carry the um-brella. In this I agree with Ernest Laclau and Chantal Mouffe's argument in "Post-

Marxism without Apologies": "As we have seen, however, outside of any discursive context objects *do not have* being; they have only *existence*" (85).

28. See Smith, esp. 9–26. One of the clearest definitions of the "impartial spectator" appears on 129, n. For analyses similar to mine of the Smithian notion of sympathy see Jonas Barish's *Antitheatrical Prejudice*, esp. 243–55, and David Marshall's *Figure of Theater*, esp. 167–92.

29. Smith writes, for example: "When I endeavour to examine my own conduct, when I endeavour to pass sentence upon it, and either to approve or condemn it, it is evident, in all such cases, I divide myself, as it were, into two persons; and that I, the examiner and judge, represent a different character from that other I, the person whose conduct is examined into and judged of" (113). The same structure of *dédoublement* is replicated in sympathizing with and judging someone else.

30. For Bakhtin's specific uses of "play," refer to *The Dialogic Imagination*, 70, 237, 277, 308, 328, 333, 343, and 367.

31. Kristeva's *Desire in Language* (particularly the chapters "The Bounded Text" and "Word, Dialogue, and Novel") provides a series of overlapping definitions of "ambivalence." It is at once a dialogue between the metonymic and metaphorical linguistic axes of language (using Roman Jakobson's categories); an overthrow of the monological binarism of "0–1 logic" by a "0–2 poetic logic," which subverts the dogmatic, patriarchal truth-claim signified by the "1"; and a "permutation of the two spaces observed in the novelistic structure: dialogical space and monological space" (Kristeva 39, 41, 43). It should be noted that in one sense I read Kristeva against Kristeva here, since I apply her reading of Bakhtin to my reading of the realist novel while she sometimes claims — reductively, I think — that realism cannot be dialogical. Kristeva's dismissal of realism is not representative of Bakhtin's assessment, which is itself much more "ambivalent."

32. My understanding of the social word comes from multiple sources, but most specifically V. N. Voloshinov, *Marxism and the Philosophy of Language*; Daniel Cottom, *Social Figures*; Mikhail Bakhtin, *The Dialogic Imagination* (which uses the phrase "materiality of language" [323–24]); and Michel Foucault, *The Archaeology of Knowledge*, 215–37.

33. J. Hillis Miller makes a related observation in *The Form of Victorian Fiction* in his description of the "Quaker Oats box effect": "Just as the novel is a verbal structure which creates its own meaning in the play of its elements, so the reality of society is its existence as a linguistic or symbolic game which has the power to create and reveal its own foundation. . . . Imagination and reality are identical. It is the same on both sides of the mirror" (36). But there is an extremely important distinction to be made between Miller's understanding of play and mine. Both sides of the mirror are not the same; one has material existence, even if the meaning of it only can be known through signification. Miller's argument posits a universalized concept of "the text" in a way that denies social materiality.

34. With the latter part of this claim I only verify my membership in a long line of recent critics who argue in different ways for the constitutive force of literary texts in contributing to the construction of their social contexts. Among those are some of the most important recent studies in this area: Nancy Armstrong's *Desire and Domestic Fiction*; Daniel Cottom's *Social Figures*; Catherine Gallagher's *Industrial Reforma-*

tion of English Fiction 1832–1867; and Mary Poovey's *Uneven Development*. Among more recent studies in this vein, Joseph Childers's *Novel Possibilities* is exemplary.

35. For example, Wolfgang Iser writes in *The Fictive and the Imaginary*: "These doublings are brought about by play, it is play that forms the infrastructure of representation, for the latter is a figuration of what play reveals as the binding together of the incompatible" (294). Iser's use of "play" verges in places on an idealization reminiscent of Kant's play concept; if Iser avoids idealization it is because he does not lose sight of the phenomenology of reading as a material practice of individual readers. In *A Likely Story: Probability and Play in Fiction*, Robert Newsom develops a related if less sophisticated understanding of the text as play space.

36. This formulation bears distant similarity to Paul Ricoeur's distinction in "Mimesis and Representation" between "mimesis$_1$," "mimesis$_2$," and "mimesis$_3$."

Chapter 2. Gambling with Fortuna

1. The novels to which I refer in particular are, for Thackeray, *Barry Lyndon* and *Vanity Fair*; for Dickens, *The Old Curiosity Shop*, *Little Dorrit*, *Dombey and Son*, and *Our Mutual Friend*; for Eliot, *Middlemarch* and *Daniel Deronda*; and for Trollope, *Can You Forgive Her*, *The Duke's Children*, and *The Way We Live Now*. This is not to mention Thomas Hardy, in whose novels the issues that the figure of gambling emblematizes are generalized to an all-pervasive fatalism. Relevant works from other nations include Balzac's *Le peau de chagrin* and *Le Père Goriot*, Melville's *Confidence Man*, and, of course, Dostoevsky's *Gambler*. The evils of gambling also were pervasively represented in the melodramatic theater of the nineteenth century, as well as in didactic tracts published by such organizations as the Antigambling League.

2. I am aware that this represents a claim on the part of rationality and the vision of hindsight to control chance and randomness, a claim precariously similar to that which I identify and critique in George Eliot's texts. As Thomas Kavanagh writes in *Enlightenment and the Shadows of Chance*, "The premises sustaining contemporary condemnations of gambling — the supremacy of a reality independent of human volition, the triumph of the rational, the value of productive work, and the necessity of self-control — represent a heritage of the Enlightenment so fundamental to our understanding of the human situation that it has become all but impossible to think outside it" (37–38). This claim should raise questions in the first place about the central premise underlying studies such as Kavanagh's and my own: that systematic, historical investigation can uncover meaningful associations between, for instance, the novel and probability theory, or the novel and gambling, that could not have been produced "by the play of chance alone." Indeed, all "research" methodologies subscribe by definition to a belief that chance can and should be controlled in the pursuit of knowledge, truth, or reality. To the extent that we write from within a society and culture that are in part shaped by Enlightenment ideologies and, more recently, by the progressive, humanist, and liberal-intellectual ideologies of the nineteenth century, we cannot but reproduce antigambling discourse in the very form of our analyses. Given this unavoidable caveat, the current study nevertheless

strives to unpack some of the ideological encoding of nineteenth-century British antigambling discourses.

3. I have in mind George Levine, "Determinism and Responsibility"; E. A. McCobb, "*Daniel Deronda* as Will and Representation: George Eliot and Schopenhauer"; Bernard J. Paris, *Experiments in Life: George Eliot's Quest for Values*, esp. 114–127; John Reed, *Victorian Will*; Thomas Vargish, *The Providential Aesthetic in Victorian Fiction*; and Felicia Bonaparte's excellent *Will and Destiny: Morality and Tragedy in George Eliot's Novels*.

4. See, for example, Eliot, *Letters*, 2:48–49 and 6:166.

5. Levine, "Determinism and Responsibility," 358, makes a similar point.

6. I draw here on Bonaparte, 115–17.

7. See Levine, "Determinism and Responsibility," 355.

8. The not infrequent use of the term lot in Victorian fiction and particularly in relation to George Eliot's deterministic doctrine may take on added significance when one considers that gambling probably originated in the casting of "lots" as part of ancient religious ceremonies. Opposition to gambling on moral or religious grounds thus has a very long history, since the casting of lots outside of the ceremonial context was considered a sin—a playing with the divine prerogative. See Reuven Brenner and Gabrielle A. Brenner, *Gambling and Speculation: A Theory, a History, and a Future of Some Human Decisions*, 1–7. Eliot uses the figure of casting or being subject to one's lot at least seventeen times in *Middlemarch* alone.

9. Gillian Beer deftly analyzes the relationship between money and gossip in "Circulatory Systems: Money and Gossip in *Middlemarch*."

10. Wilkie Collins suggests this position in "Note Addressed to the Reader," the preface to *The Lady and the Law*. Collins provides an interesting foil to Eliot in this regard. This sort of approach to realism is exemplified in the extreme by Quentin Tarantino's film *Pulp Fiction*.

11. Some modernist and postmodern narrative forms strive to escape the desire for closure by ending indeterminately, but they arguably continue to draw on identifiable narrative conventions and end at some point, which therefore cannot avoid being determinate. Peter Brooks's *Reading for the Plot*, particularly "Narrative Desire," 37–61, is relevant to these considerations.

12. See Walter Benjamin, *Illuminations*, "On Some Motifs in Baudelaire," 155–201, esp. 177, 198.

13. On British lottery legislation, see John Ashton, *A History of English Lotteries*, as well as *The History of Gambling in England*, 238–41. Also see Brenner and Brenner, 7–18, 55–63.

14. The authority on nineteenth-century British gambling clubs and on William Crockford's Club in particular is Henry Blyth, *Hell and Hazard, or William Crockford versus the Gentlemen of England*. Though a few gambling clubs existed in London in the mid-eighteenth century and the health resort at Baden-Baden, Germany, had a casino by the 1760s, it was not until the 1820s or 1830s that the gambling club became fashionable, and not until the early 1860s, which is when Monte Carlo opened, that the casino became the recognized institution that it is today. See Alan Wykes, *Gambling*, 282–98.

15. On the infamous Derby of 1844 see Blyth, particularly "The Ultimate Scandal: Death by a Derby Favourite," 158–89.

16. On the effects of the 1845 Gaming Act see John Ashton, *Gambling*, 147–49; D. M. Downes. et al., *Gambling, Work and Leisure*, 29–43; and David C. Itzkowitz, "Victorian Bookmakers and Their Customers." On the 1853 Betting Houses Act see Ashton, *Gambling*, 213–15; Peter Bailey, *Leisure and Class in Victorian England*, 23–24; and Brenner and Brenner, 73.

17. I draw here on Itzkowitz, "The (Other) Great Evil: Gambling, Scandal, and the National Antigambling League."

18. On the rationalization of leisure, see particularly Bailey. Also see Brenner and Brenner, esp. "Gambling and Other Pastimes," 63–72. Also of general relevance to the institutionalization of lower-class recreations is Chris Waters, *British Socialists and the Politics of Popular Culture, 1884–1914*.

19. The same rhetoric is found in the 1819 Parliamentary debate on the lottery, as shown in John Ashton, *Gambling* 239.

20. Also see Ross McKibbin, "Working-Class Gambling in Britain, 1880–1939," and David Dixon, "'Class Law': The Street Betting Act of 1906."

21. Vernon lends support to this general claim; see *Money and Fiction*, 194. By "exchanges of capital," I intend to allude to the theory of "symbolic capital" developed by Pierre Bourdieu, specifically his distinctions in "Forms of Capital" between economic, social, and cultural capital. It is the exchange between these forms of capital that structures the plots of many mid-nineteenth-century British realist novels, and the primary source of tension is the characters' needs to convert one form of capital to another. While these concepts inform my thinking, I have chosen not to introduce them directly into this book, because the focus here is more on gambling as a form of play than on money and the exchange of capital.

22. The authoritative source on money as commodity is Karl Marx, esp. in *Capital*, 1:188–244.

23. As Elizabeth Deeds Ermarth remarks in this regard in *The English Novel in History, 1840–1895*: "Market-*places* may be old; but the market-*system*, which *'is a mechanism for sustaining and maintaining an entire society'* is a fairly recent invention, as new as the humanist conception of the species 'man,' as new as 'the profit motive,' and as new as the idea of gain conceived in terms of capital" (121).

24. My source for these commonly known dates is Vernon, *Money and Fiction*, 25. Also see Brian Murphy, *A History of the British Economy*, esp. 510–11, 612–18. Other sources from which I draw my understanding of the financial events of this period include Jonathan Baskin, "The Development of Corporate Financial Markets in Britain and the United States, 1600–1914"; Gillian Beer, "Circulatory Systems"; Patrick Brantlinger, *Fictions of State: Culture and Credit in Britain, 1694–1994*; John Reed, "A Friend to Mammon: Speculation in Victorian Literature"; Norman Russell, *The Novelist and Mammon: Literary Responses to the World of Commerce in the Nineteenth Century*; John Vernon, *Money and Fiction*; Igor Webb, *From Custom to Capital: The English Novel and the Industrial Revolution*; and Barbara Weiss, *The Hell of the English: Bankruptcy and the Victorian Novel*. One useful nineteenth-century source is the journalist David Morier Evans, who published revealing accounts of the financial crises of 1847–48 and 1857–58 within a year of each event.

25. The forming of the stock exchange is described in these terms in Ranald Michie, "Different in Name Only? The London Stock Exchange and Foreign Bourses, *c.* 1850–1914," 51. Also see Russell, esp. 25–42.

26. The following studies — each written from a different disciplinary or theoretical orientation and each excellent — analyze that major cultural paradigm shift within modern western societies that I adopt familiar terms in describing as the "bourgeois revolution" and the formation of "civil society": Howard Caygill, *Art of Judgement*; Michael McKeon, *The Origins of the English Novel, 1600–1740*; J. G. A. Pocock, *Virtue, Commerce, and History*; and Raymond Williams, *Culture and Society, 1780–1950*.

27. See Walter Benn Michaels, *The Gold Standard and the Logic of Naturalism: American Literature at the Turn of the Century*.

28. See James Thompson, *Models of Value*, esp. the chapter "Representation and Exchange," 15–86, as well as Michaels.

29. See Ann Fabian, "Speculation on Distress: The Popular Discourse of the Panics of 1837 and 1857," and Webb, *From Custom to Capital*, esp. 35.

30. I draw here on Henry G. Bohn, *The Hand-Book of Games* (1850), "Whist, in Four Parts." The authors represented in Bohn use the term "dummy" rather than "dead" hand, but I have heard contemporary bridge players use the term "dead hand" and so am assuming a similarity.

31. The discussion here of charity in relation to the system of noblesse oblige draws on Robert J. Werlin, *The English Novel and the Industrial Revolution*.

32. Similarly, the insurance industry only began to be considered a legitimate business in the nineteenth century, though it retained its eighteenth-century reputation as "gambling proper" (John Ashton, *Gambling*, 275). Also see Russell's chapter "Insurance Promoters: Dickens, Thackeray, and the West Middlesex Fraud," 85–103.

33. For analysis of the difference between gambling, speculation, and investment, see Brenner and Brenner, "Gambling, Speculation, Insurance — Why They Were Confused and Condemned," 90–112.

34. In *The Civilized Imagination: A Study of Ann Radcliffe, Jane Austen, and Sir Walter Scott*, Daniel Cottom develops the idea of the aristocratic "criterion of disinterest" by which all but those who financially can afford to appear to be above self-interest are excluded from any test of objectivity.

35. I obviously follow Marx at this juncture, as does Igor Webb here in a similar vein: "If money appears from a bank, in a wonderful way, increasing and multiplying as if by the medium of a wonderful spell; and if money also translates into whatever one may want, also as it were by magic, then the very existence of social relationships can be ignored. The human relationship between landlord and laborer or between owner and worker gets pushed out of sight; and the wealth produced by labor similarly becomes invisible" (35).

36. For example, the first definition of play as a noun in Samuel Johnson's dictionary (1785 ed.) is "Action not imposed; not work; dismission from work," a definition that persisted at least into the dictionaries of the 1880s, such as those edited by Robert Gordon Latham. By comparison, twentieth-century dictionaries generally no longer define play through its opposition to work.

37. The language and practices of the stock exchange are interesting in them-

selves and deserve more attention than I can give them here. One buys "futures" on commodities that one generally never intends to possess. This is truly a bet on an imaginary future. "Options" on futures are even one step more removed from any tangible basis: a bet on a bet.

Chapter 3. Performing the Self

1. My understanding of theatricality is indebted to the authors mentioned. Elizabeth Burns's *Theatricality: A Study of Convention in the Theatre and in Social Life* is the most thorough theorization. It suggests the following hypotheses: (i) the difference between theatricality on the stage and in social life is one of degree; (ii) theatricality is a boundary-marking category that separates and joins social contexts, distinguishing the authentic from the "merely theatrical," the real from the unreal; (iii) what is defined as theatrical is entirely context-specific and occurs when behavior is perceived as having crossed a boundary of protocol, convention, or manners; (iv) each subject is simultaneously a performer and a spectator in society, though whether one perceives oneself or is perceived by others to be in the position of the performer or the spectator at a given time is crucial; and, by implication, (v) the inherent theatricality of social roles may be perceptible only to those who are positioned outside the context within which that behavior is "normal." These observations summarize what may be one consensus definition of "theatricality" among late twentieth-century theorists. It would be easy but misguided to assume that they describe the very theatricality toward which Victorian antitheatrical rhetoric was directed. I strive here to avoid that error — as well as the error of assuming a clichéd understanding of the Victorians as prudishly antitheatrical — by allowing Victorian reactions to and applications of the figure of the theater to speak through nineteenth-century discourses.

2. Among the many essays on theatricality and *Mansfield Park*, the most useful I have found are Joseph Litvak, "The Infection of Acting: Theatricals and Theatricality in *Mansfield Park*," and David Marshall, "True Acting and the Language of Real Feeling: *Mansfield Park*." On theatricality and *Daniel Deronda* see Carol de Saint Victor, "Acting and Action: Sexual Distinctions in *Daniel Deronda*"; John Stokes, "Rachel's 'Terrible Beauty': An Actress among the Novelists"; and Brian Swann, "George Eliot and the Play: Symbol and Metaphor of the Drama in *Daniel Deronda*." Mark Seltzer's *Henry James and the Art of Power*, 25–58, provides a reading of Henry James's *Princess Casamassima* in terms of the theatricality of surveillance. Gillian Beer's "'Coming Wonders': Uses of Theatre in the Victorian Novel" usefully discusses theatricality in George Eliot's novels.

3. Some explanation of my decision not to include Charles Dickens in this study is warranted, given the obvious suitability of Dickens's novels to my subject areas. Indeed, I could have focused the entire study on Dickens: gambling and stock speculation figure prominently in *The Old Curiosity Shop* and *Our Mutual Friend*, for instance; Dickens famously was involved with the theater, and his novels not only include many scenes of performance but are themselves highly theatrical both thematically and formally; also, *David Copperfield* is one of the great *Kunstlerroman*s of

the nineteenth century, lending itself to the sort of analysis that I apply to *Pendennis* and *Alton Locke* in chapter four. This is not to mention the continual concern in Dickens's novels with issues of children's play and with the play of the imagination. But it is in part this obviousness of Dickens as a choice that mitigated against my choosing him. While Dickens's novels are more radically theatrical than either Brontë's or Eliot's, they are in a sense less concerned with the issues surrounding theatricality. Eliot struggled with theatricality in ways that either did not trouble or simply did not interest Dickens. This also is to say that Eliot struggled more and more self-consciously with questions of realism. I was interested in the current study with identifying and analyzing that struggle. I judged Dickens to be less representative of the issues on which I wanted to concentrate. Thus I admit that Dickens may represent a boundary to the applicability of the findings of this study, or at least that his writings remain to be analyzed relative to these specific concerns. A good deal of preliminary research exists already: On Dickens and gambling see G. Cordery, "The Gambling Grandfather in *The Old Curiosity Shop*"; Robert Dingley, "Playing the Game: The Continental Casinos and the Victorian Imagination"; and Sue Zemka, "From the Punchmen to Pugin's Gothic: The Broad Road to a Sentimental Death in *The Old Curiosity Shop*." On Dickens and the theater see Jonas Barish, *The Antitheatrical Prejudice*, 369–75; Barbara Hardy, "Dickens and the Passions"; Martin Meisel, *Realizations: Narrative, Pictorial, and Theatrical Arts in Nineteenth-Century England*; Deborah M. Vlock, "Dickens, Theater, and the Making of a Victorian Reading Public"; Leigh Woods, "Dickens and Theatre: Recent Publications"; and the collection of essays in Carol Hanbery MacKay, ed., *Dramatic Dickens*. More general studies include Ella Kusnetz, "'This Leaf of My Life': Writing and Play in *Great Expectations*," and Mark M. Hennelly, Jr., "Dickens's Praise of Folly: Play in *The Pickwick Papers*."

4. As a qualification of this claim, it should be noted that certain formal characteristics of *Felix Holt* appear to have been derived from Classical tragedy, which George Eliot was studying at the time she wrote the novel. Relevant discussion appears in Fred C. Thompson's "*Felix Holt* as Classical Tragedy" and Peter Coveney's introduction to the novel. "Theatricality" as such has not been applied previously to *Felix Holt* to my knowledge.

5. Gillian Beer in "'Coming Wonders'" was perhaps the first to point out that Victorian novels frequently draw upon the very theatricality that they scapegoat. Also in this regard see Litvak, "The Infection of Acting," 348, 352.

6. See Brontë, *Villette*, 512–17. Victorian antitheatrical anti-Catholicism points back to the Puritan closing of the theaters in 1642 and to the origins of what would come to be called "Protestant individualism." The Protestant model of individual faith was necessarily antitheatrical, since salvation rested on nothing more or less than the sincerity with which the individual opened him/herself to God. To "put on" a role that was not one's own risked not only hypocrisy but damnation, since God's gaze saw *within*, presumably to the "authentic self" that He created. The only rational defense against the sins of falseness or insincerity was to develop a constantly vigilant inward gaze that might preempt God's gaze of judgment. On the other hand, early Puritans undoubtedly had more than one motive for their antitheatricalism, as Jonas Barish argues: "No doubt . . . serious economic motives underlay the

Puritan hatred for the theater. The theater symbolized, or was taken to symbolize, a whole complex of attitudes anathema to the sober burgesses from whose bands the London magistrates were elected. . . . The theater stood for pleasure, for idleness, for the rejection of hard work and thrift as the roads to salvation" (114).

7. For a genealogical analysis of the "theater metaphor," or "*theatrum mundi,*" in relation to the early-modern development of market capitalism, see Jean-Christophe Agnew, *Worlds Apart,* 14–16, 55–56. Agnew's analysis traces the historical relationship between "the practical liquidity of the commodity form and the imaginative liquidity of the theatrical form" (11–12). This thesis is a counterpoint, or logically complementary paradox, to Barish, 114. Perhaps nineteenth-century realist novels scapegoated the theatrical in part to draw attention away from the inherent parallels between theatricality and market capitalism.

8. Nancy Armstrong's *Desire and Domestic Fiction* is relevant here, especially the discussion of the use of Shakespeare in *Shirley* (214–20). Also, Marianne Novy's *Engaging with Shakespeare: Responses of George Eliot and Other Women Novelists* offers a thorough analysis of responses to and uses of Shakespeare by Victorian (and twentieth-century) women novelists.

9. For a related discussion of the reasons for the Victorian preference for reading aloud over dramatic performance, see Alison Byerly, "From Schoolroom to Stage: Reading Aloud and the Domestication of Victorian Theater."

10. As Joseph Donohue notes in *Theatre in the Age of Kean* (and quoting the language of the Licensing Act), it "stipulated a fine of £50 for anyone convicted of acting for 'hire, gain, or reward' any play or theatrical performance not previously allowed by royal patent or licensed by the Lord Chamberlain," who also exercised censorship power over any prospective dramatic production (13). The legitimate / illegitimate distinction is not limited to the eighteenth or nineteenth centuries; see, for example, Allardyce Nicoll, *A History of English Drama, 1660–1900,* 3:227, which uncritically reproduces that distinction.

11. My thesis about the cycle in British theater between the 1737 Act and its 1843 rescinding is supported by Michael Booth and coauthors in *The Revels History of Drama in English*. vol. 6, 1750–1880, which theorizes a "decline cycle" in British theater beginning in the mid-eighteenth century and concluding in the 1880s or 1890s. Of the end of that cycle Booth writes: "In a sense the wheel had come full circle again. . . . The intervening years had seen the theatre pass, for the first time since the medieval period, under a rule that was essentially popular; it then passed out again into middle-class control, and all aspects of class composition, behaviour and taste among theatre audiences, as well as of the drama itself, must be related to this primary sequence of events" (Booth et al. 28).

12. As Terry Castle is well aware, her formulation of this change echoes Mikhail Bakhtin, as in a passage that Castle cites: "On the one hand the state encroached upon festive life and turned it into a parade; on the other hand these festivities were brought into the home and became part of the family's private life. The privileges which were formerly allowed the marketplace were more and more restricted. The carnival spirit, with its freedom, its utopian character oriented toward the future, was gradually transformed into a mere holiday mood" (Bakhtin, *Rabelais,* 33).

13. My primary source on the history of private theatricals in England is Sybil Rosenfeld, *Temples of Thespis: Some Private Theatres and Theatricals in England and Wales, 1700–1820*. Also see James S. Hodson, *Private Theatricals: Being a Practical Guide for the Home Stage*, and T. H. Vail Motter, "Garrick and the Private Theatres."

14. Holcroft borrowed the plot of *A Tale of Mystery* from one of the fathers of French melodrama, Guilbert de Pixérécourt. For further reading on the apparently overnight (though of course long-prepared) rise of melodrama, see Donohue, *Kean*, 105–26. For an analysis of the French origins of melodrama and its impact on the British novel, see Peter Brooks's *Melodramatic Imagination*. I am indebted generally for details of British theater history used throughout this chapter to the following sources: Marc Baer, *Theatre and Disorder in Late Georgian London*; Michael Booth et al., *The Revels History of Drama in English*; Michael Booth, *Preface to English Nineteenth-Century Theatre*; Donohue, *Kean*; and John R. Stephens, *The Profession of the Playwright: British Theatre, 1800–1900*.

15. Brooks, *The Melodramatic Imagination*, 11–12, offers a related description of melodrama.

16. I draw here on James Naremore's *Acting in the Cinema*, esp. 52–60.

17. George Eliot also criticized melodramatic effect, as Brian Swann observes: "Writing in the *Westminister Review* in 1856 about a novel of Charles Reade, George Eliot says that 'the habit of writing for the stage misleads him into seeking after those exaggerated contrasts and effects which are accepted as a sort of rapid symbolism by a theatrical audience, but are utterly out of place in a fiction.' At once, we can see her dissatisfaction with theatrical exaggeration, and we get a hint at her own symbolic method" (191).

18. Scott is quoted here by John O. Hayden in *Scott: The Critical Heritage*, 114. The review by Scott was published anonymously in the April 1817 *Quarterly Review*. It criticizes earlier novels by a particular author by way of praising the two more recent ones. The later novels are commended for their "air of distinct reality" and rendering of events and characters "copied from nature," while the earlier novels are said to smack of "the showman," to have a "dramatic shape," and to situate the reader in the position of the "audience at a theatre" (qtd. in Hayden, 114). It is particularly appropriate that the reviewed author is Sir Walter Scott and that the reviewer is putting on a theatrical persona.

19. Also in this regard see Donohue, *Kean* (125), and Martha Vincinus, "'Helpless and Unfriended': Nineteenth-Century Domestic Melodrama" (141).

20. Beer, "'Coming Wonders,'" provides a more detailed contextualization of "the decline" from the perspective of the writers of the time than I do, citing for example an 1834 work by F. M Jones entitled *On the Causes of the Decline in the Drama*.

21. This claim is supported by Booth et al., 50, and generally by Stephens. For further documentation of economic pressures on theaters and playwrights, see Booth et al., 9, 18–19, 46–56. I also note that Victorian novelists, Charles Dickens and George Eliot among them, did pen plays, though never with success on the scale of their novels. Eliot's failed struggle to complete *The Spanish Gypsy* is instructive in this regard.

22. For discussion of Victorian attitudes toward actresses and prostitutes and

the assumed link between them, see Tracy C. Davis, "Actresses and Prostitutes in Victorian London." Also relevant is Donohue, "Women in the Victorian Theatre: Images, Illusions, Realities."

23. Baer also notes that the OP riots took on the form of the drama over which the protest was staged, themselves becoming melodramatic. Partly as a result, they failed to effect any significant, long-term change in the institutional structures controlling cultural production and consumption. It may be that any social protest recognizable as such is liable to be seen as "theatrical." Social protests that take on a theatrical character may simultaneously be subversive *and* recuperative. They may pose a serious threat to the dominant order and, at the same time, function as a safety value, ritually releasing tensions in such a way that effectively sustains the very order against which they are a protest. Theatricalization of class-based movements might represent a desire not to eradicate such movements but to perpetuate them as an archaic *style* of protest, the symbolic violence of which is more desirable than physical violence. These issues become relevant in the readings here of the riot scenes in *Shirley* and *Felix Holt*.

24. On the conditions for playwrights in the nineteenth century see especially Stephens, *The Profession of the Playwright*. Booth et al. also discuss nineteenth-century copyright law and its effects on playwrights (46–56).

25. Laura Brown, in *English Dramatic Form, 1660–1760: An Essay in Generic History* (184), is the only other critic of whom I am aware who develops this argument. According to her analysis, the need arose in the eighteenth century for a new "moral form"; drama failed as a vehicle for this form while the novel proved to be ideally suited. Her definition of "moral form" (see 145) is very similar to a prevalent definition of nineteenth-century novelistic realism. I am indebted to Brown's work.

26. At the risk of producing yet more jargon, I coin the term *distanciation* to describe a specific process of subject construction by which a cultural medium positions subjects to be the ideal receivers and consumers of that medium's ideological material. This concept obviously is indebted to Louis Althusser's theory of "interpellation" in *Lenin and Philosophy*. In one sense, distanciation is the opposite of identification, but at the same time it is the very positioning required in order for identification to take place. I draw here on the theory of "identification" as developed in Jean-Louis Baudry, "Ideological Effects of the Basic Cinematographic Apparatus." Baudry makes a distinction between "secondary identification," which is identification with the subject positions of characters, and "primary identification," which is identification with "the apparatus" itself, the seemingly omniscient, world-generating position occupied by the camera's "central location" (540). To the extent that this theory is both defensible and applicable to the realist novel, which is open for debate, then the relevant "apparatus" is the novelistic text itself.

27. To say that Felix Holt represents a "middle-class subject" is not to subscribe to a simplistic definition of "middle-class" or to a reductive formula for reading the novel's function as an ideological vehicle. As my reading of *Felix Holt* should demonstrate, there was and is no monolithic "middle class." The novel's customary model of society, with which it appears the character of Felix is aligned, can only be characterized if one is willing to break up and recombine elements of what generally are described as "aristocratic ideology," "bourgeois ideology," and "working-class ideology."

28. It is interesting in this regard to note that in *Felix Holt* the de-theatricalization of Esther by Felix appears to amount to the domestication of the female character and a demonstration of the efficacy of masculine regulatory authority. However, the effect of Felix's domestication of Esther is the domestication of Felix (and the implied reader). More accurately, the domestication of Felix is presented as Felix's domestication of Esther. In other words, domestication masquerades as the exercise of masculine power, which would be an effective way to make the figure of theatricality serve a generalized process of domestication in a way that would appear acceptable within a dominant, patriarchal order.

29. This formulation draws in familiar ways on Michel Foucault's *Discipline and Punish* and *The History of Sexuality: An Introduction*. On spectatorship and surveillance in relation to Victorian fiction, see D. A. Miller's *The Novel and the Police*, Alexander Welsh's *George Eliot and Blackmail*, and Mark Seltzer's *Henry James and the Art of Power*. But, as I argue, the original source here is Adam Smith's *Theory of Moral Sentiments*, published in 1759.

30. For an analysis of the figure of the sickroom in Victorian fiction, see Daniel Cottom, *Social Figures: George Eliot, Social History, and Literary Representation*, 141–60.

31. I use the term performative in the sense developed by Judith Butler in *Gender Trouble: Feminism and the Subversion of Identity*; see esp. 24–25, 115–16, 134–41. Butler is preceded by Barbara Johnson's "Poetry and Performative Language: Mallarmé and Austin" and, of course, by J. L. Austin's *How to Do Things with Words*. For a recent response to Butler in relation to Victorian theatricality, see Rebecca F. Stern, "Moving Parts and Speaking Parts: Situating Victorian Antitheatricality."

32. On the psychoanalytic definition of hysteria, see Joseph Breuer and Sigmund Freud, *Studies on Hysteria*, or for a more digested version, J. Laplanche and J.-B. Pontalis, *The Language of Psycho-Analysis*. Tania Modleski also works with the concept of the hysterisized text in *Feminism without Women: Culture and Criticism in a "Postfeminist" Age*. At one point she describes it as an effect of "the weight of the not-said" (137).

33. For the coming true of the "dead face" as providential sign, see *Daniel Deronda* 738, 743, 753, 756, 758, 761.

34. For a counterpoint to this last claim, see Nina Auerbach's "Secret Performances," which argues that George Eliot theatrically orchestrated a persona, "arrang[ing] her life as a continual public presentation, eliciting in its majesty a devotional awe that Dickens never received" (254).

35. Cottom, *Social Figures*, 141–60, analyzes the linkage between sympathy, suffering, and the definition of a universalized culture within nineteenth-century middle-class humanist discourse. Marshall, *The Figure of Theater*, 167–240, offers a thorough reading of the figure of sympathy in Adam Smith's *Theory of Moral Sentiments* and Eliot's *Daniel Deronda*. I am indebted both to Cottom and to Marshall. Also see Barish, 243–55.

36. One could argue that the text's uneasiness about Daniel's overabundant sympathy manifests itself as an implicit indictment of his imposition of it upon the female characters. If one adopts the logic developed by Stephen Greenblatt in *Renaissance Self-Fashioning*, then Deronda's "act of imaginative generosity" in sympathy might be interpreted as "the transformation of another's reality into a manipula-

ble fiction" and "the mystification of manipulation as disinterested empathy" (227, 228, 231). While this reading admittedly stretches Greenblatt thin, Daniel's insistent sympathy toward Gwendolen—exercised as moral instruction *and* sublimated sexual desire—might be read as a form of infiltration and domination.

37. Christian Metz, "The Imaginary Signifier," elaborates on Baudry as follows: "In other words, the spectator *identifies with himself*, with himself as a pure act of perception (as wakefulness, alertness): as the condition of possibility of the perceived and hence as a kind of transcendental subject, which comes before every *there is*" (253). Also in this regard see Metz, "Story/Discourse."

38. My primary source in this paragraph for details of theater history is Baer, but the changes I identify are noted variously by other theater historians such as Booth, Donohue, and Nicoll.

39. Support for this claim comes from Donohue, *Kean*," 105–26; Booth, *Preface*, 26–27; and Booth et al., 33–35.

40. Brooks, *Melodramatic Imagination*, describes what amounts to a melodramatization of the novel, while I am arguing for a novelization of the theater in roughly the same period. I view these positions as two sides of the same coin.

Chapter 4. Theorizing the Aesthetic Citizen

1. Aesthetic theory comes of age as a discrete area of inquiry in the eighteenth century. Representative British works include the earl of Shaftesbury's *Enquiry Concerning Virtue or Merit* (1688), Edmund Burke's *Philosophical Enquiry into the Origin of Our Ideas of the Sublime and Beautiful* (1756), David Hume's *Of the Standard of Taste* (1757), Adam Smith's *Theory of Moral Sentiments* (1759), and H. H. Kames's *Elements of Criticism* (1762).

2. See my discussion in chapter one and in footnotes 13 and 14 to that chapter of Derrida's use of play. As I argue there, one need not subscribe to a familiar, simplistic reading of his "*jeu*" as "free play" in order to observe that all of his coined words are not only play-derived but are synonyms for play as Derrida himself understands it. Such passages as this one from *Speech and Phenomena* illustrate the point: "The concept of *play* [*jeu*] remains beyond this opposition [between speculative philosophy and empirical thought]; on the eve and aftermath of philosophy, it designates the unity of chance and necessity in an endless calculus" (135). He similarly defines "*différance*" in terms of play: "What we note as *différance* will thus be the movement of play that 'produces' . . . these differences, these effects of difference [between signifier and signified]" (141). The same is true for his definition of "supplement" in *Writing and Difference*: "This field [writing, signification] is in effect that of *play*, that is to say, a field of infinite substitutions. . . . [T]his movement of play, permitted by the lack or absence of a center or origin, is the movement of *supplementarity*" (289). I handle Derrida's use of play with an awareness of his responses, in the afterword to *Limited Inc* and elsewhere, to those who would reduce his theories to an advocacy for unlimited free-play (see 115–16). My claim (following Peter De Bolla's thesis about the figure of the sublime) is that play is the necessary aporia out of which Derrida's theory produces itself.

3. Among recent studies are Peter De Bolla's *Discourse of the Sublime: Readings in History, Aesthetics, and the Subject* and Frances Ferguson's *Solitude and the Sublime: Romanticism and the Aesthetics of Individuation*. Both are excellent, though they also represent recent critical fascination with the sublime at the expense of attention to the more pervasive figure of the beautiful and the more fundamental figure of play. I also note that while theorists as diverse as Kant, Nietzsche, Gadamer, and Derrida use play extensively as an aesthetic concept, very little critical analysis of such uses of play in aesthetic theory exists. Most of the secondary analyses of play as an aesthetic concept that I have found (for instance, the essays by Hilde Hein or M. C. Nahm) are too impressionistic to be useful.

4. In this regard also see Andrew Bowie, *Aesthetics and Subjectivity: From Kant to Nietzsche*, esp. 253.

5. Caygill identifies a discourse of what is labeled "perfect rights" in Francis Hutcheson's *Inquiry into the Origin of Our Ideas of Beauty and Virtue* (1725). These rights are expressed in the eighteenth century as "respect for property and honouring of contracts" (58). I would argue that the rights *to* objects constitute, at the same time, the rights *of* objects; the parallel here is between the autonomous or "free" commodity and the autonomous or universal art object.

6. For instance, despite the transcendental strains in Carlyle's writings and the ambiguity of the author's attitude toward the idealism of Diogenes Teufelsdrockh in *Sartor Resartus*, the "editor" of that work makes statements such as this: "Thus, in answer to a cry for solid pudding, whereof there is the most urgent need, comes, epigrammatically enough, the invitation to a wash of quite fluid *Aesthetic Tea!*" (133). John Ruskin proposed the term theoria in order to distance his work from what he perceived to be the tainted sensuality of continental aesthetics; see "Of the Theoretic Faculty as concerned with the Pleasure of Sense," *MP* II 35–36. For a consideration of the debt of nineteenth-century British aesthetic theory to German thinkers and of the lag between German conception and British adoption of key concepts, see Rosemary Ashton, *The German Idea: Four English Writers and the Reception of German Thought, 1800–1860*. Ashton argues that "it was Germany, with its pioneering methods in philosophy, history, and aesthetics, which contributed most to English thinking in the later nineteenth century" (2).

7. Kant 173–74.45. Citations to *Critique of Judgment*, translated by Werner S. Pluhar, are made parenthetically throughout in the following format: the page number is listed first and is separated by a period from the section number. The section numbers are those assigned by Kant. If in lowercase roman numerals, they are from Kant's introduction; if in arabic numerals, they are from the main body of the text. The interjections enclosed in brackets within passages quoted from the third *Critique* are written by the translator unless otherwise noted.

8. Reference is made to the following pages/sections in this order: 236.61, 261–64.68, 270.72, and 282.75.

9. This claim is supported by Elinor S. Shaffer's "Illusion and Imagination: Derrida's Parergon and Coleridge's Aid to Reflection: Revisionary Readings of Kantian Formalist Aesthetics." Shaffer goes further than I do in arguing that in *The Truth in Painting* Derrida misrepresents Kant's use of the term parergon and that, in effect, Kant understood Derrida long before Derrida (mis)understood Kant.

10. The interjections in brackets in this passage are mine. For the translator's rationale for translating *darstellen* as "presentation," see 14.ii, note 17. For Kant's definition of the imagination, see 30.vii. For discussion in the third *Critique* of "determinate" as opposed to "indeterminate" concepts, see 37.ix and 152.36. Also in this regard see Pluhar's "Translator's Introduction" to the third *Critique*, xxxiv, xl, and lvii-lviii.

11. See Kant 73.15, 84.17, and 92.22.

12. My argument here is indebted to Pluhar, "Translator's Introduction," ciii.

13. The Kantian concept of "negative pleasure" bears obvious similarities to Freud's definition of the "pleasure principle," or, rather, Freudian theory owes a debt to the eighteenth-century discourse of the sublime.

14. Derrida, in "Economimesis," theorizes much more thoroughly than I do here a distinction within Kantian aesthetics between "pleasure" and "enjoyment." In the same essay, he draws out one of the secondary uses of the figure of play in the third *Critique*, which is represented in this widely noted passage: "*Art* is likewise distinguished from craft. The first is also called *free art*, and the second could also be called *mercenary art*. We regard free art [as an art] that could only turn out purposive (i.e., succeed) if it is play, in other words, *an* occupation that is agreeable on its own account; mercenary art we regard as labor" (43.171). This distinction by Kant, and Derrida's development of it, might be relevant to analysis of Caygill's *Art of Judgment*, Ruskin's anti-Kantian theories of the work of the artist, and Thackeray's portrayal in *Pendennis* of the artist's vocation, but I have chosen not to enlist it in the current study.

15. More thorough treatments of Schiller's thought are provided by Eva Schaper's "Toward the Aesthetic: A Journey with Friedrich Schiller"; Mihai Spariosu's chapter on Schiller in *Dionysus Reborn* (53–65); and Terry Eagleton's excellent discussion in *The Ideology of the Aesthetic* (102–19). Peter Brooks's essay "Aesthetics and Ideology—What Happened to Poetics?" argues eloquently for a reassessment of Schiller's liberatory poetics.

16. Schiller's recognition of the body appears in his treatment of the play drive as originating in part from animal play, which in turn is produced by an excess of physical/psychical energy. Thus his work appears to be a precursor of Herbert Spencer's theory in *The Principles of Psychology* ("Aesthetic Sentiments," 627–48) that play results from a "surplus of energy," as well as of Freud's model of the psyche in *Beyond the Pleasure Principle* (1–36) as an economy for the regulation of "unpleasurable tension."

17. For example, René Wellek's *Immanuel Kant in England, 1793–1838*, traces Coleridge's familiarity with Kant back to 1801 and identifies the specific sites within the *Biographia Literaria* and other works where Kant's influence is evident (70). Coleridge's copy of A. F. M. Willich's *Elements of Critical Philosophy: containing a concise account of its original tendency; a view of all the works published by its founder, Professor Immanuel Kant, and a glossary of terms and phrases* (1798) is preserved with Coleridge's marginal annotations in the British Museum (21). Shaffer (148) and Ashton (35–39) support these claims as well. Also see Roy Park, "Coleridge and Kant: Poetic Imagination and Practical Reason."

18. There has been an ongoing debate over Coleridge's apparent plagiarism of

the writings of German philosophers who had not yet been translated into English, particularly F. W. Schelling. Coleridge's son, Henry Nelson Coleridge, attempts to expiate his father in his introduction to the 1871 *Complete Works*.

19. Kelly's "Homo Aestheticus" carries this argument forward to the late twentieth century with a critique of postmodern celebrations of play, which Kelly likewise ties to the economics of professionalization. She relates the postmodern rediscovery of play-related concepts to the increasingly unsympathetic social and economic context for academic professionals in the humanities: "Literary critics have wrapped themselves in the flag of radical 'play,' hoping to protect the tenuous economic space reserved for poetic subjectivity through the 'magical' properties of abstract play." Her contentious conclusion is that this maneuver has backfired, leaving literary critics only more alienated from society.

20. With Walter Pater and the Aesthetes of the last quarter of the century, play recognizably returns to the theorization of art; "art for art's sake" can be understand as a manifesto for play. John Wilcox's "The Beginnings of *l'Art Pour l'Art*" traces the Continental origins of that concept, analyzing its debt to and divergence from Kant.

21. See George P. Landow, *The Aesthetic and Critical Theories of John Ruskin*, 17. For Ruskin's summary dismissal of German idealism (coupled with an effective admission that he had not read any of the major works of German aesthetics), see "German Philosophy," *MP* III, 424–26. I note that in jumping from Schiller and Coleridge to Ruskin I am choosing to exclude consideration of early-nineteenth-century theorists of art and taste, most notably Archibald Alison and Richard Payne Knight. A more complete genealogy also would have to contend with Carlyle's *Sartor Resartus*, which is one of the most important treatises on aesthetics in the period.

22. The term theocentric is from Landow, *The Aesthetic and Critical Theories of John Ruskin*, 15. In this regard, see also Michael Sprinker's *Imaginary Relations: Aesthetics and Ideology in the Theory of Historical Materialism*, 11–34.

23. I draw here on John D. Rosenberg, *The Darkening Glass: A Portrait of Ruskin's Genius*, esp. "A Gothic Eden," 46–63.

24. See, for example, *MP* III, "Of the Real Nature of Greatness of Style," 299ff. For a discussion of Ruskin's objectivist theory of beauty and allegiance to scientific factuality, see Hilary Fraser, *Beauty and Belief: Aesthetics and Religion in Victorian Literature*, 121–32.

25. Ruskin was thoroughly familiar with Edmund Burke's *Philosophical Inquiry into the Origin of Our Ideas of the Sublime and Beautiful* (1756), though apparently not with Kant's use of the sublime. On Ruskin's response to the sublime, see Landow, 145, 239, and the chapter "Ruskin's Theory of the Sublime," 183–220. David Robertson, "Mid-Victorians amongst the Alps," analyzes Victorian responses to the sublime.

26. I invoke Mikhail Bakhtin's concept of "carnival." Ruskin addresses the carnivalesque in his discussion of the Venetian festival of Fat Thursday, which originated in the twelfth century. See *SV* III, 192. For the characterization of the sportive grotesque in terms of parody, see Ruskin *SV* III, 172ff.

27. For a discussion of Ruskin's antisubjectivism, see Fraser, 122, 127–28, 182, and Landow, 89–90, 179.

28. See, for example, the opening of "The Quarry," *SV* I.

29. See Morris, particularly "How We Live, and How We Might Live" (565–87), "The Aims of Art" (587–602), "Useful Work versus Useless Toil" (603–23), and "A Factory as It Might Be" (646–54).

30. Compare Kant 43.171; Marx, *Economic and Philosophic Manuscripts of 1844*, "Estranged Labour," 70–81, and *The Grundrisse*, 252–21, 292–93.

31. In addition to Landow's thorough discussion of Ruskin's loss of faith and its effect on his writing, see Fraser, 112ff.

32. My isolation of this passage from "Work" perhaps is unfair to Ruskin, since the piece also attacks aristocratic forms of "play," such as gambling and war, and recognizes the inequality of social conditions. Indeed, "Work" offers a complex Victorian perspective on the issue of play-versus-work across classes, of which I choose not to offer a more complete reading here.

33. The only other mid-Victorian text of which I am aware that focalizes the figure of play almost to the extent that *Culture and Anarchy* does is *The Gay Science* (1866), written by Arnold's less-known contemporary E. S. Dallas. Dallas criticizes the cult of "self-culture" as selfish and alienating (304–6).

34. Ongoing debates, both within and outside academia, about multiculturalism and political correctness are testimony to the currency of issues of culture. Arnold's *Culture and Anarchy* has become emblematic in certain circles for elitism and cultural-centricism and in other circles for the type of solution to cultural anarchy that contemporary society needs more than did Victorian society. The range of these perspectives is represented, though not necessarily in a balanced proportion, in the critical essays that accompany the edition of *Culture and Anarchy* that I use here. See particularly Maurice Cowling, "One-and-a-Half Cheers for Matthew Arnold"; Gerald Graff, "Arnold, Reason, and Common Culture"; Samuel Lipman, "Why Should We Read *Culture and Anarchy*?"; and Stephen Marcus, "*Culture and Anarchy* Today."

35. For reference to the body or to animality, see *CA* 26, 38, 88, 103, 105, 127. Daniel Bivona, *Desire and Contradiction: Imperial Visions and Domestic Debates in Victorian Literature*, analyzes the nineteenth-century British "population crisis," heralded by Thomas Robert Malthus's *Essay on Population* (1798).

36. For an analysis of the Victorian metaphor of growth with particular reference to Matthew Arnold, see Lawrence Starzyk's "The Non-Poetic Foundations of Victorian Aesthetics." For a broader and more sophisticated treatment of the same issues, see Cottom, *Social Figures*.

37. An adequate treatment of Arnold's four case examples would require detailed and lengthy historical contextualization, which does not seem justified in this study and, as I argue, is not really relevant to the point I wish to make. For a more thorough analysis of the four issues, see Wendell V. Harris, "Interpretive Historicism: 'Signs of the Times' and *Culture and Anarchy* in Their Contexts."

38. There may be a relationship between the relative spate in Britain of *Kunstlerromans* in the mid-Victorian period and the fact that "between 1840 and 1855 the number of artists recorded in the London Post Office Directory had risen from 168 to 636" (Denvir 26). Among the other *Kunstlerromans* that I considered for inclusion in this study were Charles Dickens's *David Copperfield* and Elizabeth Barrett

Browning's "novel poem" *Aurora Leigh*, the latter of which is, among other things, a sustained treatise on the aesthetics of play *(The Letters of Robert Browning and Elizabeth Barrett Browning, 1845–1846*, 1:31).

39. Concerning Thackeray's own struggles with artistic ambition and conflicting aesthetic beliefs, see Judith Fisher, "Siren and Artist: Contradiction in Thackeray's Aesthetic Ideal," esp. 411ff.

40. Citations to *Aurora Leigh* are by book and line numbers, not page number. Also see Browning 3.240. Of course, unlike Pen, Aurora redeems the image of the poet.

41. I realize that in Kant's theory aesthetic judgment and taste are not synonymous; I have blurred the boundary between the two here in order to make a general point. The distinctions between the discourse of judgment and the discourse of taste are analyzed in Caygill's *Art of Judgement*.

42. For an analysis of Thackeray's engagement in the "dignity of literature" controversy and its effect on the writing of *Pendennis*, see Craig Howes, "*Pendennis* and the Controversy on the 'Dignity of Literature.'" For Pen's belated defense of artistic sensibility, see *P* 434.

43. I would argue that the level of Thackeray's' identification with his protagonist is indicated by the fact that he places the words given to Pen in the preceding quotation also into the mouth of the narrator in the concluding paragraph of the novel: "If the best men do not draw the great prizes in life, we know it has been so settled by the Ordainer of the lottery. We own, and see daily, how the false and worthless live and prosper, while the good are called away, and the dear and young perish untimely," and so on (*P* 785).

44. The concept of "ho(m)mo-sexuality" is developed by Luce Irigaray in *This Sex Which Is Not One*.

45. On the Victorian "fable of character," see Cottom, *Social Figures* 28.

46. It is paradoxical that the character of Major Pendennis contributes at one point to the definition of the "fair play" that will be turned against him. Here, for example — and significantly in relationship to the issue of gambling — the Major tells Pen that "an English gentleman should play where the fashion is play, but should not elate or depress himself at the sport" (*P* 586).

47. It is interesting that Kingsley gives his character a taste in art that is antithetical to John Ruskin's in its preference for the works of the High Renaissance, of which Guido Reni's (1575–1643) portrait of St. Sebastian is only one example in the novel. Alton's visit to the art gallery invites comparison to Lucy Snowe's in *Villette*.

48. The passages quoted in this paragraph are all from the chapter of *Alton Locke* titled "Dream Land," 334–53, esp. 343–52.

49. Bivona, *Desire and Contradiction*, argues along similar lines for "an imaginative alliance between the imperial field and a discourse on 'play,'" although his work is concerned more with imperialism than with play and not with play as an aesthetic concept (ix). The findings of this study appear to support his claim that "imperialism is not simply either the good or bad conscience of nineteenth-century Britain, but rather, in an important sense, its unconscious, lurking under the surface of a variety of discourses" (viii).

50. According to *The Oxford English Dictionary*, artisan is defined precisely between the artist and the laborer: the first definition is "one who practices or cultivates an art; an artist"; the second definition is "one who is employed in any of the industrial arts." Late Victorian socialist utopianists such as William Morris similarly call for an aesthetic solution to the problems of alienated labour. See, for instance, "How We Live, How We Might Live," where Morris writes, "I have said so much as that the aim of art was to destroy the curse of labour by making work the pleasurable satisfaction of our impulse towards energy" (598). Though Morris represented the genuine interests of the working classes more successfully than did Ruskin or Kingsley, one need only visit the headquarters of a major U.S. corporation to see how thoroughly Morris's plans for the beautiful workers' factory of the future have been incorporated by owners.

51. "Subject effect" is a variation on the Althusserian concept of "interpellation" and the concept within film theory of "suture." See Althusser, 174–75; Jacques-Alain Miller, "Suture (Elements of the Logic of the Signifier)"; and Kaja Silverman, *The Subject of Semiotics*, 194–236.

52. Bernstein further argues, "Aesthetic modernism in philosophy is not only *about* art's alienation from the critique of modernity, but equally *is* that alienation and critique; it is the attempt by philosophy to liken itself to an aesthetic object in order that it can both discursively analyze the fate of art and truth while simultaneously being works to be judged (the way poems are works to be judged)" (9). What Bernstein offers as the antidote to aesthetic alienation and as the solution to the "absence of a truly political domain" is a return to art, art conceived as the experience of social particularity among individuals within a shared community. While largely in agreement, I remain cautious of Bernstein's idealization of art.

53. Bakhtin, *The Dialogic Imagination*, "Discourse in the Novel," 259–422. For clarification of the mimesis/diegesis distinction, see David Lodge, *After Bakhtin*, 25–44.

54. In "The Word in the Novel" in particular, Bakhtin develops a definition of the novel as a dialogue between different "images of languages." R. Rawdon Wilson, *In Palamedes' Shadow: Exploration in Play, Game, and Narrative Theory*, 25–74, provides a reading of the use of the figure of play in Bakhtin that is relevant to my argument here.

55. In relation to the novel's resistance to aestheticism and the characteristics of novels that fail in this regard, see Bakhtin, *The Dialogic Imagination*, 333.

56. This thesis may be parallel to the concept of "narrative annexes" developed in Suzanne Keen, *Victorian Renovations of the Novel*. Keen writes, "Annexes provide a record of something like a conscience within the Victorian novel, a conscience insisting that differences, exceptions, and alternatives appear on the page" (14). Keen acknowledges the parallels to Bakhtinian concepts.

57. Michael Holquist makes a similar observation in "The Surd Heard: Bakhtin and Derrida": "Bakhtin's utterance articulates itself in a conceptual space somewhere between the specter of an absolute absence that animates grammatology and the dream of an absolute presence that is the hallmark of ontotheology" (147).

58. Compare this claim with those in one of the more recent (or recently translated) general studies of the form, Dario Villanueva's *Theories of Literary Realism*.

Works Cited

Abrams, A. H. *The Mirror and the Lamp: Romantic Theory and the Critical Tradition*. Oxford: Oxford University Press, 1953.

Adorno, T. W. *Aesthetic Theory*. Trans. C. Lenhardt. London: Routledge and Kegan Paul, 1984.

Agnew, Jean-Christophe. *Worlds Apart: The Market and the Theater in Anglo-American Thought, 1550–1750*. Cambridge: Cambridge University Press, 1986.

Alison, Archibald. *Essays on the Nature and Principles of Taste*. 3d ed. 2 vols. Edinburgh: George Ramsay, 1812.

Alliston, April. "Female Sexuality and the Referent of Enlightenment Realisms." In *Spectacles of Realism: Gender, Body, Genre*, ed. Margaret Cohen and Christopher Prendergast. Minneapolis: University of Minnesota Press, 1995.

Althusser, Louis. *Lenin and Philosophy*. Trans. Ben Brewster. New York: Pantheon, 1969.

Armstrong, Nancy. *Desire and Domestic Fiction: A Political History of the Novel*. New York: Oxford University Press, 1987.

Arnold, Matthew. *Culture and Anarchy*. 1869, ed. Samuel Lipman. New Haven: Yale University Press, 1994.

Ashton, John. *The History of English Lotteries*. 1893. Detroit: Singing Tree Press, 1969.

———. *The History of Gambling in England*. 1898. Montclair, N.J.: Patterson Smith, 1969.

Ashton, Rosemary. *The German Idea: Four English Writers and the Reception of German Thought, 1800–1860*. Cambridge: Cambridge University Press, 1980.

Auerbach, Erich. *Mimesis: The Representation of Reality in Western Literature*. Trans. Willard R. Trask. 2d ed. Princeton, N.J.: Princeton University Press, 1968.

Auerbach, Nina. "Secret Performances: George Eliot and the Art of Acting." In *Romantic Imprisonment: Women and Other Glorified Outcasts*, ed. Nina Auerbach, 253–67. New York: Columbia University Press, 1985.

———. "Alluring Vacancies in the Victorian Character." *Kenyon Review* 8 (summer 1986): 36–48.

———. *Private Theatricals: The Lives of the Victorians*. Cambridge: Harvard University Press, 1990.

Austen, Jane. *Sense and Sensibility*. 1811. Oxford: Oxford University Press, 1980.

Austin, J. L. *How to Do Things with Words*. 2d ed. Oxford: Oxford University Press, 1975.

Baer, Marc. *Theatre and Disorder in Late Georgian London*. Oxford: Clarendon Press, 1992.

Bailey, Peter. *Leisure and Class in Victorian England: Rational Recreation and the Contest of Control, 1830–1885*. London: Routledge and Kegan Paul, 1978.

———. "Custom, Capital, and Culture in the Victorian Music Hall." In *Popular Culture and Custom in Nineteenth-Century England*, ed. Robert D. Storch, 180–208. London: Croom Helm, 1982.

Bakhtin, M. M. *Rabelais and His World*. Trans. Hélène Iswolsky. Cambridge: MIT Press, 1968.

———. "The Word in the Novel." Trans. Ann Shukman. In *Comparative Criticism: A Yearbook*, ed. Elinor Shaffer, 2: 213–21. Cambridge: Cambridge University Press, 1980.

———. *The Dialogic Imagination*, ed. Michael Holquist. Trans. Caryl Emerson and Michael Holquist. Austin: University of Texas Press, 1981.

Barish, Jonas. *The Antitheatrical Prejudice*. Berkeley: University of California Press, 1981.

Barthes, Roland. *S/Z*. Trans. Richard Miller. New York: Hill and Wang, 1974.

———. *The Pleasure of the Text*. Trans. Richard Miller. Oxford: Basil Blackwell, 1975.

———. *Writing Degree Zero*. Trans. Annette Lauers and Colin Smith. New York: Hill and Wang, 1977.

———. *The Rustle of Language*. Trans. Richard Howard. New York: Hill and Wang, 1986.

Baskin, Jonathan Barron. "The Development of Corporate Financial Markets in Britain and the United States, 1600–1914: Overcoming Asymmetric Information." *Business History Review* 62 (summer 1988): 199–237.

Baudry, Jean-Louis. "Ideological Effects of the Basic Cinematographic Apparatus." In *Movies and Methods*, ed. Bill Nichols, 2: 531–42. Berkeley: University of California Press, 1985.

Baumgarten, Alexander Gottlieb. *Reflections on Poetry*. 1735. Trans. K. Aschendrenner and W. B. Holther. Berkeley: University of California Press, 1954.

Beer, Gillian. "'Coming Wonders': Uses of Theatre in the Victorian Novel." *English Drama: Forms and Development*, ed. Marie Axton and Raymond Williams, 164–239. Cambridge: Cambridge University Press, 1977.

———. "Circulatory Systems: Money and Gossip in *Middlemarch*." *Cahiers Victoriens et Edouardiens* 26 (October 1987): 46–62.

———. "The Reader's Wager: Lots, Sorts, and Futures." *Essays in Criticism* 40 (April 1990): 99–123.

Benjamin, Walter. *Illuminations: Essays and Reflections*. Trans. Harry Zohn, ed. Hannah Arendt. New York: Schocken Books, 1968.

Bernstein, J. M. *The Fate of Art: Aesthetic Alienation from Kant to Derrida and Adorno*. University Park: Pennsylvania State University Press, 1992.

Bersani, Leo. *A Future for Astyanax: Character and Desire in Literature*. Boston: Little, Brown, 1976.

Best, Steven, and Douglas Kellner. *Postmodern Theory: Critical Interrogations*. New York: Guilford Press, 1991.

Bivona, Daniel. *Desire and Contradiction: Imperial Visions and Domestic Debates in Victorian Literature*. Manchester: Manchester University Press, 1990.

Blyth, Henry. *Hell and Hazard, or William Crockford versus the Gentlemen of England*. London: Weidenfeld and Nicolson, 1969.

Bogue, Ronald, ed. *Mimesis in Contemporary Theory: An Interdisciplinary Approach*. Philadelphia: John Benjamins, 1991.

Bogue, Ronald, and Mihai I. Spariosu, eds. *The Play of the Self*. Albany: State University of New York Press, 1994.

Bohn, Henry G., ed. *The Hand-Book of Games*. 1850. Detroit: Singing Tree Press, 1969.

Bonaparte, Felicia. *Will and Destiny: Morality and Tragedy in George Eliot's Novels*. New York: New York University Press, 1975.

Boone, Joseph Allen. *Tradition Counter Tradition: Love and the Form of Fiction*. Chicago: University of Chicago Press, 1987.

Booth, Michael. *Preface to English Nineteenth-Century Theatre*. Manchester: Manchester University Press, 1980.

Booth, Michael, Richard Southern, Frederick Marker, Lise-Lone Marker, and Robertson Davies. *The Revels History of Drama in English*. Vol. 6, 1750–1880. London: Methuen, 1975.

Bourdieu, Pierre. "The Forms of Capital." In *Handbook of Theory and Research of the Sociology of Education*, ed. John G. Richardson, 241–58. Westport, Conn.: Greenwood Press, 1986.

———. *The Logic of Practice*. Trans. Richard Nice. Stanford: Stanford University Press, 1990.

Bowie, Andrew. *Aesthetics and Subjectivity: From Kant to Nietzsche*. Manchester: Manchester University Press, 1990.

Brantlinger, Patrick. *Fictions of State: Culture and Credit in Britain, 1694–1994*. Ithaca: Cornell University Press, 1996.

Brecht, Bertolt. "Against Georg Lukàcs." *New Left Review* 84 (March-April 1974): 39–53.

Brenner, Reuven, and Gabrielle A. Brenner. *Gambling and Speculation: A Theory, a History, and a Future of Some Human Decisions*. Cambridge: Cambridge University Press, 1990.

Breuer, Joseph, and Sigmund Freud. *Studies on Hysteria, The Standard Edition of the Complete Psychological Works of Sigmund Freud*. Vol. II, ed. and trans. James Strachey and Anna Freud. London: Hogarth Press, 1953–1973.

Brontë, Charlotte. *Shirley*. 1849, ed. Andrew and Judith Hook. London: Penguin, 1985.

———. *Villette*. 1853, ed. Mark Lilly. Middlesex: Penguin, 1985.

Brooks, Peter. *The Melodramatic Imagination: Balzac, Henry James, Melodrama, and the Mode of Excess*. New Haven: Yale University Press, 1976.

———. *Reading for the Plot*. New York: Alfred A. Knopf, 1984.

———. "Aesthetics and Ideology—What Happened to Poetics?" In *Aesthetics and Ideology*, ed. George Levine, 153–67. New Brunswick, N.J.: Rutgers University Press, 1994.

Brown, Laura. *English Dramatic Form, 1660–1760: An Essay in Generic History*. New Haven: Yale University Press, 1981.

Browning, Elizabeth Barrett. *Aurora Leigh*. 1857. In *The Complete Works of Elizabeth*

Barrett Browning, ed. Charlotte Porter and Helen A. Clarke. New York: AMS Press, 1973.

———. *The Letters of Robert Browning and Elizabeth Barrett Browning 1845–1846*, ed. Elvan Kinter, vols. 4 and 5. Cambridge: Harvard University Press, 1969.

Burke, Edmund. *A Philosophical Enquiry into the Origin of Our Ideas of the Sublime and Beautiful*. 4th ed. London: R. and J. Dodsley, 1764.

Burns, Elizabeth. *Theatricality: A Study of Convention in the Theatre and in Social Life*. London: Longman, 1972.

Butler, Judith. *Gender Trouble: Feminism and the Subversion of Identity*. New York: Routledge, 1990.

Byerly, Alison. "From Schoolroom to Stage: Reading Aloud and the Domestication of Victorian Theater." In *Culture and Education in Victorian England*, ed. Patrick Scott and Pauline Fletcher, 125–41. Lewisburg, Pa.: Bucknell University Press, 1990.

Caillois, Roger. *Man, Play, and Games*. Trans. Meyer Burash. New York: Free Press, 1961.

Carlyle, Thomas. *Sartor Resartus and Selected Prose*. 1834, ed. Herbert Sussman. New York: Holt, Rinehart and Winston, 1970.

Castle, Terry. *Masquerade and Civilization: The Carnivalesque in Eighteenth-Century English Culture and Fiction*. Stanford: Stanford University Press, 1986.

Caygill, Howard. *Art of Judgement*. London: Basil Blackwell, 1989.

Childers, Joseph W. *Novel Possibilities: Fiction and the Formation of Early Victorian Culture*. Philadelphia: University of Pennsylvania Press, 1995.

Coleridge, Henry Nelson, ed. Introduction to *Biographia Literaria*: *The Complete Works of Samuel Taylor Coleridge*, vol. 3. New York: Harper, 1871.

Coleridge, Samuel Taylor. *Biographia Literaria*. 1817. In *The Complete Works of Samuel Taylor Coleridge*, ed. H. N. Coleridge and Professor Shedd, vol. 3. New York: Harper, 1871.

Collins, Wilkie. *The Law and the Lady*. In *Three Great Novels*, 875–1159. Oxford: Oxford University Press, 1995.

Cordery, G. "The Gambling Grandfather in *The Old Curiosity Shop*." *Literature and Psychology* 33 (1987): 43–61.

Cottom, Daniel. *The Civilized Imagination: A Study of Ann Radcliffe, Jane Austen, and Sir Walter Scott*. Cambridge: Cambridge University Press, 1985.

———. *Social Figures: George Eliot, Social History, and Literary Representation*. Minneapolis: University of Minnesota Press, 1987.

Coveney, Peter. Introduction. *Felix Holt, the Radical*, by George Eliot. London: Penguin, 1987.

Cowling, Maurice. "One-and-a-Half Cheers for Matthew Arnold." In *Culture and Anarchy*, ed. Samuel Lipman, 202–12. New Haven: Yale University Press, 1994.

Craft-Fairchild, Catherine. *Masquerade and Gender: Disguise and Female Identity in Eighteenth-Century Fictions by Women*. University Park: Pennsylvania State University Press, 1993.

Cripps, Elizabeth A., ed. Introduction to *Alton Locke, Tailor and Poet, An Autobiography*, by Charles Kingsley. Oxford: Oxford University Press, 1983.

Culler, Jonathan. *On Deconstruction: Theory and Criticism after Structuralism*. Ithaca: Cornell University Press, 1982.

Dallas, E.S. *The Gay Science*. London: Chapman and Hall, 1866. In *The Victorian Muse: Selected Criticism and Parody of the Period*, ed. William E. Fredeman, Ira Bruce Nadel, John F. Stasny, vol. 1 and 2. New York: Garland, 1986.

Davis, Tracy C. "Actresses and Prostitutes in Victorian London." *Theatre Research International* 3 (autumn 1988): 221–33.

——. "Spectacles of Women and Conduits of Ideology," *Nineteenth Century Theatre* 19 (summer 1991): 52–66.

De Bolla, Peter. *The Discourse of the Sublime: Readings in History, Aesthetics, and the Subject*. Oxford: Basil Blackwell, 1989.

Deleuze, Gilles. *Nietzsche and Philosophy*. Trans. H. Tomlinson. London: Athlone, 1983.

Denvir, Bernard. *The Early Nineteenth Century: Art, Design, and Society, 1789–1852*. London: Longman, 1984.

Derrida, Jacques. *Speech and Phenomena — and Other Essays on Husserl's Theory of Signs*. Trans. David B. Allison. Evanston, Ill.: Northwestern University Press, 1973.

——. *Of Grammatology*. Trans. Gayatri Chakravorty Spivak. Baltimore: Johns Hopkins University Press, 1976.

——. *Writing and Difference*. Trans. Alan Bass. Chicago: University of Chicago Press, 1978.

——. *Dissemination*. Trans. Barbara Johnson. Chicago: University of Chicago Press, 1981.

——. "Economimesis." Trans. R. Klein. *Diacritics* 11 (1981): 3–25.

——. *The Truth in Painting*. Trans. Geoff Bennington and Ian McLeod. Chicago: University of Chicago Press, 1987.

——. *Limited Inc*. Evanston, Ill.: Northwestern University Press, 1988.

——. *The Ear of the Other: Otobiography, Transference, Translation: Texts and Discussions with Jacques Derrida*, ed. Christie V. McDonald. Trans. Peggy Kamuf. New York: Schocken Books, 1985.

Detsch, Richard. "A Non-Subjectivist Concept of Play: Gadamer and Heidegger versus Rilke and Nietzsche." *Philosophy Today* 29 (summer 1985): 156–72.

Deutsch, Phyllis Dianne. "Fortune and Chance: Aristocratic Gaming and English Society, 1760–1837." Ph.D. diss. New York University, 1991.

Dingley, Robert. "Playing the Game: The Continental Casinos and the Victorian Imagination." *Cahiers Victoriens et Edouardiens* 44 (October 1996): 17–31.

Dixon, David. "'Class Law': The Street Betting Act of 1906." *International Journal of the Sociology of Law* 8 (1980): 101–28.

Donohue, Joseph. *Theatre in the Age of Kean*. Totowa, N.J.: Rowman and Littlefield, 1975.

——. "Women in the Victorian Theatre: Images, Illusions, Realities." *Gender and Performance: The Presentation of Difference in the Performing Arts*, ed. L. Senelick, 115–40. Hanover, N.H.: University Press of New England, 1992.

Downes, D. M., B. P. Davies, M. E. David, and P. Stone. *Gambling, Work, and Leisure: A Study Across Three Areas*. London: Routledge and Kegan Paul, 1976.

Duckworth, Alistair. *The Improvement of the Estate: A Study of Jane Austen's Novels.* Baltimore: Johns Hopkins University Press, 1971.

Eagleton, Terry. *The Ideology of the Aesthetic.* Oxford: Basil Blackwell, 1990.

Ehrmann, Jacques. "Homo Ludens Revisited." *Yale French Studies* 41 (1968): 31–57.

Eliot, George. *Adam Bede.* 1859. London: J. M. Dent, 1937.

———. *Felix Holt, the Radical.* 1866, ed. Fred C. Thompson. Oxford: Oxford University Press, 1988.

———. *Middlemarch: A Study of Provincial Life.* 1871–2. New York: New American Library, 1981.

———. *Daniel Deronda.* 1876, ed. Barbara Hardy. Middlesex: Penguin, 1978.

———. *Selected Essays, Poems, and Other Writings*, ed. A. S. Byatt and Nicholas Warren. London: Penguin, 1990.

———. *The George Eliot Letters.* 7 vols. Ed. Gordon S. Haight. 7 vols. New Haven: Yale University Press, 1954–55.

Ellis, John M. *Against Deconstruction.* Princeton: Princeton University Press, 1989.

Elsaesser, Thomas. "Tales of Sound and Fury: Observations on the Family Melodrama." In *Movies and Methods*, ed. Bill Nichols, 2: 165–89. Berkeley: University of California Press, 1985.

Ermarth, Elizabeth Deeds. *Realism and Consensus in the English Novel.* Princeton: Princeton University Press, 1983.

Evans, David Moirer. *Speculative Notes and Notes on Speculation, Ideal and Real.* 1864. New York: Burt Franklin, 1968.

Fabian, Ann. "Speculation on Distress: The Popular Discourse of the Panics of 1837 and 1857." *Yale Journal of Criticism* 3.1 (1989): 127–42.

———. *Card Sharps, Dream Books, and Bucket Shops: Gambling in Nineteenth-Century America.* Ithaca: Cornell University Press, 1990.

Ferguson, Frances. *Solitude and the Sublime: Romanticism and the Aesthetics of Individuation.* New York: Routledge, 1992.

Fink, Eugene. *Spiel als Weltsymbol.* Stuttgart: W. Kohlhammer, 1960.

———. "The Oasis of Happiness: Toward an Ontology of Play." *Yale French Studies* 41 (1968): 19–30.

Fisher, Judith. "Siren and Artist: Contradiction in Thackeray's Aesthetic Ideal." *Nineteenth-Century Literature* 39 (March 1985): 392–419.

Foucault, Michel. *The Archaeology of Knowledge.* Trans. A. M. Sheridan Smith. New York: Harper, 1972.

———. *Discipline and Punish.* Trans. Alan Sheridan. New York: Vintage Books, 1979.

———. *The History of Sexuality: An Introduction.* Vol. I. Trans. Robert Hurley. New York: Vintage, 1990.

Fraser, Hilary. *Beauty and Belief: Aesthetics and Religion in Victorian Literature.* Cambridge: Cambridge University Press, 1986.

Freud, Sigmund. *Beyond the Pleasure Principle.* Trans. James Strachey. New York: W. W. Norton, 1961.

Friedman, Susan Stanford. "Spatialization: A Strategy for Reading Narrative." *Narrative* 1 (January 1993): 12–23.

Gadamer, Hans-Georg. *Truth and Method.* 2d ed. Trans. Joel Weinsheimer and Donald G. Marshall. New York: Crossroad, 1975.

Gagnier, Regenia. "A Critique of Practical Aesthetics." In *Aesthetics and Ideology*, ed. George Levine, 264–82. New Brunswick, N.J.: Rutgers University Press, 1994.

Gallagher, Catherine. *The Industrial Reformation of English Fiction, 1832–1867*. Chicago: University of Chicago Press, 1985.

Galperin, William. "The Theatre at Mansfield Park: From Classic to Romantic Once More." *Eighteenth-Century Life* 16 (November 1992): 247–71.

Gasché, Rodolophe. *The Tain of the Mirror: Derrida and the Philosophy of Reflection*. Cambridge: Harvard University Press, 1986.

———. "Of Aesthetic and Historical Determination." In *Post-Structuralism and the Question of History*, ed. Derek Attridge, Geoff Bennington, and Robert Young, 139–61. Cambridge: Cambridge University Press, 1987.

Gay, Penelope. "Theatricals and Theatricality in Mansfield Park." *Sydney Studies in English* 13 (1987–88): 61–73.

Goffman, Erving. *Presentation of Self in Everyday Life*. Garden City, N.Y.: Anchor Books, 1959.

———. *Frame Analysis: An Essay on the Organization of Experience*. New York: Harper and Row, 1974.

Gombrich, E. H. *The Story of Art*. 13th ed. Oxford: Phaidon, 1979.

Graff, Gerald. "Arnold, Reason, and Common Culture." In *Culture and Anarchy*, ed. Samuel Lipman, 186–201. New Haven: Yale University Press, 1994.

Greenblatt, Stephen. *Renaissance Self-Fashioning: From More to Shakespeare*. Chicago: University of Chicago Press, 1980.

Groos, Karl. *Die Spiele der Menschen*. Trans. Elizabeth L. Baldwin. New York: D. Appleton, 1901.

Haley, Bruce. *The Healthy Body and Victorian Culture*. Cambridge: Harvard University Press, 1978.

Hans, James S. *The Play of the World*. Amherst: University of Massachusetts Press, 1981.

Hardy, Barbara. "Dickens and the Passions." *Nineteenth-Century Literature* 24 (1970): 452–57.

Harpman, Geoffrey Galt. "Aesthetics and the Fundamentals of Modernity." In *Aesthetics and Ideology*, ed. George Levine, 124–49. New Brunswick, N.J.: Rutgers University Press, 1994.

Harris, Wendell V. "Interpretive Historicism: 'Signs of the Times' and *Culture and Anarchy* in Their Contexts." *Nineteenth-Century Literature* 44 (March 1990): 441–64.

Hayden, John O., ed. *Scott: The Critical Heritage*. New York: Barnes and Noble, 1970.

Hazlitt, William. *The Complete Works of William Hazlitt*, ed. P. P. Howe. New York: AMS Press, 1967.

Hein, Hilde. "Play as an Aesthetic Concept." *Journal of Aesthetics and Art Criticism* 27 (fall 1968): 67–72.

Heller, Peter. "Multiplicity and Unity in Nietzsche's Works and Thoughts on Play." *German Quarterly* 52 (May 1979): 319–38.

Hemingway, Andrew. *Landscape Imagery and Urban Culture in Early Nineteenth-Century Britain*. Cambridge: Cambridge University Press, 1992.

Hennelly, Mark M., Jr. "Dickens's Praise of Folly: Play in *The Pickwick Papers*." *Dickens Quarterly* 3 (March 1986): 27–46.

Heraclitus. *The Presocratic Philosophers: A Critical History with a Selection of Texts*. Trans. G. S. Kirk and J. E. Raven. Cambridge: Cambridge University Press, 1957.

——. *Fragments: A Text and Translation with Commentary*, ed. T. M. Robinson. Toronto: University of Toronto Press, 1987. 37.

Hinman, Lawrence M. "Nietzsche's Philosophy of Play." *Philosophy Today* 18 (summer 1974): 106–24.

Hodson, James. *Private Theatricals: Being a Practical Guide for the Home Stage*. London: W. H. Allen, 1881.

Holquist, Michael. "The Surd Heard: Bakhtin and Derrida." In *Literature and History: Theoretical Problems and Russian Case Studies*, ed. Gary Saul Morson, 137–56. Stanford: Stanford University Press, 1986.

Howes, Craig. "*Pendennis* and the Controversy on the 'Dignity of Literature.'" *Nineteenth-Century Literature* 41 (December 1986): 269–98.

Huizinga, Johan. *Homo Ludens: A Study of the Play-Element in Culture*. London: Routledge and Kegan Paul, 1949.

Hutcheon, Linda. *A Poetics of Postmodernism: History, Theory, Fiction*. New York: Routledge, 1988.

Hutcheson, Francis. *An Inquiry into the Origin of Our Ideas of Beauty and Virtue*. 2d ed. London: J. Darby et al., 1726.

Hutchinson, Peter. *Games Authors Play*. London: Methuen, 1983.

Irigaray, Luce. *This Sex Which Is Not One*. Trans. Catherine Porter and Carolyn Burke. Ithaca: Cornell University Press, 1985.

Iser, Wolfgang. *The Fictive and the Imaginary: Charting Literary Anthropology*. Baltimore: Johns Hopkins University Press, 1993.

Itzkowitz, David C. "Victorian Bookmakers and Their Customers." *Victorian Studies* (1988): 32 (1988): 7–30.

——. "The (Other) Great Evil: Gambling, Scandal, and the National Anti-Gambling League." In *Victorian Scandals: Representations of Gender and Class*, ed. Dritine Ottesen Garrigan, 235–56. Athens: Ohio University Press, 1992.

Jefferson, Ann. "Intertextuality and the Poetics of Fiction." *Comparative Criticism: A Yearbook*, ed. Elinor Shaffer, 2: 235–52. Cambridge: Cambridge University Press, 1980.

Johnson, Barbara. "Poetry and Performative Language: Mallarmé and Austin." In *The Critical Difference: Essays in the Contemporary Rhetoric of Reading*, 52–66. Baltimore: Johns Hopkins University Press, 1980.

Josipovici, Gabriel. "The Balzac of M. Barthes and the Balzac of M. de Guermantes." In *Reconstructing Literature*, ed. Laurence Lerner, 81–105. Totowa, N.J.: Barnes and Noble, 1983.

Joyce, Patrick. *Visions of the People: Industrial England and the Question of Class, 1848–1914*. Cambridge: Cambridge University Press, 1991.

Kames, Henry Home, Lord. *Elements of Criticism*. Dublin: Sarah Cotter, 1762.

Kant, Immanuel. *Critique of Judgment*. 1790. Trans. Werner S. Pluhar. Indianapolis: Hackett, 1987.

Kavanagh, Thomas M. *Enlightenment and the Shadows of Chance: The Novel and the Culture of Gambling in Eighteenth-Century France*. Baltimore: Johns Hopkins University Press, 1993.

Kelly, Nancy Webb. "Homo Aestheticus: Coleridge, Kant, and Play." *Textual Practice* 2 (summer 1988): 200–218.

Keen, Suzanne. *Victorian Renovations of the Novel: Narrative Annexes and the Boundaries of Representation*. Cambridge: Cambridge University Press, 1998.

Kent, Christopher. "Image and Reality: The Actress and Society." In *A Widening Sphere: Changing Roles of Victorian Women*, ed. Martha Vincinus, 94–116. Bloomington: Indiana University Press, 1977.

Kingsley, Charles. *Alton Locke, Tailor and Poet, an Autobiography*. 1850, ed. Elizabeth A. Cripps. Oxford: Oxford University Press, 1983.

Knight, Richard Payne. *An Analytical Inquiry into the Principles of Taste*. London: T. Payne, 1805.

Kristeva, Julia. *Desire in Language: A Semiotic Approach to Literature and Art*, ed. Leon S. Roudiez. Trans. Thomas Gora. New York: Columbia University Press, 1980.

———. *The Kristeva Reader*, ed. Toril Moi. New York: Columbia University Press, 1986.

Kusnetz, Ella. "'This Leaf of My Life': Writing and Play in *Great Expectations*, II." *Dickens Quarterly* 10 (September 1993): 146–60.

Lacan, Jacques. *Écrits: A Selection*. Trans. Alan Sheridan. New York: W. W. Norton, 1977.

———. *Feminine Sexuality*, ed. Juliet Mitchell and Jacqueline Rose. Trans. Jacqueline Rose. New York: W. W. Norton, 1985.

Laclau, Ernest, and Chantal Mouffe. "Post-Marxism without Apologies." *New Left Review* 166 (December 1987): 79–106.

Landow, George P. *The Aesthetic and Critical Theories of John Ruskin*. Princeton: Princeton University Press, 1971.

Laplanche, J., and J.-B. Pontalis. *The Language of Psycho-Analysis*. Trans. Donald Nicholson-Smith. New York: W. W. Norton, 1973.

Lerner, Laurence. *The Literary Imagination: Essays on Literature and Society*. Sussex, England: Harvester, 1982.

Levine, George. "Determinism and Responsibility." In *A Century of George Eliot Criticism*, ed. Gordon S. Haight, 349–60. Boston: Houghton Mifflin, 1965.

———. "Realism Reconsidered." In *The Theory of the Novel: New Essays*, ed. John Halperin, 233–56. New York: Oxford University Press, 1974.

———. "High and Low: Ruskin and the Novelists." In *Nature and the Victorian Imagination*, ed. U. C. Knoepflmacher and G. B. Tennyson, 137–52. Berkeley: University of California Press, 1977.

———. *The Realistic Imagination: English Fiction from Frankenstein to Lady Chatterley*. Chicago: University of Chicago Press, 1981.

Levine, George, ed. Introduction to "Reclaiming the Aesthetic." *Aesthetics and Ideology*. New Brunswick, N.J.: Rutgers University Press, 1994.

Lewes, George Henry. *On Actors and the Art of Acting*. 1875. New York: Grove Press, 1957.

——. "Realism and Idealism." In *Literary Criticism of George Henry Lewes*, ed. Alice R. Kaminsky, 87–90. Lincoln: University of Nebraska Press, 1964.

Lipman, Samuel. "Why Should We Read *Culture and Anarchy?*" In *Culture and Anarchy*, ed. Samuel Lipman, 213–28. New Haven: Yale University Press, 1994.

Litvak, Joseph. "The Infection of Acting: Theatricals and Theatricality in *Mansfield Park*." *ELH* 53 (summer 1986): 331–55.

——. *Caught in the Act: Theatricality in the Nineteenth-Century English Novel*. Berkeley: University of California Press, 1992.

Lodge, David. *After Bakhtin: Essays on Fiction and Criticism*. London: Routledge, 1990.

Loesberg, Jonathan. *Aestheticism and Deconstruction: Pater, Derrida, and De Man*. Princeton: Princeton University Press, 1991.

Lyotard, Jean-François, and Jean-Loup Thébaud. *Just Gaming*. Trans. Wlad Godzich. Minneapolis: University of Minnesota Press, 1985.

MacKay, Carol Hanbery. *Dramatic Dickens*. New York: St. Martin's, 1989.

MacKenzie, William Douglas. *The Ethics of Gambling*. London: Sunday School Union/Morrison and Gibb, printers, 1895.

Makaryk, Irena R. ed. *Encyclopedia of Contemporary Literary Theory: Approaches, Scholars, Terms*. Toronto: University of Toronto Press, 1993.

Marcus, Stephen. *The Other Victorians: A Study of Sexuality and Pornography in Mid-Nineteenth-Century England*. New York: Basic Books, 1964.

——. "*Culture and Anarchy* Today." In *Culture and Anarchy*, ed. Samuel Lipman, 165–85. New Haven: Yale University Press, 1994.

Marino, Adrian. *The Biography of "The Idea of Literature from Antiquity to the Baroque*. New York: State University of New York Press, 1996.

Marino, James A. G. "An Annotated Bibliography of Play and Literature." *Canadian Review of Comparative Literature* 12 (June 1985): 306–53.

Marshall, David. *The Figure of Theater: Shaftesbury, Defoe, Adam Smith, and George Eliot*. New York: Columbia University Press, 1986.

——. "True Acting and the Language of Real Feeling: *Mansfield Park*." *Yale Journal of Criticism* 3 (1989): 87–106.

Marwick, Arthur. *Beauty in History: Society, Politics, and Personal Appearance c. 1500 to the Present*. London: Thames and Hudson, 1988.

Marx, Karl. *Economic and Philosophic Manuscripts of 1844*. In *The Marx-Engels Reader*. 2d ed., ed. Robert C. Tucker, 66–125. New York: W. W. Norton, 1978.

——. *Capital*. Vol. 1, ed. Ernest Mandel. Trans. Ben Fowkes. Harmondsworth: Penguin, 1976.

McCobb, E.A. "*Daniel Deronda* as Will and Representation: George Eliot and Schopenhauer." *Modern Language Review* 80 (July 1983): 533–49.

McGowan, John P. *Representation and Revelation: Victorian Realism from Carlyle to Yeats*. Columbia: University of Missouri Press, 1986.

McKeon, Michael. *The Origins of the English Novel 1600–1740*. Baltimore: Johns Hopkins University Press, 1987.

McKibbin, Ross. "Working-Class Gambling in Britain 1880–1939." *Past and Present* 82 (February 1979): 147–78.

Meisel, Martin. *Realizations: Narrative, Pictorial, and Theatrical Arts in Nineteenth-Century England*. Princeton: Princeton University Press, 1983.

Metz, Christian. "The Imaginary Signifier." Trans. Ben Brewster. *Screen* 16 (summer 1975): 14–76. Reprint. *Narrative, Apparatus, Ideology*, ed. Philip Rosen, 244–80. New York: Columbia University Press, 1986.

———. "Story/Discourse: Notes on Two Kinds of Voyeurism." In *Movies and Methods*, ed. Bill Nichols, 543–49. Berkeley: University of California Press, 1985.

Michaels, Walter Benn. *The Gold Standard and the Logic of Naturalism: American Literature at the Turn of the Century*. Berkeley: University of California Press, 1987.

Michie, Ranald. "Different in Name Only? The London Stock Exchange and Foreign Bourses, c. 1850–1914." *Business History* 30 (1988): 46–68.

Miers, David, and David Dixon. "National Bet: The Re-Emergence of Public Lottery." *Public Law* (1979): 372–403.

Miller, D. A. *The Novel and the Police*. Berkeley: University of California Press, 1988.

Miller, Jacques-Alain. "Suture (Elements of the Logic of the Signifier)." *Screen* 18 (1977–78): 24–34.

Miller, J. Hillis. *The Form of Victorian Fiction: Thackeray, Dickens, Trollope, George Eliot, Meredith, and Hardy*. Notre Dame: University of Notre Dame Press, 1968.

———. "Narrative and History." *ELH* 41 (1974): 455–73.

Modleski, Tania. *Feminism Without Women: Culture and Criticism in a "Postfeminist" Age*. New York: Routledge, 1991.

Morris, William. *William Morris: Stories in Prose, Stories in Verse, Shorter Poems, Lectures and Essays*. Ed. G. D. H. Cole. London: Nonesuch Press, 1948.

Morrow, Nancy. *Dreadful Games: The Play of Desire in the Nineteenth-Century Novel*. Kent, Ohio: Kent State University Press, 1988.

Motter, T.H. Vail. "Garrick and the Private Theatres." *ELH* 11 (1944): 63–75.

Murphy, Brian. *A History of the British Economy*. London: Longman, 1973.

Nahm, M. C. "Some Aspects of the Play-Theory of Art." *Journal of Philosophy* 39 (March 1942): 148–59.

Naremore, James. *Acting in the Cinema*. Berkeley: University of California Press, 1988.

Newbolt, Sir Henry. "Vitaï Lampada." In *Parlour Poetry: A Casquet of Gems*, ed. M. R. Turner, 75. New York: Viking, 1969.

Newman, Otto. *Gambling: Hazard and Reward*. London: Athlone Press/University of London, 1972.

Newsom, Robert. *A Likely Story: Probability and Play in Fiction*. New Brunswick, N.J.: Rutgers University Press, 1988.

Nicoll, Allardyce. *A History of Early-Nineteenth-Century Drama 1800–1850*. Vol. 1. Cambridge: Cambridge University Press, 1930.

———. *A History of English Drama 1660–1900*. Vol. 3. *Late-Eighteenth-Century Drama, 1750–1800*. Cambridge: Cambridge University Press, 1952.

Nietzsche, Friedrich. *The Birth of Tragedy, or Hellenism and Pessimism*. *The Complete Works of Friedrich Nietzsche*. Vol. 1, ed. Oscar Levy. Trans. W. A. Haussmann. New York: Russell and Russell, 1964.

———. *Philosophy during the Tragic Age of the Greeks*. *Early Greek Philosophy*. In *The Complete Works of Friedrich Nietzsche*, 2: 71–170. Ed. Oscar Levy. Trans. M. A. Mugge. New York: Russell and Russell, 1964.

——. *Human All-Too-Human: A Book for Free Spirits. The Complete Works of Friedrich Nietzsche.* Vol. 6. Ed. Oscar Levy. Trans. Helen Zimmern. New York: Russell and Russell, 1964.

——. *The Will to Power.* Ed. Walter Kaufmann. Trans. Walter Kaufmann and R. J. Hollingdale. New York: Vintage Books, 1967.

——. *The Gay Science.* Trans. Walter Kaufmann. New York: Vintage/Random House, 1974.

——. *Daybreak: Thoughts on the Prejudices of Morality.* Trans. R. J. Hollingdale. Cambridge: Cambridge University Press, 1982.

——. *Beyond Good and Evil: Prelude to a Philosophy of the Future.* Trans. Walter Kaufmann. New York: Vintage/Random House, 1989.

Norris, Christopher. *Derrida.* Cambridge: Harvard University Press, 1987.

——. *What's Wrong with Postmodernism: Critical Theory and the Ends of Philosophy.* London: Harvester Wheatsheaf, 1990.

——. *The Truth about Postmodernism.* Oxford: Blackwell, 1993.

Novy, Marianne. *Engaging with Shakespeare: Responses of George Eliot and Other Women Novelists.* Athens: University of Georgia Press, 1994.

Nowell-Smith, Geoffrey. "Minnelli and Melodrama." In *Movies and Methods*, ed. Bill Nichols, 2: 190–94. Berkeley: University of California Press, 1985.

The Oxford English Dictionary. Ed. James A. H. Murray, Henry Bradley, W. A. Craigie, and C. T. Onions. 12 vols. 1933. Oxford: Clarendon Press, 1970.

Paris, Bernard J. *Experiments in Life: George Eliot's Quest for Values.* Detroit: Wayne State University Press, 1965.

Park, Roy. "Coleridge and Kant: Poetic Imagination and Practical Reason." *British Journal of Aesthetics* 8 (1968): 335–346.

Penley, Constance. "The Avant-Garde and Its Imaginary." In *Movies and Methods*, ed. Bill Nichols, 2: 576–601. Berkeley: University of California Press, 1985.

Petrey, Sandy. *Realism and Revolution: Balzac, Stendhal, Zola, and the Performance of History.* Ithaca: Cornell University Press, 1988.

——. *Speech Acts and Literary Theory.* New York: Routledge, 1990.

——. "Balzac's Empire: History, Insanity, and the Realist Text." In *Historical Criticism and the Challenge of Theory*, ed. Janet Levarie Smarr, 25–41. Urbana: University of Illinois Press, 1993.

Pfeffer, Rose. *Nietzsche: Disciple of Dionysus.* Lewisburg, Pa.: Bucknell University Press, 1972.

Plato. *The Collected Dialogues of Plato.* 7th ed. Ed. Edith Hamilton and Huntington Cairns. Princeton: Princeton University Press, 1973.

Pluhar, Werner S. Translator's Preface to *Critique of Judgment*, by Immanuel Kant. Indianapolis: Hackett, 1987.

Pocock, J. G. A. *Virtue, Commerce, and History: Essays on Political Thought and History, Chiefly in the Eighteenth Century.* Cambridge: Cambridge University Press, 1985.

Polhemus, Robert. *Erotic Faith: Being in Love From Jane Austen to D. H. Lawrence.* Chicago: University of Chicago Press, 1990.

Poovey, Mary. *Uneven Developments: The Ideological Work of Gender in Mid-Victorian England.* Chicago: University of Chicago Press, 1988.

——. "Aesthetics and Political Economy in the Eighteenth Century: The Place of Gender in the Social Constitution of Knowledge." In *Aesthetics and Ideology*, ed. George Levine, 79–105. New Brunswick, N.J.: Rutgers University Press, 1994.

——. *Making a Social Body: British Cultural Formation, 1830–1864*. Chicago: University of Chicago Press, 1995.

Prendergast, Christopher. *The Order of Mimesis: Balzac, Stendhal, Nerval, Flaubert*. Cambridge: Cambridge University Press, 1986.

Rastier, François. "Semantic Realism and Aesthetic Realism." *SubStance* 71/72 (1993): 74–97.

Reed, John. "A Friend to Mammon: Speculation in Victorian Literature." *Victorian Studies* 27 (winter 1984): 179–202.

——. *Victorian Will*. Athens, Ohio: Ohio University Press, 1989.

Ricoeur, Paul. "Mimesis and Representation." *Annals of Scholarship* 2.3 (1981): 15–32.

Riviere, Joan. "Womanliness as a Masquerade." *The International Journal of Psychoanalysis* 10 (1929): 103–13.

Robertson, David. "Mid-Victorians Amongst the Alps." In *Nature and the Victorian Imagination*, ed. U. C. Knoepflmacher and G. B. Tennyson, 113–36. Berkeley: University of California Press, 1977.

Robison, Roselee. "Victorians, Children, and Play." *English Studies* 64 (1983): 318–29.

Rosenberg, John D. *The Darkening Glass: A Portrait of Ruskin's Genius*. New York: Columbia University Press, 1962.

Rosenfeld, Sybil. *Temples of Thespis: Some Private Theatres and Theatricals in England and Wales, 1700–1820*. London: The Society for Theatre Research, 1978.

Ruskin, John. *Modern Painters*. Vol. 2: 25–50. 1843–60. *The Works of John Ruskin*. Vol. 4. Ed. E. T. Cook and Alexander Wedderburn. Library Edition. 39 vols. London: George Allen, 1903–12.

——. *Modern Painters*. Vol. 3: 201–20. 1843–60. *The Works of John Ruskin*. Vol. 5. Ed. E. T. Cook and Alexander Wedderburn. Library Edition. 39 vols. London: George Allen, 1903–12.

——. *The Stones of Venice*. Vol. 1. 1851–3. *The Works of John Ruskin*. Vol. 10. Ed. E. T. Cook and Alexander Wedderburn. Library Edition. 39 vols. London: George Allen, 1903–12.

——. *The Stones of Venice*. Vol. 2: 180–269. 1851–3. *The Works of John Ruskin*. Vol. 10. Ed. E. T. Cook and Alexander Wedderburn. Library Edition. 39 vols. London: George Allen, 1903–12.

——. *The Stones of Venice*. Vol. 3: 135–95. 1851–3. *The Works of John Ruskin*. Vol. 11. Ed. E. T. Cook and Alexander Wedderburn. Library Edition. 39 vols. London: George Allen, 1903–12.

——. *The Crown of Wild Olives*. 1866. *The Works of John Ruskin*. Vol. 23. Ed. E. T. Cook and Alexander Wedderburn. Library Edition. 39 vols. London: George Allen, 1903–12.

Russell, Norman. *The Novelist and Mammon: Literary Responses to the World of Commerce in the Nineteenth Century*. Oxford: Clarendon Press, 1986.

Schaper, Eva. "Toward the Aesthetic: A Journey with Friedrich Schiller." *British Journal of Aesthetics* 25 (1985): 153–68.

———. "Taste, Sublimity, and Genius: The Aesthetics of Nature and Art." In *The Cambridge Companion to Kant*, ed. Paul Guyer, 367–93. Cambridge: Cambridge University Press, 1992.

Schiller, Friedrich von. *On the Aesthetic Education of Man*. 1795. Trans. Reginald Snell. New York: Frederick Ungar, 1983.

Seltzer, Mark. *Henry James and the Art of Power*. Ithaca: Cornell University Press, 1984.

Shaffer, Elinor S. "Illusion and Imagination: Derrida's Parergon and Coleridge's Aid to Reflection: Revisionary Readings of Kantian Formalist Aesthetics." In *Aesthetic Illusion: Theoretical and Historical Approaches*, ed. Frederick Burwick and Walter Pape, 138–57. Berlin: de Gruyter, 1990.

Shaftesbury, Anthony Ashely Cooper, Earl of. *An Enquiry Concerning Virtue or Merit*. 1688. Manchester: Manchester University Press, 1977.

Shell, Marc. *The Economy of Literature*. Baltimore: Johns Hopkins University Press, 1978.

———. *Money, Language, and Thought: Literary and Philosophical Economies from the Medieval to the Modern Era*. Berkeley: University of California Press, 1982.

Silverman, Kaja. *The Subject of Semiotics*. Oxford: Oxford University Press, 1983.

Singer, Alan. *The Subject as Action: Transformation and Totality in Narrative Aesthetics*. Ann Arbor: University of Michigan Press, 1993.

Smith, Adam. *The Theory of Moral Sentiments*. 1759, ed. D. D. Raphael and A. L. Macfie. London: Clarendon Press, 1976.

Spariosu, Mihai I. *Literature, Mimesis, and Play: Essays in Literary Theory*. Tübingen: Gunter Narr Verlag, 1982.

Spariosu, Mihai I., ed. *Mimesis in Contemporary Theory: An Interdisciplinary Approach*. Philadelphia: John Benjamins, 1984.

———. *Dionysus Reborn: Play and the Aesthetic Dimension in Modern Philosophical and Scientific Discourse*. Ithaca: Cornell University Press, 1989.

Sparshott, F.E. "Work—The Concept: Past, Present, and Future." *Journal of Aesthetics and Education* 7 (1973): 23–38.

Spencer, Herbert. *The Principles of Psychology*. Vol. 2. New York: D. Appleton, 1897.

Sprinker, Michael. *Imaginary Relations: Aesthetics and Ideology in the Theory of Historical Materialism*. London: Verso, 1987.

Stang, Richard. *The Theory of the Novel in England 1850–1870*. New York: Columbia University Press, 1959.

Starzyk, Lawrence J. "The Non-Poetic Foundations of Victorian Aesthetics." *British Journal of Aesthetics* 26 (summer 1986): 218–27.

———. "'The Coronation of the Whirlwind': The Victorian Poetics of Indeterminacy." *Victorian Newsletter* 77 (spring 1990): 27–35.

Stephens, John. *The Profession of the Playwright: British Theatre, 1800–1900*. Cambridge: Cambridge University Press, 1992.

Stern, Rebecca F. "Moving Parts and Speaking Parts: Situating Victorian Antitheatricality." *ELH* 65 (1998): 423–49.

Stewart, Susan. *Nonsense: Aspects of Intertextuality in Folklore and Literature*. Baltimore: Johns Hopkins University Press, 1979.

Stokes, John. "Rachel's 'Terrible Beauty': An Actress Among the Novelists." *ELH* 51 (winter 1984): 771–93.

Swann, Brian. "George Eliot and the Play: Symbol and Metaphor of the Drama in *Daniel Deronda.*" *Dalhousie Review* 52 (1972): 191–202.

Tanner, Tony. *Adultery in the Novel: Contract and Transgression.* Baltimore: Johns Hopkins University Press, 1979.

Thackeray, William Makepeace. *Vanity Fair: A Novel Without a Hero.* 1848, ed. Geoffrey and Kathleen Tillotson. Boston: Houghton Mifflin/Riverside, 1963.

———. *The History of Pendennis.* 1850. Ed. Donald Hawes. London: Penguin, 1986.

Thompson, Fred C. "*Felix Holt* as Classical Tragedy." *Nineteenth-Century Fiction* 16 (1965): 47–63.

Thompson, James. *Models of Value: Eighteenth-Century Political Economy and the Novel.* Durham: Duke University Press, 1996.

Trollope, Anthony. *The Duke's Children.* 1880. Oxford: Oxford University Press, 1990.

———. *The Last Chronicle of Barset.* 1867. London: Penguin, 1993.

Ulmer, Gregory L. "The Object of Post-Criticism." In *The Anti-Aesthetic: Essays on Postmodern Culture*, ed. Hal Foster, 83–110. Seattle: Bay Press, 1983.

Vargish, Thomas. *The Providential Aesthetic in Victorian Fiction.* Charlottesville: University Press of Virginia, 1985.

Vernon, John. *Money and Fiction: Literary Realism in the Nineteenth and Early Twentieth Centuries.* Ithaca: Cornell University Press, 1984.

Victor, Carol de Saint. "Acting and Action: Sexual Distinctions in *Daniel Deronda.*" *Cahiers Victoriens et Edouardiens* 26 (1987): 77–88.

Villanueva, Darío. *Theories of Literary Realism.* Trans. Mihai I. Spariosu and Santiago García-Castañón. Albany: State University of New York Press, 1997.

Vincinus, Martha. "'Helpless and Unfriended': Nineteenth-Century Domestic Melodrama." *New Literary History* (1981): 127–43.

Vlock, Deborah M. "Dickens, Theater, and the Making of a Victorian Reading Public." *Studies in the Novel* 29 (summer 1997): 164–90.

Voloshinov, V. N. *Marxism and the Philosophy of Language.* Trans. Ladislav Matejka and I. R. Titunik. New York: Seminar Press, 1973.

———. "Appendix 1: Discourse in Life and Discourse in Art (Concerning Sociological Poetics)." In *Freudianism: A Marxist Critique*, trans. I. R. Titunik, ed. Neal H. Bruss, 93–116. New York: Academic Press, 1976.

Waters, Chris. *British Socialists and the Politics of Popular Culture, 1884–1914.* Manchester: Manchester University Press, 1990.

Watt, Ian. *The Rise of the Novel: Studies in Defoe, Richardson, and Fielding.* Berkeley: University of California Press, 1957.

Webb, Igor. *From Custom to Capital: The English Novel and the Industrial Revolution.* Ithaca: Cornell University Press, 1981.

Weiss, Barbara. *The Hell of the English: Bankruptcy and the Victorian Novel.* Lewisburg, Pa.: Bucknell University Press, 1986.

Wellek, René. *Immanuel Kant in England 1793–1838.* Princeton: Princeton University Press, 1931.

Welsh, Alexander. *George Eliot and Blackmail.* Cambridge: Harvard University Press, 1985.

Werlin, Robert J. *The English Novel and the Industrial Revolution: A Study in the Sociology of Literature*. New York: Garland, 1990.

White, Hayden. *The Content of the Form: Narrative Discourse and Historical Representation*. Baltimore: Johns Hopkins University Press, 1987.

Wilcox, John. "The Beginnings of l'Art pour l'Art." *Journal of Aesthetics and Art Criticism* 11 (June 1953): 360–77.

Wilde, Oscar. *The Artist as Critic: Critical Writings of Oscar Wilde*, ed. Richard Ellmann. New York: Vintage, 1970.

Williams, Raymond. *Culture and Society, 1780–1950*. New York: Columbia University Press, 1983.

Wilson, R. Rawdon. *In Palamedes' Shadow: Exploration in Play, Game, and Narrative Theory*. Boston: Northeastern University Press, 1990.

Wise, Jennifer. "Marginalizing Drama: Bakhtin's Theory of Genre." *Essays in Theatre* 8 (November 1989): 15–22.

Woods, Leigh. "Dickens and the Theatre: Recent Publications." *Nineteenth-Century Theatre* 19 (winter 1991): 130–38.

Wykes, Alan. *Gambling*. London: Aldus Books, 1964.

Zemka, Sue. "From the Punchmen to Pugin's Gothic: The Broad Road to a Sentimental Death in *The Old Curiosity Shop*." *Nineteenth-Century Literature* 48 (December 1993): 291–309.

Acknowledgments

I am grateful to the professors and mentors who became friends and colleagues in the English Department at the University of Florida, especially Daniel Cottom, Alistair Duckworth, Caryl Flinn, Elizabeth Langland, and David Leverenz. For the institutional and financial support that East Carolina University provided, I would like to thank Bruce Southard, Michael Poteat, Keats Sparrow, and especially Thomas Feldbush, Vice Chancellor for Research and Graduate Studies. I am grateful to my colleagues and friends in the English Department at East Carolina University for continuing to remind me with jokes and hugs that "career" is a shared experience. I thank Peter Stallybrass, who stood up for this book at the University of Pennsylvania, Jerome Singerman, my forbearing editor at the University of Pennsylvania Press, and two readers for the Press who provided much-needed encouragement and honest criticism, Sheila Emerson and Joseph Childers. The one person without whose intellectual example, unflagging support, and acid wit this book probably would not have been written is Daniel Cottom. Finally, to my wife, Judy Lucas, and our children, Tyler and Emma — no thanks would be sufficient, so my love will have to do.

An earlier version of a portion of Chapter 2 appeared as "The Victorian Discourse of Gambling: Speculations on *Middlemarch* and *The Duke's Children*," *ELH* 61 (winter 1994). An earlier version of my reading of *Felix Holt* from Chapter 3 appeared as "The Victorian Novel's Performance of Interiority: *Felix Holt* on Trial," *Victorians Institute Journal* 26 (autumn 1998). My thanks to these journals for their permissions to reproduce this material.

Index